THE HOUSE OF DEATH

Piero della Francesca, Adam (with Eve standing behind him) announces his
death to a group of descendants; detail from the *Death of Adam* (after 1452).
Church of San Francesco, Arezzo.

THE
House of Death

Messages from the English Renaissance

ARNOLD STEIN

THE JOHNS HOPKINS UNIVERSITY PRESS
Baltimore and London

*This book has been brought to publication with the
generous assistance of the National Endowment for the Humanities.*

© 1986 The Johns Hopkins University Press
All rights reserved
Printed in the United States of America

The Johns Hopkins University Press
701 West 40th Street   Baltimore, Maryland 21211
The Johns Hopkins Press Ltd., London

The paper used in this publication meets the minimum requirements
of American National Standard for Information Sciences—
Permanence of Paper for Printed Library Materials, ANSI Z39.48-1984.

Library of Congress Catalog Card Number 86-45448
ISBN 0-8018-3296-9

Library of Congress Cataloging in Publication data
will be found on the last page of this book.

201800

To Bess

Contents

Contents

Preface

A *soldier on leave,* I was in Paris the day the city mourned the death of Paul Valéry. I listened to the soliloquy of a great city remembering the honor of poets just after a long war lost and won. I was thirty years old and had become acquainted with battlefield death.

A few years later, in a world that paid special attention to important public funerals, usually preceded by carefully edited hospital bulletins and then coordinated with the publication of full obituaries, reviews, and feature articles, the products of foresight—in that world, entirely familiar to me, I was surprised to observe a very different order in the deaths of popes. My instructive examples were those of Pius XII and John XXIII, and these reminded me in part of some Renaissance deaths. It was plain that the dying, the daily reported "events" of the approaches to death, were themselves of considerable interest and were followed intently, at least in Italy, but elsewhere too. Each death had a shape of its own, a consciously ordered one, I thought, and wondered in passing how much was due to intermediaries. But however individual the deaths, as they seemed to answer in brief a purpose of representing the spiritual life by the arrangement of the extreme business of life, whatever else they were intended to express, these deaths mainly emphasized their thoughtful sameness within a clearly framed order.

Some interests have changed, others not, since I began to think that I might try to write this book. I remember the first question that fully gripped me: How, with what seemed to be a few prescriptive ways of regarding death, and on the other side much that was unsayable, perhaps unthinkable, did Renaissance writers manage to say such marvelous, unforgettable things?

The English writers most drawn upon come from a period of about one hundred years, from the late sixteenth to the late seventeenth century. During that time the life of the nation experienced more than usual conflict, violence, change, loss, and growth. To mention literature: one of the world's great ages of drama came and went; other masterpieces of poetry and prose appeared. In religion conflicts smoldered and raged, but the ways of thinking and speaking of death were for the most part spared the rancor of systematic public dispute. For instance, it was a common truth that death was feared; the answer least likely to stimulate troublesome questions was the master goal of turning fear of death into love of the divine. Similarly, a value that seemed to be inherent in the good death, trusted by pagan philosophers and articulate Christians, was the wisdom of reasoned and therefore peaceful and controlled acceptance of death. Admired and desired, it was another generally untroubled answer. Though a kind of tolerated stability of agreement concealed major changes beginning to take shape, these were not in doctrine itself.

There are several ways to tell the story. When I choose to do so from the evidence of serious imaginative literature, I find the poets conserving, remembering, restoring, even in the midst of change. The sameness of death and the unchallenged rules for thinking about death do not prevent good writers from discovering and showing, in any instance, what is distinct and individual—not through new ideas, principles, or methods, but through observed or imagined details that search, illuminate, question. As Montaigne testifies concerning one aspect of the relationship between the universal and the particular: "I saw death nonchalantly when I saw it universally, as the end of life. I dominate it in the mass; in detail it harasses me."

After the introductory essays in background, the two central sections concentrate on poems anticipating the poet's own death and poems responding to the death of another. The first of these (Part 2) develops its demonstrations from major examples and from interpretations of the individual practice of such figures as Raleigh, Donne, and Herbert. Much of Part 3 is developed through contrasting examples, such as Marvell's lines on the execution of Charles and those in response to viewing the dead body of Cromwell; poems by Henry King and John Donne on a dead wife; Ben Jonson on the death of a first son and a first daughter. Some of the problems evident in the writing of public elegies contribute to a sense of the difference and advantage of the more personal poems. Throughout, as in Part 2 and again in Part 4, the imagination of time is a recurrent theme. Finally, there is a consideration of some efforts, in jest and earnest, to imagine death as a kind of abstract idea.

Part 4 concerns in various ways problems involving the expression of thoughts, feelings, and beliefs in response to death. The path leads from Aristotle and thinking "along with an image" through human and "divine" rhetoric. This latter is illustrated by the exemplary expression of the Holy Spirit (as in Scripture); according to Donne, that language works directly upon the human soul and conscience but indirectly and figuratively upon the reason and understanding. My study takes me through some different kinds of images and into some particular characteristics of the language of devotion, and to a survey of three basic images related to death: sleep, time, and love.

A large chapter, "Intricacies," looks for paths among complex relations. These paths will not always conclude as boulevards of triumphant connection. Some of the subjects explored are the ways of the certainty and uncertainty, the known and unknown, and the mysteries of death (with selected references to the same, of life). Other matters touched on include the charged spaces between memory and not-thinking, and include the kinds of self and other which make talk of death worth hearing. Toward the end of the chapter some connections are made with the present, and in the concluding chapter for purposes of comparison the perspective is consciously modern, and the author allows himself a different range of voice.

I began by remembering the death of Valéry in 1945. Forty years later I remember that it has been a long time since I saw quoted Valéry's famous, haunting sentence after World War I, reminding France (and Western civilization) that now we too have glimpsed the mortality of our civilization. The confident grace of his writing cannot have yielded much to the passage of time, yet surely something has happened to the novelty of that first shiver of recognition many once felt. But then, for the past forty years it has begun to look possible, and to some observers probable or worse, that man might succeed in killing everything on earth. If it does not happen but still could happen, our responses to concepts of mortality are sure to reflect changes, and the present rules for contemplating the certainty and the uncertainties of death will need to accommodate some new relations. But at least some of that process will already be in motion, perhaps even along the edges of the present book, though it arrives late in the surge of modern attention and draws most of its material from literature written three or four centuries ago.

I began with a detail of personal history which was part of the remote beginning of this book. How past and present speak to each other is a question that a student of Renaissance literature lives with regularly. In any case, I have not tried to keep out of this book about the past everything learned from personal experience and from a normal interest in the present. My chief sources, however, and what I most value, are those that become the "messages" of individual poets as they express and renew some of our best knowledge and self-knowledge.

Acknowledgments

John Hollander read the manuscript of this book with a quality of attention and insight most authors in their right senses crave. This is to acknowledge my professional gratitude. I wish to thank next Ronald Paulson for his frank, severe, and accurate judgment of a dozen pages I asked him to read.

This book, no doubt intending to be the product of mature deliberateness, has enjoyed the favor and support of two academic institutions. For their help in many ways I am grateful to the Johns Hopkins University and the University of Illinois at Urbana. I wish to express my appreciation to the staff of the Johns Hopkins University Press and most particularly to Eric Halpern and Carol Ehrlich.

I have reached the place to thank the following friends who did not know they were helping me to finish this book: Sharon Cameron, Jackson Campbell, Margaret Dickie, Coburn Freer, Hugh Kenner, Keneth Kinnamon, Richard Macksey, Claude Rawson, Robert Penn Warren.

As houses that stand in *two Shires,* trouble the execution of Justice, the house of death that stands in two worlds, may trouble a good mans resolution. As death is a sordid *Postern,* by which I must be thrown out of this world, I would decline it: But as death is the gate, by which I must enter into Heaven, would I never come to it?

DONNE, *Sermons*

PART ONE

Three Essays in Background

Darknesse and light hold interchangeable dominions, and alternately rule the seminal state of things. Light unto *Pluto* is darknesse unto Jupiter. . . . Light that makes things seen, makes some things invisible: were it not for darknesse and the shadow of the earth, the noblest part of the Creation had remained unseen, and the Stars in heaven as invisible as on the fourth day, when they were created above the Horizon, with the Sun, or there was not an eye to behold them. The greatest mystery of Religion is expressed by adumbration, and in the noblest part of Jewish Types, we finde the Cherubims shadowing the Mercy-seat: Life it self is but the shadow of death, and souls departed but the shadows of the living: All things fall under this name. The Sunne it self is but the dark *simulachrum,* and light but the shadow of God.

BROWNE, *Garden of Cyrus*

"O Teacher, some great mischief hath befall'n
To that meek man, who well had sacrificed;
Is piety thus and pure devotion paid?"
    T' whom Michael thus, he also moved, replied:
"These two are brethren, Adam, and to come
Out of thy loins; th' unjust the just hath slain. . . ."
    "Alas, both for the deed and for the cause!
But have I now seen Death? Is this the way
I must return to native dust? O sight
Of terror, foul and ugly to behold,
Horrid to think, how horrible to feel!"
    To whom thus Michael: "Death thou hast seen
In his first shape on man; but many shapes
Of Death, and many are the ways that lead
To his grim cave, all dismal; yet to sense
More terrible at th' entrance than within."

MILTON, *Paradise Lost*

CHAPTER ONE

What Renaissance Poets Would Have Known

People *think about* death and their own death, and they necessarily use familiar materials and habits of thinking on the subject. This truism is a foundation of everything that will follow. In Renaissance England, original ways of thinking about death, even if they had been forthcoming, were hardly suitable for the many occasions that required public expression. And even personal expression responding to the unique experience of irrecoverable loss might well have found itself repeating the familiar lessons that come to mind when the rawest feelings and the thoughts they release prove inadequate. Death was a frequent, expected, and familiar experience; the general and particular aspects of the subject were thought of in advance by means of private and public exercises of meditative anticipations and retrospections. By the sixteenth century poets had available, from the history of thinking about death, a rich vocabulary of feeling and representation and an extensive literature to draw from.

Death spoken of in a crisis of feeling, as that of a lyric occasion, will necessarily traverse familiar grounds but will not therefore be predictable or trite. For example, Macbeth's "Out, out, brief candle" is and is not the light of Othello's "Put out the light, and then put out the light."[1] Macbeth's contemptuous judgment of life—"a walking shadow . . . a tale / Told by an idiot, full of sound and fury, / Signifying nothing"— differs from what a theologian might have said chiefly in being more vivid and precisely timed and in being final rather than a threatening alternative, a judgment resembling a curse, the poetry of a self-characterizing tragic figure caught in the last stages of an action. The difference is terrible, and the power of the tragic statement continues unabated, though subsequent audiences will have lost touch with some of its tortured but customary usage.

Our understanding will be improved if we are able to recognize that which is traditional and how it is used. In imaginative expression the unprecedented is not limited to identifiable "thoughts." We may be faced with apparently spontaneous or apparently deliberate selections made from or omitted from traditional materials. Even a highly literate

3

citizen of an age may respect the difficulties in comprehending the subtle juxtapositions of the spontaneous and the deliberate, and their timing and relationship to each other and to the whole discourse. What has been omitted, and is noticed, is always a special problem. The same literate reader must pause, as we must do, over materials that are made prominent or inconspicuous and must emphasize, or not, the significance of their relative excesses and deficiencies. These are frequent features of imaginative expression, baffling if one does not know the language and the habits of thought from which they derive. The difficulties are such that we may reasonably doubt that all effects are thoroughly understood by able contemporaries.

These observations are intended to suggest conditions that neither stifle nor overdetermine individual responses by good poets. The subject is one that I shall return to for special and general illumination. In the meantime, I wish to emphasize the existence of certain ways of thinking about death which are characteristic of an age and will therefore shape what can be said. What cannot be said has a different kind of existence, useful in the study of this subject mostly as a defining limit, a kind of boundary and barrier which makes it own contributions to the shape of what can be said. The more elusive parts of what cannot be said may require extraordinary alertness and some intricate apparatus to detect and explain them. The subject is attractive, but I am now chiefly concerned with the discovery of what can be said, for it has been said, though one perhaps did not realize that it could be said.

Some modern examples illustrate briefly how circumstances and time affect what can be said of death. Pope John XXIII, late in his preparations for dying, was reported as saying, "My bags are all packed." The common image of life as a journey provided the secondary image by which John concisely expressed the individual style of his own life and death. His wry displacement glanced at the familiar knowledge that there were no things to pack for this trip; all one could take to the point of the departure was the proper state of spiritual readiness. On the other side of his expression, but effectively canceled by it, was the state of imminent death haunted by a long history of troubled apprehensions. The good humor, insofar as it entered the public record, added a comment to his own personal example of how to die. One cannot conceive of Pius XII saying these words, or if by some miracle he had, of their appearing in newsprint, for the shape and style of his death (at least as I read the daily official reports) was carefully composed to represent his own life and concept of office. My point is a simple one to illustrate the difference in time as well as person. For by the end of

4

John's pontificate a new age had begun, and the pope understood himself as well as his own position in time.

Not long ago, in the *Times* of London, I saw the quoted words of a dying person which were most unusual even if the thought behind the words cannot be imagined as entirely novel. At least it is certain that the *Times* would not have printed "the last words" a little while ago. The account marked the occasion of Marilyn French's second novel, *The Bleeding Heart,* which was reviewed in connection with a promotional interview granted by the visiting author:

> Recently, men have taken to writing her. "Their letters fall," says Dr. French, "into two categories. There are those who say, 'My wife got me to read your book and now I understand much more.' The worst was when a man wrote and said that his wife had just died, and that her last words to him were: 'Gee whizz Tom, 30 years bullshit.' Then he had heard a voice guiding him to the bookstore to buy my book."[2]

We seem to be invited to recognize in "Tom's" letter the modern subgenre of hoax. We may also observe an interesting verisimilitude of stunted growth or regression conveyed by the passive echo of a juvenile euphemism for the name of Jesus; at the same time there is an active assertiveness in the emancipated argot which offers a pronouncement on the worthlessness and illusionary nature of life, in this case a particular married life. In their way the attitudes back of the expression are as traditional as Macbeth's speech on the death of his wife. As "Tom's" wife puts it, her existence is to be despised; it has been full of show and contrived illusion, and at the last the speaker can no longer keep up the efforts to deceive and to be deceived. The stripped stage reveals the inept actors, one of whom has also been an uncritical spectator. The example is a convenient if unusual example of how traditional attitudes can be reworked into the individual expression of a person and a time. Even the exaggerations of a probable hoax are supported by present conventions and their acceptability, including the come-on of a revelation leading the way to personal salvation by purchase. What is new we may acknowledge as not likely to have been said so under other conditions, in another time.

These examples, and even the triviality, are reminders that responses to death are not without limits and not without a history that influences what can and cannot be said.

What would Renaissance poets have known of the thinking about death? The main ideas were few, but in their implications, when brought to bear upon individual experience, they were of inexhaustible interest. The records are voluminous, and the history of circumstances, issues, and their potential meaning is a proper subject for many branches of specialized knowledge. I shall need to return to certain items more than once in later discussions and also to remark upon the existence of historical changes. For the most part, however, the knowledge of poets and their readers was a present knowledge, possessed by historical process and repetition but in general acquired without the conscious historical study that is a normal way by which we expect to learn from the past. The Renaissance could assume that, except for a few changes made by the Reformation, the most important knowledge concerning the subject of death had already been collected and systematically organized. Studious theologians, to be sure, would have been more interested in selected issues involving historical knowledge, and some of them were poets, but I shall make no effort to give them special consideration in what follows.

Much of the basic knowledge could have been learned without reading—by word-of-mouth instruction, attending church services, being present at the deathbed, witnessing some scenes in the public theaters, looking at pictures. The educated had the Bible, commentaries, treatises, books of devotion. There were also the sources in classical literature and philosophy, important bits and pieces that had been quoted for centuries, and now whole texts edited in print. What would have been current knowledge included the wisdom literature recorded in arguments of grief and consolation, in which the ancients had said almost everything that could be said on the subject. The greatest personal example from the pagan world was that of Socrates, and especially the moral optimism of his reasoned acceptance of death. Theologians would not forget to annotate the commanding advice of Ecclesiasticus 7:40 ("In everything you do, remember your end and you will never sin") with Socrates' definition of the philosopher's life as a rehearsal for death. The general bent of Platonic dualism, the fruitful antagonism between appearances in this world and the truth of supernatural reality, became a permanent part of Christian thought. The image of God in which man was made became the endowment of reason and the power to know and apply the laws of reason. Plato's doctrine that held memory to be immortal could be transformed, and then largely forgotten, in Christian thoughts of the life of eternity and the Communion of Saints, and in the practical exercises by which the individual helped prepare himself for salvation.

The Stoics both repeated and altered some aspects of Platonic thought, but they were also the great practical schoolmasters in furnishing lessons that fortunately accorded with many inclinations of Christian moral thought. They acquired the authority of ready usefulness by their shrewd observations on the uncertainty and brevity of life, by their insistence on the necessity of controlling one's own life upon the pivot of consciously remembering death, and by their many portable *sententiae*. To live "as though every hour the last" could be regarded as a useful supplementary means of avoiding sin and of applying moral reason to the practical decisions of life. Seneca, like Cicero, acquired great personal authority; the moving eloquence of both could be regarded as a book of natural man's wisdom, a reassuring phenomenon of Providence that validated odd and detached contributions by various pagan figures, including poets whose moral integrity and stature did not need to be judged if the particular quotation was apt: as, for instance, Catullus, Propertius, Ovid, Martial.

Though Christian philosophy could handle or assimilate parts of the pagan tradition while consciously rejecting other parts, the providential meanings of Christ's death introduced some radical differences in the orientation toward death as a final test of life. The test now involved salvation or damnation in the life of eternity and required effective penitence for sins and effective faith in Christ as Redeemer. Faith and reason made certain accommodations: for instance, if the whole design of salvation required using some of the attributes of a cyclical concept of history, this was not allowed to intrude upon the commitment to thinking of Christ's death as an actual, unique event in a linear conception of history.[3] Furthermore, the new orientation toward death, as if responding to some latent necessity that could be answered only by the mental work of a special joy, sought full and clear explanations of why everything that had to be so was so.

The durable phenomenon of human fear is an instructive example and one I shall return to in later pages. Aristotle had described the fear of death as the greatest of human fears (*Ethics* 3.6.1115a), and that quotable judgment was supplemented by a psychological observation made in his *Rhetoric*: "We do not fear things that are a very long way off; for instance, we all know we shall die, but we are not troubled thereby, because death is not close at hand" (2.5.1382a). Donne illustrates a typical application when he attributes "the first accesses" of sickness to God's reminder "that I must die" and then adds the personal apprehension, "By this further proceeding therein, that I may die now."[4] Death, which pagans could endeavor to understand as a law of nature, Christians interpreted as a direct punishment for Adam's disobedience. Since the punishment was imposed by God, it could not be explained by reasoning based upon the natural order of things; furthermore, the pains were believed to be unique, appropriately exceeding all other natural experiences. In Augustine's influential expression, death was "a sharp, unnatural experience" (*City of God* 13.2). *Timor mortis* was then a natural response to a divinely ordained "unnatural experience," and religious instructors did not neglect stimulating the fear of imminent death while balancing that personal fear, variously, with doctrines intended to provide the support of reason and faith, and finally to transform the fear into acceptance and the purified desire of eternal good.

Not to experience fear was to risk depriving oneself of the full advantages of penitence. Since fear was a stage that existed for the purposes of transition and change, it also provided an opposing element for dialectical conversion. If death was a punishment and not a law of nature, it was nevertheless a punishment for breaking divine law, and the case could be argued with all the resources developed in legal practices—not with the thought of winning the case, but in order to explore all contingencies so that the case could be lost with dignity and full awareness. Peter Lombard could praise fear as one of the seven gifts of the Holy Ghost, a means of turning the sinner toward the noble fear of losing eternal good.[5] The opposite direction for fear to take led in the direction of despair. But the human endowment of fear, though linked in simple ways to the nature of moral being, retained some intricate, ultimately mysterious affinities with God's providential purposes. Keen observers had noted, at least since Origen, that in spite of the acknowledged rules of rational order conversions often came when the excesses of sin reached a sudden climax, the progress of which was not discernible by the rules of reason.[6]

Though in Stoic thought the last hour was installed as an authoritative measure of life, it was a moral measure that did not subdue the nature of life to the nature of death. Instead, the relationship preserved a kind of openness in which the claims of life were disciplined by the necessity of death but were not diminished in importance or dignity. By constant reference to a fixed standard of judgment, the Stoics heightened the stress on personal responsibility for shaping one's life according to the laws of reason. One consequence was the accepted duty of living well; dying well was not so much a purposive climax as a natural conclusion of reason. The stress on free will in the service of reason was admired by Christians, but not the relative autonomy that allowed no room for human weakness and little need for God. Though attractive, the doctrine was plainly not an adequate substitute for Christian ways of dying. But since thinking about death inevitably faced the necessity of trying to explain what could not be known by reason, though never to the point of demonstrating why human beings no longer had reason to think of the subject, good minds continued to be attracted by the implications of the Stoic concept, and in the Renaissance the problems of living well raised questions that began to require special attention, most pronouncedly after the Reformation.

Centuries of Christian thought based on the warnings and promises of Scripture, and also based on the observation of human nature, developed a great body of knowledge, ordering sins and their classes, characteristics, dynamic interrelations, and resourceful vitality. To see these from the perspective of the connections between sin and death was to acquire the means of new insights and the means of bringing these insights into a rational organization. For example, lust, the natural sin of youth, could not be expected to terminate naturally; rather, in later life the depleted energies of sexual desire renewed themselves in the dominant sin of age, avarice. (By their emphasis, medieval preachers and poets seem to be expressing, not a detached doctrinal point, but a lesson based upon the observation of contemporary behavior, and recognizing that loss of possessions was in a particular way a chief impediment to the final letting go of life.)

Remembering death was a practical instrument of control, and its larger purposes licensed the effective means and rhetoric for developing the subject of death in ways that would cancel its imagined remoteness and would bring it home to the individual in all the feeling immediacy that art and spiritual conviction could command. Any excess might be justifiable because of the stubborn cunning of the enemy within. Remembering death included remembering its unpredictability, the human certainty of uncertainty, which had its communications with the secret maneuverings of sin and the fallibilities of conscience. Thought of uncertainty could loosen related uncertainties and quicken conscientious doubts behind the rational assurances of personal salvation. The duty of training people how to die always ran some risk of overtraining them.

"Remember your end and you will never sin" seemed to offer an answer that oversimplified the better knowledge of theology and to the less well educated was directed toward a single stage of prevention. The maxim worked best as a training device that sharpened one edge of thought while blunting another. For example, all minute consideration of death and of the sins to be prevented or repented served to intensify conflicts—as between the idea of death as "unnatural" and the rhetoric of warning which exploited both natural and supernatural terrors in picturing punishments and in expounding the loathsomeness but insidious power of sin. Fighting fear with fear authorized the dangers of excess within a restrictive narrowness and often ignored, postponed, or slighted the higher goal of turning fear into the calm peace of faith and love of God. But the effectiveness and memorability of "Remember your end" were beyond dispute.

Many texts from Scripture supplied lessons that answered the purposes of elevated and less excitable contemplation—for instance, the words of Psalm 39:4–7: "Lord, make me to know mine end, and the measure of my days, what it is; that I may know how frail I am. . . . And now, Lord, what wait I for? my hope is in thee." The concluding petition of verse 13 is to "recover strength before I go hence, and be no more." The way to that strength is the knowledge of the brevity of life, the acknowledgment of human vanity as a law of being, and the expression of dependence on God. The implied fear of natural reluctance ("what wait I for?") is subdued in expressed humility and is followed at once (as if a set form of religious reasoning were now fulfilled) by the affirmation of hope "in thee." The words present a religious paradigm in which the knowledge of death leads to the felt knowledge of humility and ends in the renewal of faith before death.

The most authoritative pattern for Christian death was the history of Christ's death, the first formal stage of which could be interpreted as beginning with the agony in the garden, where he prayed, "O my Father, if it be possible, let this cup pass from me! nevertheless, not as I will, but as thou wilt" (Matt. 26:39). This could be taken as representing the exemplary human experience of hesitation before the knowledge of death. The loud voice that cried from the cross, "My God, my God, why hast thou forsaken me?" could signify all the human fears of abandonment by God—as part of the established laws of dying, all of them fulfilled by the sinless Redeemer, including the climax of a human struggle, dark before dawn, death becoming a second birth, and perhaps expressing the pain of the "sharp, unnatural experience." Clearly, both of these events required and lent themselves to exegesis, both for Christology and for the purpose of instructing Christians in what to expect and imitate in their own deaths. Only the last words, as reported by Luke 24:46 ("Father, into thy hands I commend my spirit"), expressed the unquestionable assurance of faith, and these entered the prescribed ritual of Christian dying. The essential design became a settled part of the thinking about death and authorized the expectations of reluctance and fear on the way to the final peace of overcoming all uncertainties.

Familiar rules prescribed the right way to die and anticipated and corrected individual errors likely to be discovered on the way, but they could not prevent, cure, or fully understand manifestations that seemed to lie outside or would not respond to established methods. In the fifteenth century the phenomenon of the dance of death released a range of expression that ecclesiastical authorities could not have anticipated or directed. A new art form satisfied particular desires and flourished at once: a dance in which living figures represented surprise and reluctance while their partners, decaying corpses, showed an extreme liveliness. I want to emphasize chiefly the limited, and obvious, point that the new artistic invention, and the astonishing success that greeted its appearance, reveal the existence of feelings that were not being contained by the acknowledged methods of handling fear, penitence, and faith. Some of the grotesque elements extended in their own ways the familiar lessons taught in the numerous discourses arguing the case for rejecting the world and the things of the world (*contemptus mundi*). One may also recognize features related to the common advice, *memento mori,* and its many elaborations and to the less common subgenre, the "triumph of death." Perhaps there was an oral or visual tradition surviving in ways we cannot follow from a strain of pagan humor that provided messages from the tomb, salutations and reminders to passersby, to which might be added the Socratic advice askew, "Know thyself." In any case, the wit and wisdom of personal messages from a corpse or ghost, frequent in medieval writing and slow to lose their appeal and bite for purposes of satire in later writing, reached one fruition in the widely popular aphorism from the grave, "What you are I was, what I am you will be."

Perhaps these feelings, at least in their demonstrated character, belonged chiefly to one period of time, the fifteenth century, which was also notable for its increased interest in depicting the details of bodily putrefaction. But though the strange intensity and relish might never reappear on a similar scale, the effects on the imagination and memory of others would not disappear. Sir Thomas More did not forget the pictures of the dance of death he saw in the north cloister of St. Paul's,[7] and John Donne's imagination of death certainly was influenced by late medieval developments. In brief, to the established ways of thinking about death something was added that might need to be resisted or taken into account.

A related phenomenon was the sudden rise of a new genre, the *ars moriendi,* which commanded instant attention and created a lasting influence of considerable power. The systematic concentration on one period of time, the final getting ready for death, was new and provided the sense of a structured scene and design. Because of the concentration, the systematizing, and the potentialities of the form, much of the counsel and wisdom, though collected from familiar sources, could produce effects not quite like those available from advice offered in other circumstances and arranged more casually, according to different principles of selection. As the genre developed, its affinities to a dramatic action brought into use other potentialities. Those assisting the protagonist, *moriens*—his friends, counselors, and witnesses—took part in dialogues and were alternately an immediate audience who could also represent a larger audience of readers. The sequence of conflicts and temptations instructed the living, added suspense to the plot, and could furnish vivid scenes. Within the familiar rules for understanding the physical and spiritual process of dying, the analytical dramatizing of an imagined situation discovered new kinds of flexibility in the distribution of emphasis. At the right time in the right form, old knowledge becomes the presage, forerunner, grounds of new knowledge. In fact, the popular genre proved capable of reflecting shifts in the approach to live theological issues and could explain in its handling of details many shades of post-Reformation emphasis and doctrine.[8]

From one point of view it may appear that the *ars moriendi* provided a soberly entertaining substitute for the stronger excitements of the dance of death. Centering the scene on the deathbed and its fascinations would probably have engaged some of the interests satisfied by the dance of death but would have brought them into an aesthetic and rational order capable of internal development and closure. For the dance of death created and remained a memorable image drawn from the traditions of threat and instructive fear, while the *ars moriendi* became a literary genre and entered a period of growth. The image of the dance represented communal participation by the living of all social classes and by the classless dead. Whatever its darker side, the image was wryly celebratory and offered a strange expression of the spirit of Christian triumph over death, a triumph resembling something of the spirit of those ancient eccentrics who mourned birth and celebrated death. But the *ars moriendi* was a literary form that moved with varied rhythms through episodes, some of which were expected and could therefore evoke the peculiar effects of partly reluctant, partly relieved recognition, with room for other feelings as well. The dramatic elements produced their own sense of participation, but the form also kept and exploited the dramatic advantage of being able to move readers attending an imagined action that threatened with strange pleasure their own conscious sense of personal separation. The most memorable part of its image was that protracted concentration on *moriens,* the center of intent spectators. The fully shared message was the old one, that all must die, but the protagonist was the person acting out the story, and he was set apart. From that image and from the individual experience of the story in which he figured, every reader might receive his own personal message.

No doubt the rapid spread of editions and translations and a continuing stream of new books on "the art of dying well" answered a deep, emerging need that signaled a change in the response to death.[9] That the need and the change did not require a definitive clarity of recognition we may take for granted. The privilege of a historical perspective may also acknowledge that "recognition" for contemporaries may express itself, and perhaps do so best, without the kind of reasoned awareness justly esteemed in other intellectual enterprises. Besides, the privilege of historical perspective is better able to observe need and change than to distinguish with assurance between the relations of cause and effect in those difficult areas where change may produce the recognition of need by increasing it, and where successful expression becomes an effect that also acts as a cause.

In part the popularity of the subgenre resembles that of works advocating *contemptus mundi,* though the *ars moriendi* lasted less than half as long in a vital tradition before dwindling into the reduced existence of a practical manual for those who wanted to know more about how to do it. Unlike the *contemptus mundi,* however, the *ars moriendi* attracted new feeling and art that were sensitive to changing conditions—economic and social in the larger sense—and to the particular influences of Reformation and Counter Reformation and the new humanism.

The major change in the response to death, a constant among other changes brought on by the crises of the religious struggles, was general acceptance, in spite of differences in doctrine, that the individual death was a subject worthy of close attention. It would be absurd to think that the interest was altogether new, but something happened when the interest was discovered and spread. The available records would seem to say that for centuries the individual death, once it was about to happen, was governed by a set of rules ready for the occasion, and these took over the act of dying without encouraging any scrutiny of the process that might detect individual and distinctive features. The center of interest shifted in a normal way to hope in the Resurrection; anxieties concerning personal salvation did not thrust themselves into the moment of death, but the dying were content to wait with optimistic faith in the Day of Judgment. One could die well enough without worrying whether one was dying as well as possible. When Sir Thomas Browne wrote that he would be satisfied to bring up the rear and be the last person admitted to heaven, he was whimsically recovering part of the spirit of an age long departed.[10] Or, to cite a modern instance that may speak more directly to a modern reader's recognition, in some recent candid words about the fear of death, Irving Howe darts across the intervening centuries to illustrate the calm force of a promise that can move from life to life without fixing on death itself as a heightened episode one must imagine and experience fully:

> I think about death because I fear extinction, total and end-less. . . . no one would mind a thousand-year sleep if at the end . . . there were a prospect of waking.[11]

Concentration on the individual death became a fact of history and an emphatic departure from the subdued emphasis that had lasted for many centuries. I am not equipped to untie the historical knots with expert knowledge of the order and patterns in which they were made, but it may be enough to observe that the growing emphasis on the individuality of death was reinforced by a growing belief that a kind of preliminary judgment concerning salvation occurred at the time of death. If salvation was not exactly dependent upon or determined by the quality of the individual death, still there might be an omen at the least, and at the best a personal message of encouragement or approval com-municated to the dying person. For Protestants committed to the pri-macy of faith, death was a crucial moment for testing the efficacy of a lifetime of faith; they were of course indignant at the easier techniques of warranting salvation ratified by Roman practice. The Counter Refor-mation, while sharing the increased emphasis on individual death, could in its *artes moriendi* draw with renewed energy upon its own traditions of renouncing the world, seeking penitence, and affirming faith. If candidates for immortality could be made to raise their own standards by instruction in the art of dying well, the old wisdom (most of which it was unthinkable to tamper with anyway) could continue with all its authority. In addition, hostile arguments against the in-terpretations of "good works" and against the validity of uncritical absolution would be reduced to annoying impertinence. The Roman church had never minimized the importance of death, and without altering anything but the emphasis it could employ its rich traditions to meet the changing interest in the individuality of death.

Freely moving across the drawn lines of Reformation and Counter Reformation, certain other currents of shared interest appeared on both sides and have some bearing on the new emphasis given the individual death. A new literature of meditation sprang up, Jesuit in origin and applied purpose but quietly adapting successful methods from other traditions of thought and expression. The genre proved itself adaptable to changes in doctrine, emphasis, and religious sensibility. Many of the topics and effective methods of meditation led outward, the mind disciplining itself to gain a desired end of devotion. But though the Jesuit handbooks prescribed the content and goals of meditation, they also deliberately left room for individual application of details, and however closely the routines were followed, success or failure could be felt as a personal experience. The Ignatian model emphasized a rigorous mode of analytical reasoning; Calvinists would not find themselves wholly unprepared or uncritical, and in practice Protestants had small difficulty in adjusting and redirecting the congenial parts of the Ignatian discipline. In the seventeenth century, Protestant meditation was an individual and inward act characteristically given a public hearing. While the process of meditation expressed the movement of a single guiding religious conscience, it could in printed or spoken words draw an audience to participate in a course of mental and spiritual experience which moved them as individuals, with their own souls to save, but also as members of a community.[12]

Moral theology awakened to a neglected and timely branch of its learning, the detailed and practical problems of casuistry, that reasoning upon moral problems discoverable in daily life but too particular in their circumstances to be treated well by the direct application of the larger moral laws. Again the Reformation side was late in starting but soon discovered that casuistry filled a gap left by the decline (which was to be applauded) of speculative theology, and that Protestants had inexhaustible resources for cases of conscience.[13]

In another development, the ancient system of typology was given a new and practical emphasis. As the New Testament revealed and realized the meanings obscurely anticipated in the Old Testament, the newer times saw themselves as part of the continuing story, now consciously reliving the history of salvation. A dying person and the assistants, revising and modernizing the old, smoothly running mental machinery, could discover and interpret many comforting parallels to give assurance that this death conformed with the true history of God's will. Protestants introduced their own interpretations, carefully pruned of the excesses and outmoded habits of mind which could be identified and disliked in medieval traditions, but did not feel it necessary to justify their own efforts by the practices of the primitive church. The new typology was not brought under formal rule, *de jure,* but expressed a distinctly Protestant piety, giving the individual faith and death the right kind of emphasis: not a binding tradition imposed by authority, but rather a *de facto* practice that grew by agreement. The reformed typology contributed to the individuality of death while assisting the candidate to join, not the *all* of the standard medieval emphasis, an indiscriminate throng under a compulsion leveled upon them, but a select community of the faithful. [14]

The most instructive historical study of death in Western civilization is that of Philippe Ariès. [15] Though I began writing before I became acquainted with his work, I have been influenced by his demonstrations and have made specific use of one basic pattern that he identifies and traces. In brief: the medieval centuries develop their acceptance of death in ways that do not self-consciously intensify and explore the passage from life to death; the characterizing expression is that you/we/all must die. The break occurs when death becomes more dramatic, an episode of heightened experience, the death of an individual, a self. In my last chapter I undertake a brief critique of Ariès' book in order to clarify some of the differences that emerge from a study of literary evidence.

When *observing the* work of imaginative writers, including their use of the old pattern "all must die" and the new scene of the individual death, one notices differences that are characteristic of literary tradition, which has a long memory. One may also observe that individual writers have their own ways of responding to the old and the new. What to the historian is an attitude irreversibly in decline, as the various and cumulative evidence demonstrates, may possess another life in literature, where the old and the new may combine in irreducible ways. For the old may not only be unforgettable, it may continue to speak with and against the new and the newer and prevent the mind from closing its books on what has been and can be convincingly felt.

CHAPTER TWO

Answers and Questions

A Dialogue between two Infants in the womb concerning the state of
this world, might handsomely illustrate our ignorance of the next,
whereof methinks we yet discourse in *Platoes* denne, and are but
Embryon Philosophers.

BROWNE, *Urne Burial*

The process of dying was, everyone was encouraged to understand, lifelong. To think of the matter so was to possess a ready source of practical
and contemplative lessons. Actual death at hand, imagined dying, images of death, a process of deriving images from images—if one
thought of any of these in the right way, one could insert the first
thought into standard stages of living-and-dying, or into any chosen
moment, and the thought would begin to flower and bear fruit in kind.
The field was large, its temporal borders were open, and one might
review, revise, or refine one's thoughts. But the last phase of dying,
even when it conformed in all important ways with the practiced
thought of a lifetime and the accepted rules of tradition, could not but
be different. The basic symptoms were definite and unmistakable to
trained observers. It was an exact event in time, and whatever one might
wish to think then or later, this event required some practical application of thought.

The last phase of dying was customarily presided over by the best
wisdom of the church in the person of a clerical representative or,
depending on the church or circumstances, one or more lay representatives or, if need be, by the dying person following remembered instructions. A standard death in Reformation England would be attended by
three interested parties: the dying person, the church representative,
and various others—family, friends, mourners-to-be. Let us glance
briefly at the situation from the perspective of each party.

In the Anglican Order for the Visitation of the Sick, the minister
had considerable latitude, depending upon circumstances and his judgment of the physical and spiritual condition of the sick person. His main

purpose was the traditional one of encouraging a dying sinner to understand and accept the conditions of Christian death. The first prayers concern the forgiveness of all the community of the redeemed. Then for the sick the minister prays for God's mercy, comfort, "sure confidence in thee," and defense "from the danger of the enemy." The comfort enters a rational development in identifying the sickness with "fatherly correction" and in praying "that the sense of his weakness may add strength to his faith, and seriousness to his repentance"; so that if God restores his health,

> he may lead the residue of his life in thy fear, and to thy glory: or else give him grace to take thy visitation, that after this painful life ended he may dwell with thee in life everlasting, through Jesus Christ our Lord.[1]

Then an exhortation to the sick person touches on possible causes of God's visitation: to try his patience "for the example of others," and his faith, so that the latter may be found "laudable, glorious, and honourable, to the increase of glory and endless felicity." On the other hand, the visitation may have the purpose of amending in you "whatsoever doth offend the eyes of your heavenly Father." This is followed by the assurance that true repentance, patience, trust, and submission will "help you forward in the right way that leadeth unto everlasting life."

The relationship to others is confirmed by the first prayer and remembered again by the suggestion that the trial of patience is also "for the example of others." And after the sick person has answered to each of the Articles of Faith, the minister will examine the sincerity of his repentance, including the state of his relations with others. If he has neglected to make his will, he must be admonished to do so—"for the better discharging of his conscience, and the quietness of his executours." If practicable, he is to be urged to be liberal to the poor.

Though the Order contains particular suggestions for extending or contracting the service, the briefest form, as in a pressing emergency, illustrates what is essential: true repentance, steadfast faith, and gratitude for redemption through Christ. Here comfort and consolation quickly assimilate penitence, though in a standard death consolation would also serve to support and direct the "right way" of dying. One knows that the traditional value of reasoned acceptance, connected as it was with the deep claims of free will, remained important. The purposes of Christian dying aimed at a prepared and active state, one of responsible and rational dying. Circumstances permitting, the conscientious minister would wish to assure himself and the sick person that the sins reported were clearly understood and rejected for the right reasons, lest they rankle and secrete obstructions to faith. The brief mention of Satan, temptations, and fear reflects the underlying sense that the approaches to death are filled with danger and conflict between the enemies and the friends of the soul. Psalm 71, prescribed for reading to the sick, begins, "In thee, O lord, have I put my trust, let me never be put to confusion." Trust, longing, hope, praise, and patience are re-affirmed. Deliverance is from others "that are against my soul":

> For mine enemies speak against me, and they that lay wait [*sic*] for my soul, take their counsel together, saying: God hath forsaken him, persecute him, and take him; for there is none to deliver him.

The human friends of the soul are the minister and those who are included in the opening prayer for God's mercy. If the trial of patience is to be "for the example of others," they are the witnessing others. Only "at the point of departure," in the "commendatory" prayer, are those present formally included in their own persons:

> And teach us who survive, in this and other like daily specta-cles of mortalitie, to see how frail and uncertain our own condition is, and to number our days, that we may seriously apply our hearts to that holy and heavenly wisdom, whilst we live here.

That teaching was part of the lifelong process of dying, by means of which the examined life might be spared the unknown spontaneities of an unexpected death. People thought of death, their own death, and witnessed deaths. What one learned from the deaths of others was easily summarized and reduced to rule and practice. But not everything was so surely ordered. The experience of awe and sympathy, being immedi-ate and personal and entering into the flow of both voluntary and spontaneous memory, could not but begin with and develop qualities of individual distinctness. Nor could the powerful sense of identification with the dying other retain, then or later, its highest level of intensity. While present one might well remember, intermittently and with con-flicting emotions variously acknowledged, that the present was a true image of but not yet the future, and that the drama of the engaged spectator still possessed a privileged dimension that separated him not only from the actor but from his imagination of the actor's experience. And again, later memory would reconstruct, develop, and change the experience, perhaps to interpret, perhaps to criticize what it was doing. So however authoritative they were, the instructions of what to think and feel would not surely correspond at all significant points with the experience of the witness and mourner. When one brought the lessons home and resumed one's life, the unquestionable answers were not likely to divert all questions arising from grief. There was much to be learned, and some of it could be written out in direct language or written into the words of poetry. Most of what we can learn will come from such sources.

As for the protagonist, the dying person who was the center of attention—if well prepared he, like the witnesses, would know the ruling expectations and to some degree the nature of possible interference and the correct means of overcoming such. His relationship with others, like the extent of his dependence, might vary with the individual and his effective state of readiness. Farewells might be formal or implicit. The emotions directed toward others were regulated by choice and capacity, but also by the ultimate need to direct emotions toward oneself and God. There was room for the play of personal strength and weakness, for hope and fear, and for the specific grief caused by regretted acts and failures to act, by personal and general sins. Helped by guidance and by pressure of the personal time drawing toward its absolute conclusion, in the expected course of dying the protagonist would raise regret to active understanding and cross the threshold of penitential rejection once and for all. Helped by an intensified sense of gratitude toward the Savior and free of all anxieties of the past, the dying person would be released into the faith of trusting and desiring only God, that ideal condition of religious life now ready to be achieved and to be validated by feeling divine acceptance in the joy of the answering assurance of faith.

The design so described, while allowing room for individual and intervening variations and developments, presents an ideal conclusion that cannot be known. The design itself, however, bespeaks that knowledge and may be advanced further by the testimony of witnesses. One recognizes that a protagonist may retain some of the detached view of a spectator, by force of keen intellectual capacity, but he may also resemble an incompetent spectator and suffer from a numbing disablement. (One sees and hears of the blurred disjunctions that make the dying wonder whether and how what is happening is happening to them.) It is clear that much of one's knowledge must come from actual spectators and their reports in prose and poetry.

The formal design I have sketched, though widely subscribed to, was not an absolute necessity for a good death. All of the preparation may have been done in advance, as by the soldier entering battle, or by the person submitted to a public execution. Though death makes all equal, one does not ordinarily expect the formal design to be very prominent in reporting, say, the recent death of a monarch. So Donne delivers a sermon at Denmark House in the presence of King James's body and concludes with dignified and measured praise. On the death itself an invisible curtain is drawn; other things hold all the attention. To illustrate with a single example, Donne offers a carefully wrought image from which all distracting details are excluded: the dead king is an admirable crystal glass, but we can see ourselves in him because it is a glass "darkned on the backside" by our human nature, by natural infirmities by original and actual sin.[2] When William Camden writes of Queen Elizabeth's religious death, he does so with carefully selected and interpreted details:

> Then being admonished by the Archbishop, to have her thoughts onely upon God. *I doe,* said she, *neither goeth my minde astray from him.* And when she could not use her tongue as an Instrument of prayer, with her hands and eyes, she directed to God the devotion of her heart; praying even in this, that she seemed to grieve because she could not pray.
>
> Shortly after, upon the 24. of March, being the Eve of the Annunciation of the blessed Virgin *Mary,* (being the very same day whereon she was borne) being called out of the prison of her flesh, into her heavenly Country, she quietly departed this life, in that good manner of death as *Augustus* wished for himself. . . . let her live in the very hearts of all true Englishmen. . . . Being that she was a Queene, who hath so long, and with so great wisedome governed her Kingdomes, as (to use the words of her Successour, who *in sincerity confessed so much;) the like hath not beene read or heard of, either in our time, or since the daies of the Romane Emperour* Augustus.[3]

Bacon is interested in defending the piety, moderation, constancy, and steadiness in Elizabeth's religious conduct; though he partly masks his own position, these virtues are presented as admirable, and they appear in her whole conduct of the affairs of state (which affairs include those of the established religion). He too records the resemblance between her death and that of Augustus, but he seems to prefer the trope of singularity to the expression of mental habits akin to those of typology. The necessary praise of James he handles with grace and dignity, like a statesman. As for Elizabeth, only time can praise her truly: "which, so long a course as it has run, has produced nothing in this sex like her, for the administration of civil affairs."[4] His main argument is her happiness, "for praise is the tribute of men, felicity the gift of God" (p. 461).

She obtained at last by an easy and gentle death that *euthanasia* which Augustus Caesar was wont so earnestly to pray for; and which is noted in the case of that excellent Emperor Antoninus Pius, whose death wore the appearance of a sweet and placid sleep. . . . She was not tormented either with desire of life, or impatience of sickness, or pangs of pain: none of the symptoms were frightful or loathsome; but all of that kind which showed rather the frailty than the corruption and dishonour of nature. For a few days before her death . . . she was struck with paralysis; and yet she retained her powers of speech . . . and of mind and of motion; only somewhat slower and duller. And this state of her body lasted only a few days, as if it were less like the last act of life than the first step to death. For to continue long alive with the faculties impaired is a miserable thing, but to have the sense a little laid asleep, and so pass quickly to death, is a placid and merciful period and close of life. (pp. 451–52)

Before I go on, I want to suggest how Camden and Bacon help to illustrate some of the purposes of my present discourse. Camden is a sincere eulogist emphasizing what he believes to be most important for the historical record. He wishes to move others who are pious like himself and will respond to the essentials of "the right way of dying," who are accustomed to receiving, uncritically, the indirect evidence of witnesses, the direct eloquence of the eulogist, and the supplementary evidence of God's design to be noted by analogies drawn from the sacred calendar of events in time. He is conservative with no sense of strain. But he also writes like a "progressive" contemporary by noting a prestigious secular analogy that praises the new king by quoting his praise.[5]

Bacon's "essay" is more reserved and is presented as an act of rationally admiring judgment. He is careful to bring up many of the matters of pious expectation, but he does not follow them through in ways that would fulfill the established expectations. The right words ring out like bells, but the full satisfactions of their consonance will be heard only by uncritical readers who supply what they expect and do not closely attend the apparently casual divarications. The interpretations that advance his sense of Elizabeth's historical character and his values are managed in a diplomatic syntax and rhetoric that appeal to those conscious that they are living in a new age with more exacting standards of rational judgment—and he does all this under the flexible theme that her successful reign, and other evidences of her happiness, were the gift of God. The distinction between the last stage of life and the stage of death—however mild-mannered, or even suggesting intellectual humility in its tentativeness—is radical in its implications, for it suggests that one *can* (perhaps *may*, perhaps *should*) think of life and death apart from each other. Yet both Camden and Bacon seem to agree upon the general criteria for acknowledging a "happy death."

The *Phaedo* recorded an unrivaled story of happiness in death and, as if by accident, scattered some unforgettable standards. It showed how a happy death might also be thought of as the last act of life and did not require an uneasy imagistic separation to mark "the first step" to death. "Whether it is better to live or die, God knows, but I think no man knows, as Socrates, about to die, said in Cicero's book." Thus Petrarch in 1371, having left a sickbed over which the physicians had concluded that he was to die about midnight. In Petrarch's own summing up, no friend "should have any other thought or hope than that of making a good end."[6] Toward the close of a long life the proximity of death gave his own previous questions and answers the distaste of an alien luxury, and he preferred simpler answers. Writing to Boccaccio he defends, against friendly advice, the uses of the intellectual life and its pleasant labors. He will not complete his work with his life and therefore, perhaps, can express the wish to do so.

> But since that is too much to hope for, I hope that death may find me reading or writing, or, if it be Christ's will, praying and weeping. (p. 302)

The happy death will "find" him doing what he has always done as part of the normal course of living. Though the choice and timing are not his, the simple hope is.

An earlier letter, reviewing the personal history of his "deep consciousness of the brevity of life," acknowledges surprise "that with such thoughts and cares I should have been so led astray by youthful loves and errors."

> Now, looking both forward and back, I recognize the truth of what I read; I experience what then I imagined. I see myself rushing to my end with such speed that I cannot describe it or easily imagine it. I need no authority of poet and philosopher. I am my own witness, my own author. (p. 202)

Wondering what further to say or not say, he tapped at the paper with his pen top:

> I reflected how in that brief interval time was flowing on, and I was flowing with it, slipping down, departing, or to use the

23

right word, dying. We are continually dying; I while I am writing these words, you while you are reading them, others when they hear them or fail to hear them, we are all dying. I shall be dying when you read this, you die while I write, we both are dying, we all are dying, we are dying forever. (p. 203)

The element of surprise finds its way back, though it is not now directed toward the personal state of youthful inadvertence. The power of surprise becomes part of the imaginative experience and its expression. All must die; all are on the course or will be. The old message is explored and turned as if it were a free-standing object of beauty, one representing rigorous truth but to be handled with free pleasure. One is reminded of Petrarch's conviction (and consolation) "that of all earthly delights none is more noble than literature, none longer-lasting, sweeter, more constant, none that so readily endows its practitioner with a splendid cloak for every circumstance, without cost or trouble" (p. 302). The correspondent reading the letter will appreciate the discourse on time and dying. The others who will hear these words represent the power of literature to last, and the vital force of the voice of an author who is read. When others "fail to hear" the words, the alternative state of personal oblivion slips with a quiet wrench into a discourse on universal dying. But the man reading the eloquence, and its masterly flow through the linking and relinking of its members, may well be startled by that literal application of his own temporal place in the correspondence: "I shall be dying when you read this, you die while I write."

When Petrarch's Laura responds to the monster Death by saying, "Do thou unto me as thou doest to all men,"[7] we are surprised by the simple perfection of her answer. May we think that she speaks better than the author can speak for himself while enjoying the nimble weight of the pen in his hand, while not forgetting the noble delights of literature and the availability of "a splendid cloak for every circumstance"? When the dying Lady Jane Pawlet in Jonson's elegy ministers with brief precision to the distraught feelings of husband, son, sisters, parents, friends,

> And, in her last act, taught the Standers-by,
> With admiration, and applause to die![8]

we may find our admiration encumbered by surprise. Lady Jane is embarrassing, at least if we discover ourselves to be casual visitors to her performance. She does everything in the book with the hurried ease of a consciously perfect hostess; in comparison, the greatest masters of dying seem like inspired but clumsy pioneers, or like narrow specialists who have studied and need to be studied if we are to admire them properly. Still, in this abundance of right doing there is at least some latency, in addition to Jonson's reporting only the effect of her "last act." For her sympathetic interest in the feelings of the witnesses also represents a large gesture of assurance that her own interests are well in hand and will meet her schedule.

Other protagonists, as the records amply illustrate, will find their own ways to go beyond the considerate decencies acquired by the habits of living and will leave "for the example of others" not only the trial of their patience but some unexpected flower springing from that solemn ground. Last acts and last words are memorable and are sought out by the persistent human interest that absorbs ordinary and eccentric details indifferently. "Late" and "last" may be remembered as one, along with transitions, like "the first step" to death.

As part of his biographical duty Izaak Walton gives particular attention to the art of describing death. He admires the lives of his subjects, and he admires all their deaths. Let us look at Sir Henry Wotton's end, but notice first that Walton puts on the record, early, certain facts that interest him: that Henry's father Thomas and Thomas's Uncle Nicholas both (while "in perfect health") foresaw "the very days of their own death."[9] If we expect those facts to be recorded for the sake of an echo that we may then hear, it is plain that we are not quite in tune with the nature of Walton's interest. As for Sir Henry, "finding some decays of health" he made his will "about two years before his death" (p. 141). The document is a remarkable one, and the formal schedule of dying begins here.

The summer before death he revisited Winchester College and confided some striking observations to his companion on the journey. After his return (about five months before death), "he became much more retir'd, and contemplative" (p. 149). What he said then to "learned Mr. *John Hales*" in summation of his life and coming death is very strong in its answer to death. But in what he mentions in his brief review of a full and active life one can see matters left ajar, but pronounced upon, as wonder takes the place of troubles and questions, as in a drawing composed of strangely quickened, austere lines. So the view of the life receives its particular shape and resolution from the position of looking back on it and closing it in preparation for death. Though only a reported personal speech spoken to a friend and answering the impulse of particular circumstances, it has qualities that may challenge Petrarch's definition of "literature." It does not, and does not wish to, display "a splendid cloak for every circumstance, without cost or trouble."

> I have in my passage to my grave met with most of those Joys
> of which a discoursive soul is capable: and, being entertain'd
> with more inferior pleasures then the sons of men are usually
> made partakers of: nevertheless, in this voyage I have not
> always floated on the calm Sea of Content; but have often met
> with cross winds and storms, and with many troubles of mind
> and temptations to evil. And yet, though I have been and am a
> man compass'd about with humane frailties, Almighty God
> hath by his grace prevented me from making shipwrack of
> faith and a good Conscience; the thought of which is now the
> joy of my heart, and I most humbly praise him for it; And I
> humbly acknowledge that it was not my self but he that hath
> kept me to this great age, and let him take the glory of his great
> mercy.—And my dear Friend, I now see that I draw near my
> harbour of death: that harbor, that will secure me from all the
> future storms and waves of this restless world; and I praise
> God I am willing to leave it, and expect a better; that world,
> wherein dwelleth Righteousness, and I long for it. (p. 149)

About a month before the end he became weaker and began the
burning of some writings from his youth and from "the busie part of
his life." "These and several unusual expressions to his Servants and
Friends, seem'd to foretell that the day of his death drew near." There
are no more quotations or transitions reported, but only the testimony
(unquoted) of "many friends" and of his last letters, which all agree in
showing him well prepared, patient, and "free from all fear." At last, in
the tenth attack of a quotidian fever,

> his better part, that part of Sir *Henry Wotton* which could not
> dye, put off mortality with as much content and chearfulness
> as human frailty is capable of; being then in great tranquillity
> of mind, and in perfect peace with God and man. (p. 150)

One must conclude that his belonged among the happy deaths, and
must note the absence of the detailed matters that characterize the life
and are energetically brought forward to mark the approaches to death.
We are told which recurrence of his fever was the fatal one, but we are
not invited to be curious about the individual process by which a dynamic state ("as much content and chearfulness as human frailty is
capable of") is composed into an ideal moment, partly veiled. Wotton's
life and character are presented as a coherent whole; he shares virtues
with worthy ancestors who are singled out for suggestive description,
but his life does not mirror theirs and his death is not a summation of his

own life but a heightened moment of departure. Its qualities are derived from the life and character; so we are encouraged to believe but are spared argument and demonstration. The death has a shape of its own and also answers to the traditional standards of the good religious death. Walton presents a moment of unified equilibrium, but the coherence is reduced to essentials, and the art of the biographer depends upon our remembering, but not obtruding, such details as Wotton's declaration of faith, good conscience, and willingness to die.

While *preparing for death* an unusual protagonist might participate in the preparation of his death and act as if he were author of the scene, or, from another perspective, both subject and collaborator of biographers and elegists to come. Such a protagonist might seem indifferent to the art of arranging transitions between the shape of the life and that of the death. He would nevertheless wish to convey signs that the life maintained its coherent shape and that the death did not lack the proper assurance.

Sir Thomas More knowingly put his life in jeopardy while defending himself with skill and determination. He also fully prepared himself to die—that is, he intensified and deepened a process that was a regular part of his conscious life. Though his writings in the Tower go well beyond the purpose of shaping himself to the experience at hand, they establish, as well as art, argument, and devotion can, a record of settled personal conviction. In all that lay within the reach of reason, faith, and will, he was the author of his own death. In addition to the written record, among the last reports, pieced together as they had to be, were these accounts: More's welcoming the "good tidings" of the final messenger, Thomas Pope, and comforting him in the best personal and religious form; sending some of his last money to the executioner; being mocked on the way to the scaffold by an angry woman; saying merrily of the weak condition of the scaffold stairs, "I pray you Master Lieutenant, see me safe up, and for my coming down let me shift for myself"; kneeling in prayer; and finally addressing the executioner "with a cheerful countenance," encouraging him with a courteous jest intended to remind him of his duty, which included the art of aiming well.

The reported actions fit the life and seem a believable account of More's intentions concerning the true appearance of his death. One or two matters may perhaps deserve a second look. If More had been able to arrange any personal revisions, he might, one imagines, have sent the executioner thirty pieces of gold, after the example of St. Cyprian. But a wise biographer might have wanted to persuade him that things were very well as they were. Yet one fortuitous occurrence introduces a potentially dissonant note. The woman who taunted More on the way to his death can have had no place in the harmony of his own planning and should have surprised him. (Perhaps that is why son Roper happens not to include the episode in his story.) But a self-controlled, quick-witted man used to profound searching must have soon recognized what his own meditations on Christ's death had fully explicated. This event, beyond the power to control if things are happening on their own and not yet slipping into the rule of story and legend, may be welcomed as a true sign of grace, bringing the candidate for a worthy religious death a short step closer to the inimitable shame and loneliness of Christ's death.

One may look differently at More's impromptu witticism addressed to "Master Lieutenant." That it expresses part of the character of More's life as he and others knew it, and a part he enjoyed expressing as an author, one may acknowledge at once. Questions will emerge slowly, for the moment itself is inviolable, even when it is but recreated by first reports or by the first reading of such. Nor do questions lend themselves to a swift and simple answer—one, say, that refers to the category of gallows humor. The inspired wit is immediately winning and admirable to those conscious of their own human frailty—that is, to anyone able to imagine himself in More's position, trusting his courage and faith perhaps, or even his acting ability, but surely not trusting the ready inspiration of his wit. Subsequent reflection may reasonably ask whether the wit is inspired or only quick, impromptu, and detachable from this unique scene, like a joke that may be borrowed, revised, and applied to a similar occasion. It expresses a strange, individual freedom within a ceremony governed by fixed expectations. It does not, however, as late or last words might do, go straight to the heart of meaning to sum up the life or the death. It is markedly individual and spontaneous, and yet both the immediate and the reflective response may also ask whether the wit does not strongly suggest the authority and import of a sign.

Insofar as the humor represents his cheerful acceptance of death, one may relate the merriment to an assurance that has purged fear and is rejoicing at the nearness of his entrance into eternal life. That would be another way of celebrating the "good tidings" he received from the weeping Thomas Pope. Perhaps it is also another way of postvalidating that still earlier stage—when conflicts involving a good cause were carefully tested by all honorable means of opposition, so that death was in conscience not desired until it was officially pronounced. (Though intricate, these were well-charted conditions that More needed to master with a clear head and conscience.) This is no lingering deathbed achievement of "as much content and chearfulness as humane frailty is capable of." More's cheerfulness is unqualified, not a tranquil state but an active one, and there is no trace of frailty. The kneeling prayer is addressed to God; the expressions of a merry heart are addressed to the world, however we want to understand this puzzling state.

To the world the witticism may appear to be a clear achievement of courage and self-control, recognizable virtues of life, and may be the believable outward sign of the inner assurance of faith as well as a moving argument that the good man's cause is indeed a true one. More will obey the king and speak no more than a few words from the scaffold, but he cannot be unaware that, though he has reluctantly accepted advice not to put on his best apparel, "as one that had been invited to some solemn feast," his conduct will make the right impres sion. If this is not the chief and last business of his soul, the line of demarcation must be a very fine one, for here the divine and the human touch, or almost do. His death will also serve as an example to others— family, friends, others who may be persecuted for their faith, on- lookers, and the enemies he has forgiven. If the witticism does not sum up the life, does not speak to God or "imitate" Christ; if it may seem to regard death as only a law (as pagan philosophers taught), or as here only the instrument of law and not the last step of affliction and punish- ment decreed by a loving God; if the witticism registers its effects in the highly individual, exuberant expression of a carefree man about to die—how are we to understand it so that all of the careful obligations of a good Christian death may be judged as perfectly and harmoniously fulfilled? My purpose is not to answer these questions but only to indicate that they may be raised without denying the formal rules and conditions More accepted when he went about preparing his own death.

Some of the difficulty may inhere in the anomalous case, the happy death, further complicated by the fact that it is imposed by man on man and that the victim has chosen to reject the words of the binding script which would have released him from the sentence against his life. But if we think that Socrates' dying words in the *Phaedo* are touchingly witty, we think so because we find them strange and surprising—an urbanely wry summing up by the hero who has just made a full display of his character and of the arguments that concern the philosopher's life, death, and immortality: "Crito, I owe a cock to Asclepius; will you remember to pay the debt?"

In 1618, after the complete failure of the Guiana expedition, fol- lowed by a quick trial and the decision to execute the suspended judgment of 1603 which had found him guilty of treason, Sir Walter Raleigh threw himself into a concentrated effort to accomplish—what? The only place and time available to him were those of his public execution. If one may venture to name ends, he sought, for one thing, a kind of honorable defeat. In political terms this involved some diplomatic and carefully indirect show of resistance against the powers that had defeated him and to which he was by law submitting—a resistance free to act within the customs, decorum, and traditions of dignity allowed by open justice to a proved and defeated enemy of the state. His actions could not affect his peace with those who held him in their power, not in any practical and immediate ways, but his actions could affect his peace in personal, or religious, or unknown future ways. To name another end, he sought to change a brief episode in the political life of the nation into a skirmish and then into the decisive battle of a major personal campaign to determine the final shape of his life as he prepared his death.

If the difficult category of happy deaths may embrace generous margins, "it was (you may say) satisfactory." Faced with necessity and little time, Raleigh accomplished most of what he seems to have intended. That is not a sure category of happiness, or even of pleasure, but it would take some effort not to believe that Raleigh enjoyed most of what he was doing. With a small amount of recovered knowledge we can imagine the anger and other passions of those who wanted his death; only deliberate scholarship can piece together the intricate play of national and international interests and their dubieties of conception, analysis, and timing. But Raleigh's death is easily remembered, the striking details and the general effect of heroic dignity to the last, a solitary figure presenting himself to the eyes and ears of those assembled for the spectacle, his advantages being those of character and skill and the unique attention commanded by a scene only the conclusion of which was certain.

The normal requirements of a religious death were satisfied, though fixed enemies (less well remembered) would protest that the notorious pride continued unabated under hypocrisy. Sir Lewis Stukeley, smarting from having been forgiven on the scaffold by Raleigh (who nevertheless felt obliged by "charity" to warn the world of Stukeley's treachery, "that all Men may take good heed of him"), wrote his own "Appologie":

> I could not but abhorre his hipocrisie; which the better to unmaske, I seemed to condisent unto him after I was out of hope . . . by perswasion to rectifie his affection and iudg-

ment, which feare had over strongly infatuated in him to his ruine. . . . nor were his benefittes any thinge ever to me, much lesse his desert, or the opportunitie of his favour such as could induce any man that hath the conscience to love him selfe to partake with his ruine.[10]

Stukeley may speak with personal conviction, but any wise advocate would know that the opponent had already seized the right moment and platform and was therefore practically irrefutable.

Dr. Robert Tounson, dean of Westminster, who confessed Raleigh, left a more impartial and professional account. When he "began to incourage him against the feare of death," he found that established part of his office, contrary to the settled rules of procedure, brushed aside as not needed:

And when I told him, that the deare servants of God, in better causes than his, had shrunke backe and trembled a little, he denyed not, but yet gave God thanks, he never feared death . . . with much more to that purpose, with such confidence and cheerefulnesse, that I was fain to divert my speach another way. . . . If it ["this extraordinary boldnesse"] sprong from the assurance he had of the love and favour of God, of the hope of his Salvation by Christ, and his own innocency, as he pleaded, I sayd he was an happy man; but if it were out of an humour of vain glory or carelessnesse or contempt of death, or senselessnesse of his own estate, he were much to be lamented, &c. For I told him, that Heathen Men had sett as little by their lives as he could doe, and seemed to dye as bravely.[11]

In any event though not happy, the minister was at last satisfied enough, though worried again after Raleigh took his last Communion on the morning of the execution, for Raleigh was "very cheerfull and merry."

After a long speech that held and moved his audience while answering the main charges against him and affirming his honesty ("to call God to Witness a falsehood at the time of Death, is . . . impious, and there is no hope for such an one. . . . If I speak not true, O Lord, let me never come into thy Kingdom"), he concluded with a public prayer:

And now I intreat you all to join with me in Prayer, that the Great God of Heaven, whom I have grievously offended, being a Man full of Vanity, and have lived a sinful Life, in all sinful Callings, having been a Souldier, a Captain, a Sea-Captain, and a Courtier, which are all places of Wickedness and Vice; that God (I say) would forgive me, and that he would receive me into everlasting Life. So I take my leave of you all, making my Peace with God.[12]

The prayer, intended to be heard and not read critically, was at least adequate to the occasion, though by the standards of the times mild in its fervor and remarkably general in the terms of confession. By unspoken agreement, however, and because of the trained charity of listeners who know themselves to be vain and sinful, nothing in the prayer may be adduced against the speech defending himself to the world. That remains intact and unaffected. Furthermore, the peace with God does not have to be felt as made in the public prayer but only as sealed; presumably, a deeper personal transaction has occurred elsewhere. A sinner about to die is acknowledging and rejecting the sinful state of having lived as all men do in a sinful world. Anyone present could make, or begin, his own repentance thus, needing only to substitute his particular "calling." But a Dr. Tounson would not find his deeper doubts and hesitations resolved.

Tounson's fears at Raleigh's denial of fear were well grounded, and if More had been an expert consultant he would surely have agreed. "Heathen Men had sett as little by their lives as he could doe," but Christians had the benefit of better knowledge and sounder doctrine. Not valuing one's life, like not fearing (though God be thanked for the gift), suggested a concealed or unconsidered opposition to God's will, and perhaps a "contempt of death" which dishonored Christ's own sacrificial fear and pain. But other witnesses, not privy to the confessional and perhaps less interested in the fine points of theological criticism, responded to the eloquence and perfect calm as proof that a sincere and noble man was at peace with his conscience and with God. Even the unexpected individual gestures of the man, though they must have excited sudden responses, would also have been drawn back from their strangeness and would have served to confirm the main impression. I think of these gestures: Raleigh's merry witticisms, his requesting to check the sharpness of the axe and his quasi-religious joke ("sharp Medicine . . . for all Diseases"); his refusing the blindfold; his needing to command the executioner, who, as if collaborating with the spirit of legend, failed to respond to Raleigh's signal and had to be spoken to directly: "What dost thou fear? Strike, man!"[13]

The audience was public and not a judicial body of scholarly theologians; nevertheless, even the critical observers and professionals alertly studying the performance detected not the slightest sign of imperfect composure. In a publication forty years after the event Francis Osborne sums the matter up in a compact equilibrium:

His death was by him managed with *so high and Religious a resolution,* as if *a Roman* had acted *a Christian,* or rather *a Christian a Roman.*[14]

To us the judgment may seem to quiver in its delicate balance, but we are likely to be more interested in the implications of "managing" and "acting," which lead to familiar aesthetic and psychological problems and to the assumption that Raleigh's "resolution" was shallow albeit impressive. If it was not shallow but simple and complete and beyond our ken and that of some orthodox contemporaries, we have a different kind of problem. But at least we can dismiss one possible ambiguity of interpretation. Osborne's language seems to have things under pressure and may expose the trace of strange news, but we cannot mistake his admiration for Raleigh and contempt for James. The sentence on Raleigh's death is followed by an account of James's setting forth in print

a Declaration, which according to *the ordinary successe of such Apologies, rendered the condition of that proceeding worse in the worlds opinion:* It begins thus, *Though I take my selfe bound to give no other account of my actions but to God; yet* etc.

As I suggested of questions concerning More's management of his death, especially the exuberant show of wit—though answers (culminating in canonization) are not lacking, they do not simply abrogate the recognition that legitimate questions can be raised about the acting out of a death that certainly fulfilled all obligations required of an unquestionably devout Christian. Raleigh's case, to be sure, is different, but the legitimate questions are not altogether different. More's death was, I say with some bating of breath, a happy one that did not intend to stray into the precincts of the tragic; such a death is a wonder that may stir deep satisfactions but not stifle questions. Raleigh's death may be too complicated and strenuous to be felt as "happy," creating as it does the fascinating air of conflicts-in-resolution, not unlike the spell of a tragic scene well acted. Yet many onlookers, responding to natural feelings and to the thoughts deemed appropriate to the occasion, would have considered their own deaths in his. From what one knows of the scene, of its effects, and of the audience, one may surmise that many would have felt that if they should be able to act "with so high and religious a resolution," their deaths would be "happy."

To think of death continually was the traditional teaching, supported by many and varied arguments (and with no opposing school of thought in the field), but Montaigne, who thought, also noticed the easy freedom of peasants dying without the benefit of much thinking. If not to think of death is indeed a divine gift, one might have better enjoyed the possession by not venturing to debate the issue with authorities.

If *at the end* Raleigh had the gift, he managed it most astutely by concealing it while prominently exhibiting a more ambiguous virtue but one that men, their feelings aroused by a death scene, find it hard to sift and question, the ability not to fear. Whatever Raleigh's conscious and unconscious motives and their margin of error as seen from above, he managed his death while using all the great advantages of the scene— less, I think, to shape his death as an episode apart than as a final act of life, presenting himself before others in a departure and farewell asserting dominance over and a favorable judgment of his life. It is an example, however different from More's, also directed toward others. How much that tells of the whole story no one can say.

Raleigh makes a spectacular case and may obscure the main purpose of this stage of the discourse. To glance back for a moment: the rules for dying were derived from accepted traditions of religious thought and from the good and bad examples that were supplied by Scripture and by history (loosely defined). The rules necessarily responded to a "higher" and a "lower" consideration. On the one hand, the recurrent fact of dying had to be brought into a steady and elevated relationship with God's design as interpreted by Christian faith and reason. On the other hand, individual Christians had to be instructed and helped in the practical difficulties of dying. The main features of agreement remained remarkably stable. To be sure, changes in doctrine occurred, and the changes reflected altering conditions of historical experience. Together these brought about shifts in emphasis—in the long view, of discernible importance, but less so in the short view. For nothing in the long history of thinking about death was likely to be quite disproved or forgotten. Besides, the main features were simple and of proved efficacy.

And yet—a main subject of this book—even within the established habits of thought and response, individuals could think, feel, say, and do things not exactly predictable by or conforming to standard expectations. Though such phenomena could always be explained after the fact, the explanations were not likely to achieve the same degree of simple agreement possessed by the traditional pattern of fear-repentance-acceptance-joy. To digress for a moment, even here one may notice that joy, though the last stage on the schedule of dying, was also the immediate experience of entering eternity and was not always demonstrated before death. Joy may perhaps be thought an ideal realization, one that perfectly completes a pattern answering to religious, logical, and aesthetic desires. There were examples of demonstrated joy, and also others where joy might be imputed, but also very good examples that did not visibly progress beyond the stage of reasoned acceptance. To consider my own catalogue of examples, Petrarch seems to aim no higher than the decent good end of acceptance. Camden emphasizes the peace of Elizabeth's death and her release into subsequent joy. The account of Wotton's admirable death rests on his acceptance, though he was quoted earlier as feeling joy in his gratitude toward God's grace in bringing him through the serious perils of life. More's visible exhilaration may be believed to express an invisible joy. One may or may not believe that Raleigh felt authentic religious acceptance, but one would not know how to go about believing that he felt religious joy.

To return to the subject of departures from the standard expectations: aspects of Platonic and Stoic thought on dying had long been assimilated into Christian thought, especially the central rationalistic emphasis, that the dying person understand his preparation for death. But the Renaissance brought about a new and wider acquaintance with the original sources, and at a time that favored some new kinds of interest. There was increased attention to observing what men actually do and to regarding such small facts as not simply and unquestionably aberrations from what they ought to do. Nor were the powerful institutions of church and state exempted from such attention. This is intended as a general reminder that the protagonists and witnesses of dying who did not exactly conform to the standard expectations were not therefore isolated from other precedents and supports of the times. When we come to consider some views of Bacon and Montaigne, the issue will exhibit more practical dimensions.

There is also a side of orthodox thought on dying which may be emphasized at this point. For in spite of the confidence and stability of established doctrine and practice, it was understood, more by tactful implication than public debate, that the very moment of death retained an unknowable core of mystery—if not what the dying individual ought to think and feel, what he actually thought and felt, and what God thought. In the resonant words of Psalm 68:20, "And unto God the Lord belong the issues from death." Though this is the God of salvation who delivers His people from the dangers threatening physical death, He is also the God who watches over, decides, and receives all the "issues of death," including the final judgment of salvation. So far as one could observe, not all good deaths were identical, not even all "happy" ones. God's will contained attributes of reservation and latency best acknowledged by the active devotion of prayer and praise. So

whatever a Dr. Tounson might reasonably conclude of a Raleigh's behavior, he could never deny that God might, for unquestionable reasons, have dispensed with both natural and supernatural fear and its
normal functions in Christian dying. And therefore orthodox thoughts
on death might remain confident and stable—the best and only practical guide for an ecclesiastical representative supervising a Christian
death, even while not denying his personal and ecclesiastical limitations. But still the dying man might find himself thinking, feeling,
saying, and doing things not exactly conforming to the authorized
advice for the occasion. And the witnesses would have still greater
latitude to observe and respond to what they thought they saw and felt.

I conclude this part of my discussion of matters not always and
fully in accord with the standard answers by looking more closely at
some answers and questions concerning fear. If Raleigh's exceptional
death alerts us to the special problems of fear and its absence, we should
now be in a better position to consider the ordinary problems.

Fear of God is "the beginning of wisdom" (Ps. 111:10; Job 28:28;
Prov. 9:10; Ecclus. 1:15). In Ecclesiasticus that fear is called a "holy
knowledge" (1:16) and will lead to favor and blessing at the day of death
(1:13,18). That fear also "maketh a merry heart" (1:12) and leads to
"glory, and gladness, and rejoicing, and a joyful crown" (1:11). Add to
these the weighty injunction, "In everything you do, remember your
end and you will never sin." (In omnibus operibus tuis memorare
novissima tua, et in aeternum non peccabis—7:40.) This was for centuries the most familiar redaction of the wisdom of dying daily, as St.
Paul said of himself (1 Cor. 15).

The wisdom could be illustrated by reference to the reasoning of
ethical philosophers relating fear to the moral restraint of evil and defining the end of happiness and confirmed and elaborated by the numerous
comments of authoritative doctors of the church. Fear death, fear judgment, fear hell, fear the loss of eternal good; fear your own deception,
your pride, vanity, attachment to life and possessions, your luke-
warmness, your insufficient anxiety, and so forth. Utter loss of fear was
a recognizable symptom of despair and the acceptance of damnation.
But fear was the beginning of wisdom, leading from avoidance of evil
to "holy knowledge," to the glad acceptance of death and judgment,
and to the certitude of eternal life.

Though appointed to serve wisdom, fear was a passion and therefore an unreliable servant that might veer from the path. Instead of
remaining true to the elevated end of fearing the loss of eternal good (a
positive state in which fear proved itself prepared to be transformed into
love), the passion might revert to or fix on any of the many lesser and

transitional objects of fear. Fear of death, while only in the first stage of the progress, might poison the beginning by violent perturbations. "Timor mortis conturbat me." "Conturbat" signals the kind of disturbance that disables the quiet necessary for the proper function of reason. Nevertheless, the traditions according to which reason understood its own nature and its accepted responsibility for the errant will would not regard such occasional wavering of reason as proof that it had really left its office. For even the mind disabled by fear of some lesser object would not lose its capacity to recognize and judge the subject of its own inadequate performance, though such an experience might both increase the fear and diminish the regulating function of reason.

The sickness was considered a dangerous one for which there were standard remedies, but these did not always succeed. A good man expecting a good death, toward which he had long traveled with reasonable encouragement and assurance, might still find himself bewildered when his latest preparations did not proceed as they were supposed to. By the bookkeeping of Puritan experts, a troubled mind and fear of salvation should not have suddenly crept in upon a John Knox or an Increase Mather.[13] Yet no one, however thorough in his preparations, could regard himself as surely immune to late revelations of an ominous kind. If acceptance did not erase all tracks of the progress guided by fear, and if late thoughts were not delivered from the efforts of rising above death, judgment, and hell, to be filled only with the plenitude of eternal life, then the habits of a lifetime of training might have to ask whether a calm certitude long possessed was not premature. For such a state of assurance was not without its own dangers, as wise fear was supposed to understand.

The last revelation at the time of death could not be known in advance, and when it was known it could not be communicated. Against the unthinkable, faith had to depend upon solemn, authorized forms of thinking to know that it was faith and was immune to the discovery of any flaws in the transition from reason to faith. The alternative was unthinkable.

For troubles of this kind the older forms of devotion were better equipped. Sir Thomas More can always treat fear by meditating on the "great horror and fear that our Savior had in his own flesh against his painful Passion." Unburdened by the dignities and responsibilities of "election," More can observe that feeling the fear of death does not need to presage failure. Such men can stand "for all that fear full fast" and endure "the brunt" better than those who begin by feeling "no fear at all." And there is always the word of comfort based on the assurance of scriptural promise, that God "will not suffer us to be tempted above our power" (More, *Dialogue of Comfort against Tribulation*, pt. 3, chap. 17; Ps. 91:5–6; 1 Cor. 10:13).

It was Luther's brave discovery to push fear beyond the safer limits, even to immerse himself in the experience of despair.[16] His reasoning was based upon the sound precedents of belief in man's inherent sinfulness, but the heroism of Luther's spiritual adventure did not need to be followed literally, and with his emphasis, to produce accepted benefits to Reformation doctrine. If the old law forced man to know his sins thoroughly, that was a necessary stage for the proper acceptance of the new covenant and the transfer of hope in salvation from works of moral law to faith. Like penitence, the purpose of such a stage was preparation for ascending to a higher stage. Saints and others of acutely sensitive conscience might not be able to satisfy their sense of personal obligation without proceeding as far as they could, even to the extreme of despair. It was also a way of testing personal faith in one's utter dependence upon God and saving grace. But the full intensity of Luther's choice was not binding as a principle. In *Samson Agonistes* Milton will make full use of the potentialities of Samson's heroic religious despair, but in *Paradise Lost,* summarizing through the prophetic Michael the evolution of Christian doctrine, he keeps the main lines brief and clear while suggesting that the "works" of Roman Catholic tradition are still burdened by "shadowy types" of the old law, but that the "works" of the true covenant are those of faith:

> So law appears imperfect, and but giv'n
> With purpose to resign them in full time
> Up to a better cov'nant, disciplined
> From shadowy types to truth, from flesh to spirit,
> From imposition of strict laws to free
> Acceptance of large grace, from servile fear
> To filial, works of law to works of faith.
>
> (PL 12.300–306)

Luther's personal contribution did, however, have its lasting effects on theological thought and temperament, but my purpose in mentioning it is a limited one. The strong insight and its emphasis challenged the rational optimism tirelessly applied to the problem of fear but not much interested in questioning itself or its methods. Luther added to the known problems of faith and to the stresses of the individual conscience, and thus to the individuality of death.

Bacon calls fear one of the two "predominant" emotions, but he prefers to apply his mind to those aspects of the "characters of men's natures" "which are within our own command, and have force and operation upon the mind to affect the will and appetite and to alter manners." Still, knowledge of "the diseases and infirmities of the mind" is useful in moral and civil matters, and the poets and historians are "the best doctors of this knowledge." Civil states are built upon the foundation of reward and punishment, "employing the predominant affections of *fear* and *hope,* for the suppressing and bridling the rest."[17] Nature itself is the source of the fundamental fear that seeks to preserve life and to avoid the harmful.

> Nature knows not how to keep just measure—but together with salutary fears ever mingles vain and empty ones; insomuch that all things (if one could see into the heart of them) are quite full of Panic terrors; human things most of all; so infinitely tossed and troubled as they are with superstition (which is in truth nothing but a Panic terror), especially in seasons of hardship, anxiety, and adversity.[18]

Fear of death is influenced by ignorance and superstition, "as Children fear to go in the Dark," and also have their natural fear increased by "tales" (*Selected Writings,* p. 9). He acknowledges that a proper contemplation of death is "holy and religious," but he dismisses the fear that derives from nature as a "weak" passion. Religious fear is not his subject, and he limits himself to observing how other passions—such as love, revenge, grief—master the natural fear of death. But fear is enlarged, he says, echoing Montaigne, by the human contributions to a grimly ceremonial atmosphere:

> Groans and convulsions, and a discoloured face, and friends weeping, and blacks and obsequies, and the like, shew death terrible. (p. 10)

Bacon avoids seeming to argue with religious doctrines, except when he cites general materials from the safe periods of the past. He can make his own points against the philosophers such as the Stoics, who gave too much attention to death "and by their great preparations made it appear more fearful." Or, with more detail and scope:

> And it seemeth to me, that most of the doctrines of the philosophers are more fearful and cautionary than the nature of things requireth. So have they increased the fear of death in offering to cure it. For when they would have a man's whole life to be but a discipline or preparation to die, they must needs make men think that it is a terrible enemy against whom there is no end of preparing. . . . So have they sought to make

men's minds too uniform and harmonical, by not breaking
them sufficiently to contrary notions: the reason whereof I
suppose to be, because they themselves were men dedicated to
a private, free, and unapplied course of life. (p. 327)

Bacon deliberately limits his discourse to the "science" of man's
life in this world, and thus death can be viewed unemphatically as not
the aim of but the end to life. Consequently, fear is made to lack those
functions other observers have noted—functions that Bacon, one infers, would have found "too uniform and harmonical," unable to deal
with the "contrary notions" (though there seems to be a good supply of
these in the history of thinking about the certainties and uncertainties of
death). Bacon's own use of "contrary notions," however, is often more
politic than philosophical. For example, we read that "all the works of
Divine Providence in the World are wrought by winding and round-
about ways—where one thing seems to be doing, and another is doing
really—as in the selling of Joseph into Egypt, and the like." He then
translates that familiar notion of God's mysterious ways from one
sphere of discourse to furnish a metaphorical insight for another circuit
of discourse. In the wise conduct of the state, those at the helm can
"insinuate what they desire for the good of the people more successfully
by pretexts and indirect ways than directly."[19] If Bacon had been moved
to apply such "contrary notions" to the nature and uses of fear and
death, he would not have lacked materials for saying more than he is
content to say.

The "discreet and profitable" fears that nature also produces are
not neglected, but Bacon usually observes them acting under other
names than those belonging to "the diseases and infirmities of the
mind." So "boldness," he writes with some asperity, often prevails
when it would not if men were not foolish or weak. Boldness is blind
and cannot see "dangers and inconveniences" (which, one may add,
fear would never miss). But boldness is therefore "good in execution."
To see "dangers" is a kind of wise fear: "For in counsel it is good to see
dangers; and in execution not to see them, except they be very great"
(Selected Writings, p. 34).

The model behind Bacon's thought here is that of the traditional
tripartite soul, in which the executive will receives its orders from the
high command of judgment. Therefore, what may appear to be an
example of "contrary notions," or even, more surprising, a suggestion
that seems to concede some positive value to a form of not-thinking, is
instead a shrewd and useful translation of received ideas to practical
circumstances. The case is, I think, instructive—an illustration of

Bacon's general conservatism toward "contrary notions" that are not useful for exercising and strengthening his chosen programs of thought, but that might instead be dangerous to the whole "harmonical" enterprise he conceives. His own "contrary notions" are more often alternative notions that seem to challenge and test the discourse by the acuteness with which he unexpectedly matches the familiar idea and the concrete application. Thus in the following (and my last) example, his alternative notion directs us from errant thoughts of fear and death, or from considering the limits of boldness, or from the exotic thought of not-thinking, and instead follows the proved method of directing the mind, with optimistic encouragement, toward better and more desired results:

> He that dies in an earnest pursuit is like one that is wounded in hot blood; who, for the time, scarce feels the hurt; and therefore a mind fixed and bent upon somewhat that is good doth avert the dolours of death. (p. 11)

Turning to Montaigne, as Bacon and other Englishmen certainly did, one encounters immediate differences. Death is a subject of major and continuing interest to Montaigne, and his choosing to write as a private thinker and to avoid encroaching on religious topics does not itself separate him from the broad traditions of thought. He does not feel obliged to limit his views, or to repeat the church's privileged wisdom, or to seem to challenge that. He sets himself up as one of no authority, expressing his own peculiar mind, which is free to change, in essays that evolve in part from the genre of personal letters. He can claim not to teach but to report. In any case, he can and does affirm many accepted values; he is a trained master of the commonplaces of thought and argument, which he knows how to review in summary and apply, but he also in his own way seeks the odd angles of perspective, studies interstices, and cultivates "contrary notions." In taking up the old philosophical theme that life is a meditation on death, he declares that the last day of our life "is the master day, the day that is judge of all the others."[20] When that last day is to be acted, "there is no more pretending" (1.19.55). In judging other men's lives, he writes:

> In judging the life of another, I always observe how it ended; and one of my principal concerns about my own end is that it shall go well, that is to say quietly and insensibly. (1.19.55)

> And there is nothing that I investigate so eagerly as the death of men: what words, what look, what bearing they main-

tained at that time; nor is there a place in the histories that I note so attentively. (1.20.62)

His basic early advice is the familiar counsel of making rational preparations:

> Let us learn to meet it steadfastly and to combat it. . . . Let us rid it of its strangeness, come to know it, get used to it. Let us have nothing on our minds as often as death. (1.20.60)

When it does come there will be no surprises for him; he will be ready, with nothing to do except the personal business of dying. In the meantime, the true felicity of philosophical virtue, tranquillity, will be conferred by "disdain for death" (1.20.57), which frees us "from all subjection and constraint" (1.20.60). Indeed, "Our religion has no surer foundation than contempt for life" (1.20.64).

The last two statements begin moving toward "contrary notions." "The thing I fear most is fear," he writes, for fear "is even more unwelcome and unbearable than death itself" (1.18.53). He has in mind the "panic terror" that Bacon also mentions, but this is a disease of the mind that may sweep like an epidemic and so cannot lend itself to a rational discourse on the wisdom of preparing for death.[21] Other odd angles of perspective are more playful; they leave the doors of contradiction slightly ajar, as if by personal candor or carelessness. So the despised remedy of the vulgar sort, not to think of death at all (1.20.57–58), needs to be answered directly by resolute thinking of death. But he is not unaware, as we shall see in a moment, that simple folk often die with remarkably little personal trouble. He ends his main essay on the subject ("That to philosophize is to learn to die") by mocking the ceremonies that have grown up around death and give it a terrifying new form of life:

> I truly think it is those dreadful faces and trappings with which we surround it, that frighten us more than death itself: an entirely new way of living; the cries of mothers, wives, and children; the visits of people dazed and benumbed by grief; the presence of a number of pale and weeping servants; a darkened room; lighted candles; our bedside besieged by doctors and preachers; in short, everything horror and fright around us. (1.20.68)

Then his last illustration includes, as if unawares, the fact that there are some benefits in not thinking about death. For death is always the same, and under the mask of our ceremonies "we shall find beneath only that same death which a valet or a mere chambermaid passed through not long ago without fear." (It may be worth noting that this last point, alien to the general argument for heightened consciousness and reasoning oneself out of all fear of death, injects into an up-to-date context, but with a difference, the old-fashioned portable wise sayings that all must die and that death is the great equalizer.)

To add some further examples of a playful kind· he would prefer death to come unannounced, but he avoids the dignity of his being engaged in an "earnest pursuit," as Bacon recommends. Rather, he nominates the time when he is planting his cabbages and declares that he will be unconcerned, and even more so by the unfinished state of his garden (1.20.62). In one of his extreme examples, the "luxuriousness" of the preparations for death quite discredits them (2.13.459–60). In another place he clearly enjoys the unacknowledged denial of Aristotle's famous truism, that death commands our attention when near but not when it seems remote. For he has found himself more afraid of sickness when in perfect health than when actually sick; in his experience (confirmed by Caesar's), "things often appear greater to us from a distance than near" (1.20.63).

These may serve as a modest sampling, to which I would add some "contrary notions" deeper and more strenuous than Bacon admits. Though death is "the master day" that tests and judges the life and admits no "pretending," still, when it comes to judging the deaths of others, he observes that "few men die convinced that it is their last hour; and there is no place where the deception of hope deludes us more." Indeed, true "assurance" in dying "is the most noteworthy action of human life" (2.13.458). One remote mystery perhaps is "that Fortune sometimes lies in wait precisely for the last day of our life, to show her power" (1.19.54). A more familiar mystery is the power of personal hope and its resourcefulness. The master deception, one infers, is that of fear acting as hope; a lesser one, though impressive, is that exception to the rule of no "pretending" in death. In judging "assurance" one must examine the whole situation, for

> it happens to most men to stiffen their countenance and their words in order thereby to acquire a reputation that they still hope to enjoy alive. (2.13.459)

A theologian might simply label this behavior ordinary pride of life and extraordinary vainglory. Perhaps Montaigne would have agreed, though a late addition at this point suggests that he had other things in mind as well: "Of as many as I have seen die, fortune, not their design, has disposed their countenances." (Judging death is difficult, and if it is finally not man's but only God's sphere of concern, still, if the "strangeness" of death is to be removed and rational preparation is to be made, these cannot be done well without the exercise of judgment.) In any case, perplexities abound.

> There are gallant and fortunate deaths. I have seen death bring a wonderfully brilliant career, and that in its flower, to such a splendid end that in my opinion the dead man's ambitions and courageous designs had nothing so lofty about them as their interruption. He arrived where he aspired to without going there, more grandly and gloriously than he had desired or hoped. And by his fall he went beyond the power and the fame to which he had aspired by his career. (1.19.55)

The preceding paragraph begins, "God has willed it as he pleased," and continues:

> But in my time three of the most execrable and most infamous persons I have known in every abomination of life have had deaths that were ordered and in every circumstance composed to perfection.

To die while setting out cabbages may be a welcome stroke of fortune and delivers a kind of message under the breath, but it is a message of desire that must find a place, if it can, outside the formal courses of judgment. Montaigne likes to see men continue the normal actions of their lives as long as they can. He would have considered Bacon's example of "earnest pursuit" to be an inauthentic resolute action and an opportunistic example with some adroit light-handedness in transferring the insensible concentration of the body wounded in battle to the mind fixed on the pursuit of a genuine good. (See the examples and discussion in 3.4.632–34.) The truly admirable death is for Montaigne the resolute one: "No one can say that he is resolved on it who fears to negotiate it, who cannot sustain it with open eyes" (2.13.460). (Montaigne might well have become one of the admirers of Raleigh's assurance.) As for the "pretending" of resolution:

> Those whom we see at executions running to meet their end, and hastening and urging the carrying out of the sentence, do not do so out of resolution; they want to deprive themselves of the time to consider it. Being dead does not trouble them, but dying does indeed. (2.13.460)

Only a slow, deliberate death can prove what it proves, and Socrates, therefore, is one of his true heroes. He had a whole thirty days to think it over, and then he carried it off with convincing ease and modesty:

> with a very certain expectation, without emotion, without alteration, and with a tenor of actions and words rather lowered and relaxed than strained and exalted by the weight of such a reflection. (2.13.461)

Returning to Socrates in another context, and for a different illustrative purpose, Montaigne discovers a secondary motive to explain, but certainly not to discredit, the acceptance and the deportment of Socrates' death:

> Seeing the wisdom of Socrates and several circumstances of his condemnation, I should venture to believe that he lent himself to it to some extent, purposely, by prevarication, being seventy, and having so soon to suffer an increasing torpor of the rich activity of his mind, and the dimming of its accustomed brightness. (3.2.620)

He sums up an account of the many personal virtues of Socrates:

> We have material enough, and we should never tire of presenting the picture of this man as a pattern and ideal of all sorts of perfection. There are very few full and pure examples of life. (3.13.852)

For Montaigne, one may think, the purity and the perfection were all the more authoritative because they allowed room for common, unexpected virtues:

> And he never refused to play at cobnut with children, or to ride a hobbyhorse with them, and he did so gracefully. (3.13.852)

By the time he thought himself old, Montaigne had reversed much of the emphasis that gave thinking about death its central position. "In my opinion it is living happily, not as Antisthenes said, dying happily, that constitutes human felicity" (3.2.619).

> We wrong that great and all-powerful Giver by refusing his gift, nullifying it, and disfiguring it. . . . There is no part unworthy of our care in this gift that God has given us; we are accountable for it even to a single hair. And it is not a perfunctory charge to man to guide man according to his nature;

it is express, simple, and of prime importance, and the creator has given it to us seriously and sternly. Authority alone has power over common intelligences, and has more weight in a foreign language. (3.13.855–56)

There is nothing so beautiful and legitimate as to play the man well and properly, no knowledge so hard to acquire as the knowledge of how to live this life well and naturally; and the most barbarous of our maladies is to despise our being. (3.13.852)

In his main essay on the subject (1.20) Montaigne accepts the basic premise that it is best to make rational preparations for death, and he therefore repeats, as anyone must, the good arguments and wise sayings on record. His interest in the subject continues and indeed keeps breaking into other quite different discussions, but the questions he is motivated to discover acknowledge no obligation to an all-sufficient answer.

I saw death nonchalantly when I saw it universally, as the end of life. I dominate it in the mass; in detail it harasses me. The tears of a lackey, the distribution of my old clothes, the touch of a well-known hand, a commonplace phrase of consolation, make me disconsolate and sorry for myself. (3.4.636)

If, unlike that "one and only Socrates," we cannot consider and judge our own death, and not as proposition of thought or "in the mass," but directly, in itself and in all its real details, we must have recourse to a more common answer. For instance, "The most ordinary remedy for ailments of the soul" is to divert the mind *to other interests, preoccupations, cares, business* (3.4.632). Montaigne's most radical act is to shift the governing rule of measure from the happy death to the happy life. This would seem, however, to be more than a grand diversion—rather, an alternative intuition that enables his acceptance and celebration of life and his anger at the savage rejection of existence.

He honors the gift of life by the mental discipline of observing, interpreting, and arguing from books, experience, and reflection. His own credentials are strengthened by his acute searching into human faults and concealments; toward himself he is an explorer distinguished by his personal openness and flexibility. But he seems to have little interest in seeking to disprove his previous answers. In youth he is determined to take an active part in preparing for death, in order to be free of "subjection and constraint" in living; it is also plain that he detests passive submission—even to an experience so difficult that almost no one "fixes his gaze precisely on it, and makes up his mind to it, without looking elsewhere" (3.4.632). But to speak practically of his enterprise: his questions and his answers, though surely intended to vex, delight, and challenge, were not designed to displace the systematic bulk of traditional thought on the subject.

As for his emphasis on living well, his contribution is distinctive and adds an unforgettable voice to an attitude still emerging and not yet sure of where it is going. One may say much the same about his contributions to the growing esteem for the wisdom of daily life. Both kinds of emphasis find their own way into the English Reformation and by different ways into the development of Puritanism, but do so without directly challenging the main traditions that concern Christian death.

The attention to Montaigne, as to Bacon, is intended to illustrate a background of unconventional thought widely available to writers on death but clearly more pertinent to questions than to answers. The background was there and known but exerted little direct influence on expression. The "messages" to be heard in the best English poems are rooted in their lyric occasions, for which the most reliable sources of thought, feeling, and imagining continued to be the Scriptures and religious traditions, and poetic traditions reflecting religious thought.

But Montaigne's ways of proceeding also take me back to my earlier subject—the observed and imagined experiences of the dying person, fully accounted for by the conceptual and applied wisdom of ecclesiastical traditions, yet allowing for certain limitations of merely human knowledge and for the possibility of exceptions and muted questions. Similarly, the expected presence of witnesses was an important matter that was taken for granted and did not invite analytical study. A poet writing on death, his own or another's, takes on the extended functions of a witness, and he will have a poet's freedom to observe and respond to the surfaces and depths of the occasion. Yet a poet's freedom is privileged only in special ways. He is bound by some uncommon restrictions as well, and he is not likely on the sensitive subject of death to violate the general decorum of established expectations. He is not writing one of many essays that touch the same subject variously, but must be as true as he can be to the immediate situation. Therefore, in writing on death much of what he can say will need to rest upon the tried-and-true. Not everything is so limited, however, for the privileged speech of poetry rests upon the laws of custom, and these were often extended and revised by the influential history of new invention and accomplishment. The right poet might find himself shaping that history.

The importance to poets and their readers of Montaigne, and Bacon as well, lies in part in their useful exhibition of what can be thought but may not yet be quite ready to be said, and certainly cannot be said in poems on death. But in spite of the settled ways of thinking about the subject, there is much that is unexpected in the poems to be considered. It is not useless knowledge to be aware that questions existed under the standard answers, and that there were other ways of approaching both questions and answers.

CHAPTER THREE

Donne's Pictures of the Good Death

In *what follows* I narrow the area of attention to a single topic: the good death as conceived and described by a single author. Dying well is a practical answer of the *artes moriendi* and speaks to the heightened contemporary interest in the movements and details that present death not only as what happens to everyone but as a singular framed event that a particular person experiences. The sameness of death is not denied. It is, rather, the musical ground bass that may recede or advance or undertake small modulations but is felt as ever present below the free movement of the upper parts. In the good death and its kinds of emphasis we may expect to recognize additional matters that are characteristic of the interests and concerns of the age. We may also expect that older elements, formerly but no longer felt as "sufficient," yet still desired, will be admitted in special ways. In some respects, therefore, the answer of the good death will also bring into view some underlying questions.

My purpose is limited to observation of and commentary on particular aspects of the chosen materials. Difficulties and apparent contradictions will emerge. Donne will continue to be a major source of information throughout the book, and some of the problems brought forward in the following pages will reappear in different contexts, finally in Chapter 18. Having chosen the materials, I might reasonably pursue questioning, interpreting, and explaining them, and go on to translate Donne's personal story by systematic reference to chosen magisterial answers. I prefer another course. Insofar as Donne exemplifies certain problems in thinking and writing about death, his varying degrees of success and failure (which I am willing to identify and discuss) provide instructive materials for the kind of story I shall try to tell.

Donne's examples are public and optimistic, mindful of the established laws concerning penitence and alert to the practical wisdom of disciplining listeners and readers in the art of mortification, but turned finally and emphatically toward the goals of justified consolation and hope.

For much of his life Donne's imagination was greatly hospitable to the images of death as a strenuous struggle, a long preparation for a contest of resolute hopes and resourceful fears. As preacher he could make fitting use of all bad examples in the open, meditational parts of a sermon—as in the weight of "stupefaction" that overcomes a man dying a bad death, seeing and foreseeing helplessly (*Sermons* 8:189). That fear expresses a deep personal anxiety, for the horror of stupefaction is not necessarily restricted to the convenient example of someone deserving a bad death. The last sickness of anyone may be a lethargy in which one forgets one's own name as well as that of one's religion and its founder. One hears more than a detached comment when Donne says, "For, as in bodily, so in spiritual diseases, it is a desperate state, to be speachlesse" (5:233).

Donne struggles not so much to end his struggles as to win from them gifts that can be possessed (at least as he understands himself) only on the other side of persistent efforts. In his descriptions of the good death we have a specialized subject, the end and purpose of antecedent struggles. The stage is public, the words intended for delivery from the pulpit or intended, at least permitted, to appear in print.

In the third part of Devotion 17 he breaks out of the elaborate restrictions of his thoughts to express gratitude toward the unknown benefactor whose bell he has heard tolling. His prayer, a deeply felt release, is that the other man may have the gift of a good death. These are the conditions: that the dying man be able to "perfect his *account*" by seeing his sins in such a way "as that he may *know* what thou [God] forgivest, and not doubt of thy *forgivenesse*"; that he may overcome the knowledge of "the *infinitenesse* of those sinnes" and his own *"demerits"* by dwelling on God's infinite mercy and Christ's *"merits"*; that God may "Breath inward *comforts* to his *heart,* and affoord him the power of giving such outward *testimonies* thereof, as all that are about him may derive comforts from thence, and have this *edification*" (Raspa, p. 90).

The inward and outward experiences meet in the effect upon others, and their presence is clearly important to Donne. What the audience may give is not mentioned. If the prayer is effective the witnesses will receive testimony of great spiritual benefit to themselves, and hence they will be able to testify that the death *was* good and hence—though this exceeds the due purposes and concerns of prayer—they will be able to testify that the prayer was effective. To narrow the issues, however, the witnesses are deliberately linked to the dying man by Donne's prayer, which brings him out of his own strenuous isolation to participate in the scene that he has already responded to with imagination and prayer. He turns outward in effective charity and realizes the crucial moment of a spontaneous act toward which he has groped, guiding his thoughts and restraining them, but also following them and pursued by them in passages of oblique advance and retardation. Indeed, the last sentence of the Seventeenth Expostulation anticipates the spontaneous act of his prayer by expressing a suddenly felt but unexplained sense of joy and glory: "I that aske why thou *doest* not, finde even now in *my self*, that thou *doest*." (The unexplained moment is a rare one in the *Devotions*.)

Donne's prayer is composed of certain standard steps in a clearly recognizable pattern. The developing stages consist of a penitential review, swiftly fulfilled in God's time, followed by the knowing acceptance of God's mercy and Christ's "merits"; finally, the prepared heart receives directly from God the grace of inward comforts which are so felt by "all that are about him" that they receive, indirectly, their own spiritual instruction. The recipient of the prayer is an unknown man, and the conditions must fit a general case, as that of an average sinner. Though the description lacks the kind of specificity we shall notice in some later examples, it does aim at all that is central in the achievement of felicity. It is a good death, and in this matter language discreetly refuses to acknowledge degree. The positive "good" is all-sufficient, and the superlative, introducing as it must unmanageable concepts of an ideal in an experience where such thoughts are alien, will encounter exotic difficulties.

This is what happens when Donne formally presents an ideal death deliberately held back until the last moments of a sermon when, he takes pains to notice, there is no sand left in his glass. The set description is general, with almost no particularized content. The peaceful conscience "understands Gods purpose upon him" (*Sermons*, 8:190), but there is no mention of sins or penitential review. The "holy thoughts" of his life are simply directed toward the same subjects, in death as in life. There is no scene sketched, no framing of the approach to death; there are no witnesses noted. All sense of evolving movement is eliminated as Donne deliberately translates the complete integrity of a holy life into a holy death. The example is an extreme one, but it will permit us to see the finer differences in Donne's presentation of the art of dying. I shall need to return to this perfect death for reference and contrast. In the meantime, I need a third example, a good death related to both of these but in some ways different and occupying a kind of middle range of felicity.

Let us consider what he tells us in the commemorative sermon he preached for his good friend Lady Danvers, the former Magdalen Herbert.[1] Donne follows his customary practice of beginning with a full-length sermon on a text, and thus consciously honors the dead and the living by bringing the individual aspects of the occasion into conformity with the regular church service and, beyond that, the history of the faithful. The exposition of the text is divided into six carefully articulated parts, which constitute a history of salvation and the assembling of the community of faith directed toward expectations that will reaffirm that community. The pattern thus molded is clearly one that provides a place for Lady Danvers. Furthermore, an elevated tone of calm at times, and a flow of reassurances, though with no mention at all of Lady Danvers, would affect those listening to the lesson with their minds while receiving intimations of comfort—preconsolation, as it were.

The sermon is not a piece of commanding eloquence, except for the final drawing together of the expectant community of the faithful—past, present, and future. One cannot bridge the differences between printed page and living voice, but the powerful last paragraph of the sermon lends credit to Walton's report: "I saw and heard this Mr. *John Donne* (who was then Dean of *St. Pauls*) weep, and preach her Funeral Sermon" (*Lives,* p. 267). For the most part, however, Donne's eloquence points beyond itself, and beyond his own feelings, to the purposes and obligations of the sermon. And yet, at least once, the living voice may perhaps be heard in a remarkably personal inflection. In developing the argument that we have no inherited claims on God, as part of a general list of our disqualifications Donne cites an unusual text in passing: *"My mother was an Hittite,* (as the *Prophet Ezechiel* speaks.) I am but of the *halfe bloud,* at best; More of the first, then of the second *Adam"* (8:72). For "Hittite" understand "member of a misguided religion" and translate "Roman Catholic." Donne was a faithful adopted son of the Church of England, but also a faithful son. His mother, the granddaughter of Elizabeth Rastell, sister of Sir Thomas More, had kept to the old religion and was then living with him in the dean's house at St. Paul's. The personal intimacy of the wit hardly ripples the surface, but it honors the memory of Lady Danvers's wit, and one imagines that some of those present in church (George Herbert certainly) would have recognized that.

When the regular sermon was completed, Donne turned as expected to his eulogy of Lady Danvers. Here he consistently emphasizes the pattern of her virtues. When amplifications are offered—as in the matter of her second marriage, her personal comeliness, her elegant and expensive taste in clothes, and the deliberate character of her charity—these are intended to serve purposes of clarification and not to be memorable. A seventeenth-century Protestant emphasis on candor does not ignore the conspicuous difference between her age and that of her second husband, or the potentially critical symptoms of depression (mel-

ancholy) which affected her in later life. But all the individual facts of
her person and life, and especially the sound virtues she possessed and
practiced, are assimilated to the general pattern that her life illustrates.
The details of her personal distinction are carefully but lightly drawn,
to touch and satisfy (as much as they properly can) the memories of
those who mourn her—yet everything personal is firmly subdued to
the general effect. The task of achieving that balance and subordination
is one that Donne clearly set for himself. In a commemorative sermon,
by a preacher not free to conduct the services a month earlier, and by an
old friend, the recipient of direct help when desperately needed and of
later extended hospitality—the efforts, and the side-efforts too, are
more visible than they might have been if Donne's personal relationship
to the task had been less involved. She is not sentimentalized, and even
the visibility of Donne's efforts to master the materials of the portrait he
wishes to draw—the proportions, balance, and movement—creates an
unexpected and affecting dimension, like hesitant eloquence.

The last recorded family scene occurs within two hours of her
death:

> But in the *doctrine, and discipline* of that *Church,* in which, *God*
> seal'd her, to himselfe, in *Baptisme,* shee brought up her chil-
> dren, shee assisted her family, she dedicated her soule to *God*
> in her life, and surrendered it to him in her death; And, in that
> forme of *Common Prayer,* which is ordain'd by that *Church,*
> and to which she had accustom'd her selfe, with her family,
> twice every day, she joyn'd with that company, which was
> about her *death-bed,* in answering to every part thereof, which
> the Congregation is directed to answer to, with a *cleere under-*
> *standing,* with a *constant memory,* with a *distinct voyce,* not two
> houres before she died. (8:90–91)

The scene is presented so that the tenderness may be felt but still subordinated to the continuity of her character and role: she does what she
always did, leading by example but at the same time simply participat-
ing in the regular order of the service, while incidentally demonstrating
the precious gifts of clear understanding, memory, and voice. The
perfect regularity of her spiritual life is a modest equivalent of the "holy
thoughts" in the ideal death of my previous example, and the clear
possession of her faculties may stand in part as evidence that her accounts are in order, for Donne quietly omits that formal stage of a
penitential review of sins and the assurance that they are forgiven.

As for the death itself, there are witnesses, but they have neither
shape nor outline in the space that Donne composes for our vision. We

see only Lady Danvers. "How may we thinke," Donne said in that little church in Chelsea, invoking the memory and imagination of those who were at the bedside, and the imagination of those who like himself were not:

> How may we thinke, shee was joy'd to see the face, that *Angels* delight to looke upon, the face of her *Saviour,* that did not abhor the face of his fearfullest *Messenger,* Death? Shee shew'd no feare of his face, in any change of her owne; but died without any change of *countenance,* or *posture;* without any *strugling,* any *disorder;* but her *Death-bed* was as quiet as her *Grave.* (8:91)

We see only Lady Danvers, but we apprehend a sensitive line reaching from the implied presence of those watching and responding to the figure on the bed, a line touching their solid, conscious, remembering presence a month later in the church. They *were* there at the bedside. They know, and we can know by the description of what was seen. And Donne completes his verbal art of vision—its open form, its delicate ordering of the perceptions of implied presence—by creating, out of what they did not see, the shape and substance that love and faith may be permitted to think they see.

One consideration almost untouched in my three examples is any support directed toward the Protestant argument that a proper preparation for the next world included the effective performance of domestic, civil, and religious actions in this world. The doctrine produced its own difficulties, and these are reflected in the tangled oppositions, rigid claims, and self-adjusting compensations of the religious conflicts of the times. There were changes in the conduct of dying, too, though that history does not, I think, lend itself to exact coordination with other histories. Some of the established wisdom concerning death provided the kind of foundation and continuity that left only matters of emphasis and arrangement subject to alteration within a relatively short span of time. Perhaps a single example may serve to illustrate some of the difficulties involved in the general attitude that came to prevail. Even without the sensitive problems concerning faith, good works, and election, and the issues of their priority and timing—as the moral justifications of significant activity in the world were strengthened, there was a correlative weakening of the old explanations of the sudden catastrophes and the slow-paced disintegrations that rewarded imprudent confidence in the illusions of a world infected by chance and time. Those who accepted the old assurances were not likely to be satisfied by current redefinitions of prudence and duty, or to think any of the new answers were as full and accurate as the old option of disengaging the desires of the heart from the contests and prizes of daily life.

As preacher Donne accepts as right and does his best to assure his listeners that properly tempered activities in the world are good; they may help or hinder salvation, but to avoid them is out of the question or can be dismissed with brief scorn. In my three examples of the good death, the activities of life are all treated differently. For the unknown benefactor of Devotion 17 the sins acquired by living are given prominent acknowledgment; that their actuality must be taken for granted is both an irreducible fact of life and a manageable fact of religious doctrine. The sins and their forgiveness constitute the first action in preparing for death and final salvation—first, necessary, but transitional. The second figure, idealized with scarcely a detail, seemed to have no sins, not even flaws. Yet the actions as well as the thoughts of his life apparently produced wealth and good name; he educated his children, discharged the duties of his "place," contributed in thought (and presumably in actions) to "the safety of the state, the happinesse of the King" (8:190). All of Lady Danvers's actions move from the center of domestic virtue; the civil virtue of her charity and her religious virtue move out but circle that center. No sins are mentioned, but potential flaws are brought up in passing, and careful discriminations answer and dissipate questions that are never quite formed.

She is not sentimentalized, but I do think Donne sentimentalizes that paragon of death whose continuity of good thoughts (and wholly generalized actions) in life simply pass into unchanged dreams in his "blessed Sleepe, [in which] all his devotions in heaven shall be upon the same Subjects" (8:190). The public and private actions of that imagined figure are the "lights" and "shadows" of his picture, a fine metaphor that deflects interest from any specific content in the life itself, the subject that has been freely translated into a picture.

Donne's difficulty here is one that he struggles with honorably in expressing from the pulpit visions of the essential, incomparable bliss of heaven. Sometimes the incomparable needs comparisons, if it is to be expressed. Some of the content of dying may also be thought incomparable. The weight of centuries of speculative attention and repeated explanation was not produced by the assurance that the last moment resembled other moments. If the very act of dying was not, by the criteria of faith in eternity, essential and incomparable, it was, by the common criteria of experience in the world and by the convincing effect of recorded commentary, like nothing else. Insofar as dying is believed to have content, it must be imagined, by invention of comparison or inspired leap beyond it. Or the content may be imagined by reflection, by what others see or feel they see. Or the content may be suggested in the open form of a negative description—the absence of struggle, change of countenance and posture—into which the prepared listeners and readers may pour what their own willing hopes signify, and so complete the form, but without speech or writing and the fixed, questionable record they produce.

Donne seldom undertakes anything like that picture of the perfect death, which seems to me sentimentalized. There we find a combination of unspecific content and assertive comparisons that are declared to be fully identical in heaven as on earth, and a closed, fixed completeness of the form. As for his invented comparison, it is brilliantly, boldly, swiftly drawn, and casually interprets itself:

> Bee pleased to remember that those Pictures which are deliv-
> er'd in a minute, from a print upon a paper, had many dayes,
> weeks, Moneths time for the graving of those Pictures in the
> Copper; So this Picture of that dying Man, that dies in Christ,
> that dies the death of the Righteous, that embraces Death as a
> Sleepe, was graving all his life. (8:190)

It is a tour de force on a subject so constituted that to produce the sense of having given full satisfaction is to invoke the echo of a hollow ring.

A surer practice of Donne's art is to create a sense of movement and the suggestive equivalent of comparison by marking, or shading in, stages; and to reserve for the approach to death a sense of full inwardness at the last stage. That inwardness may reflect its peace or joy to onlookers, but it is also directed away from them and from the world they still inhabit, though what they see may bring them to the threshold of a joy overcoming grief. In the reflected peace there is an implied judgment—the acceptance by the dying person, and the acceptance by God that this was a good life, that this is a good death. Yet under the peace, insuppressible for those inclined to receive it, there is another implied judgment, one involved in the disengagement from a lesser existence that may, as some have thought, be enchanted by illusions and instructed by pain.

That second judgment was the inheritance of centuries and too deeply rooted in thought, experience, and language to be discarded or effectively sterilized by the reformation of doctrine or of social or other philosophy, or by the ruling ideas of new men in a new age. At moments of crisis, disaster, or death, the retrospective sense of life as the sport of illusions, as the revels and bad spells of time and its mockery, needed no special prompting to be remembered or coaching to be rehearsed. And up to a point that retrospective sense and felt revelation was a proper discipline for religious disengagement from worldly concerns, a kind of leverage simply justified by its power to move the soul from what was made to be abandoned and toward a full and positive assent in the passage to the triumphant church in heaven. The fulcrum could and did shift, for guidance in the individual art of dying might need to search for the right point of balance, at least in any full and prolonged development, and especially if any felt changes in attitude were being accommodated.

In referring to a shifting point of balance and the varying weight and duration of the retrospective sense that conveys an adverse judgment of life and its illusions, I have begun to turn toward my next subject—that of a model for good dying which increases the particularization and is less remote from daily life. In the changing times of the English Reformation, a new consciousness of the proper uses of reason adjusted itself to a sense of recovered value in the "literal" meaning of Scripture; and accorded the facts of human experience a dignity in the pursuit of wisdom which corresponded to an enlarged interest in those facts; and encouraged the expression of some kinds of plain directness and candor by which the thoughts and beliefs of the age could distinguish themselves, in their new liberation, from the customs of older and rival practices now discarded. (The wise adage of speaking only good of the dead was too old and right to be much tampered with, but new minds could recognize the undeveloped territory that lay in validating the credible by admitting more of the common truth of human imperfection.) Any man putting off the old life in which he had struggled commendably toward salvation might have a good death. The old life, without needing much overt emphasis, would already have its good, bad, and doubtful actions; in a ceremonial speech the good, of course, would receive full emphasis.

We observed in Donne's portrayal of Lady Danvers the turns toward openness and candor, but all potential flaws are carefully explained and defended; like the virtues they are brought forward and then assimilated into a pattern. What was individual, and recognizably so, is gradually transformed in the review of the life, and she becomes a representative character: simply a good woman dying a good death. Let us consider another example, a sermon delivered about six months earlier, one in which we can also observe Donne working hard at his task, the portrayal of Sir William Cokayne's death.

Cokayne was, in part of the view Donne presents, a kind of statesman among investors, one who made money in ways that deliberately increased the wealth of the state and its capacity to enlarge the foundation of its wealth. There were and are other ways of describing

Cokayne's private motives and public consequences,[2] but Donne aligns himself at once with the economic doctrines that he praises and relates to Cokayne's career. He singles out the businessmen in the congregation to make his point: "And you have lost a man, that drove a great Trade, the right way in making the best use of our home-commodity" (7:274). The right way is by increasing exports, "to vent our owne outward." For that purpose the most beneficial imports are not luxuries to be consumed, like wine, silk, and spices, but those "Arts, and Manufactures, to be imployed upon our own Commodity within the Kingdome." Cokayne "did his part," Donne says, backing away but not conspicuously so, for he is to begin a new subject (or perhaps he prefers to separate his own convictions from the objective truth of the personal performance that he does not want to praise uncritically): "He did his part, diligently, at least, if not vehemently, if not passionately." The diligence represents conscious public duty and is good, or good enough; the lack of vehemence and passion suggests that duty was not the wholehearted and primary motive, but also that the man was prudent: that he obeyed the laws of managing money for profit; that he maintained his obligation to the money he inherited and increased by personal effort; and that he fulfilled his obligations to the estate he would pass on to his many children, in number and "quality . . . fit to receive a great Estate" (7:275).

These implications are ones that may be drawn out of Donne's preparatory remarks. Cokayne's "industry" was not slackened by the estate he expected to inherit, "which is a Canker . . . that hath eaten up many a family in this City. . . . And truly, it falls out too often, that he that labours not for more, does not keepe his own" (7:273).

Donne's emphasis and standards in fulfilling the duties of a funeral oration are not, and could not be, exactly the same as in the formal part of the sermon, which he presents as he understands his office, with a certain detached and disciplined exposition of a sacred text. There he could raise a question not to be asked at the funeral of a rich man, though if it is raised before that part of the service it may still have some life in the memory of critical listeners. He said earlier that we survey land we are about to buy, "But who thinks of taking so exact a survey of his Conscience, how that money was got, that purchased that Mannor?" And, further, that in common usage "meanes" is the word for wealth: "But that is truly his meanes, what way he came by it" (7:260). This is, perhaps, the conscious or habitual diligence of the preacher and may or may not be intended to linger in the memory.

But some of Donne's preparation for the funeral service may lie in the text he has chosen and in a major part of his exposition. There he develops the imperfect state of all our experience in the world. Everything "falls within this Rule . . . even in spiritual things, nothing is perfect" (7:261). And he moves in a famous passage from "We" to "I," to a personal demonstration, speaking for all when he acts out the vivid, trifling distractions that intervene when "I throw my selfe downe in my Chamber" to pray (7:264–65). Even in the passage quoted above, redefining "meanes," he goes on to the point that the wealthy seldom have an exact survey of their worth. They may have more than they think, or "We have seen great Wills" intended for "pious uses," but the estate was unable to provide the necessary funds (7:261). The theme of imperfection may have some preparatory purpose, and I, at least, regard the topic as a discreet justification for the special circumstances of eulogizing a dead man for the merits he had while subordinating all that could be said on the other side if the occasion required taking an "exact survey." Yet this last example, if at all pertinent, surely works to reinforce Cokayne's claims upon our respect. There is no merit in the ineffectual handling of money, and Cokayne's prudent management seems to have kept his affairs well surveyed.

In his transition to the personal part of the service, Donne both separates the two parts and at the same time makes a significant concession to the funeral and to the whole congregation:

> As we have held you, with Doctrine of Mortification, by extending the Text, from *Martha* to this occasion; so shall we dismisse you with Consolation, by a like occasionall inverting the Text, from passion in *Martha's* mouth, *Lord, if thou hadst been here, my Brother had not dyed,* to joy in ours, *Lord because thou wast here, our Brother is not dead.* (7:273)

In the four "steps" Donne is to take in his discourse (the life, the death, the funeral, and the resurrection), "The Lord was with him" and in the last "shall be with him." This is the "text" that orders each part and connects the whole.

Of the life, to what has already been quoted I add a few brief items. God gave him a "comprehensive understanding" and a "publique heart." To what degree his "way of education" is to be attributed to God is less clear, but in any case it was extraordinary in its "largenesse," and to be contrasted with the products of "our narrow and contracted times, in which every man determines himselfe in himselfe, and scarce looks farther" (7:274). This last begins the account of his public life and his distinguished ability in and comprehension of "businesses." The pinnacle of praise is reached when Donne quotes the highest authority in any land (past, present, and future), King James, on the style and content of Cokayne's expression when handling businesses. As we approach the "step" of his death we are informed that along with the "brightnesse of prosperity" there were also "many darke, and sad, and heavy crosses." They are not named, but "he had them," was "the steadier for them," and they "as well as his blessings established his assurance in God" (7:275).

In his final sickness he displayed, according to witnesses, "a religious and a constant heart towards God," and, further, refused to be dissuaded from kneeling in spite of his weakness. Then Donne enters a personal testimony of Cokayne's behavior in church, and this digresses into the remarkable "diligence" of the preacher defending the practice of honoring the worthy (of whom Cokayne was one) with privileged seating in church. We return to the one day's "labour" in his sickness, and this he spent in business. Calling friends and family together, he acknowledged God's blessings, "and his owne sins as penitently" (7:276). Then he made some last recommendations concerning charitable bequests. This was his "Valediction to the world." A specific time schedule now enters the account, beginning with the last two days. Cokayne seems to have had that legendary sense of knowing exactly when he was to die—conveying, no doubt, a special validation to educated seventeenth-century listeners, though in the standard accounts as they had appeared for centuries this particular knowledge was characterized by a simple and unself-conscious normalcy. Two days before the end he said, *"Help me off with my earthly habit, and let me go to my last bed."* During the second night following this he said, *"Little know ye what paine I feele this night, yet I know, I shall have joy in the morning;* And in that morning he dyed." Toward the end the special form of his obsecration was always this: *"Christ Jesus, which dyed on the Crosse, forgive me my sins; He have mercy upon me."* The last words he spoke were "the repetition of the name of Jesus" (7:276).

In his last two "steps" Donne is brief. The grandeur of the funeral, which may have been embarrassing, is acknowledged and explained away by reasoning not unlike that which defends Lady Danvers's expensive taste in clothes. As God is not absent when the proper forms of burial are lacking, "neither must we deny it, to be an evidence of his favour and presence, when he is pleased to afford these" (7:277). (The calculated double meaning of "afford" has been punished by time, not unjustly.) The main argument, however, that God is with Cokayne in the funeral, is the evidence that Donne marshals through all four "steps," to an extraordinary degree, as he shows that this life and death conform to the written design of God's will by the weight of scriptural parallels that can be adduced. For the funeral, in one paragraph Abraham, Jacob, Joseph, Christ, and Joseph of Arimathaea testify (7:277). To confirm that God was with him in life, such evidence is more sparingly deployed, more space being allotted to the reports and commentary on the activities themselves. But he was enlarged and filled to capacity, like David. And God "seemes to have made that Covenant with him, which he made to *Abraham . . . I will multiply thee exceedingly*" (7:274). The prosperity was *"a Pillar of Fire,"* the adversity and "heavy crosses" were "the *Pillar of Clouds* too" (7:275). In the approach to death Cokayne echoes to wife and children "Christs last commandment to his Spouse the Church, in the Apostles, *To love one another*" (7:276).

After the death Donne invokes a small flood of support from the blood of Abel and the prayers of saints and martyrs, and in the last "step" he draws all present into a community of witnesses that begins in the Old Testament and looks toward the last day:

> That which *Moses* said to the whole Congregation, I say to you all, both to you that heare me, and to him that does not, *All ye that did cleave unto the Lord your God, are alive, every one of you, this day;* Even hee, whom we call dead, is alive this day. In the presence of God, we lay him downe; In the power of God, he shall rise; In the person of Christ, he is risen already. (7:277–78)

And as spokesman for the whole congregation, Donne continues, "beseeching his blessed Spirit, that as our charity enclines us to hope confidently of his good estate, our faith may assure us of the same happinesse, in our owne behalfe." So the listeners are drawn together, though without the fervor and sweep of evocation that concludes the sermon on Lady Danvers. Indeed, the last prayer for Cokayne seems to negotiate diplomatically between hope for the dead and the spiritual self-interest of the listeners. If there are any hesitating stragglers among the flock, they will hear a prayer from which no one would choose to exclude himself. In its four "steps" the story of Cokayne has been reinforced by a typological demonstration of considerable volume and insistence by which the dead man is brought into the design of sacred history. Yet we may also observe that, as part of the general endeavor, the individual significance of the man is also heightened. For while Donne deliberately includes items appropriate to a good, old-fashioned death familiar for centuries, he is also portraying a "modern" death that serves the needs of his own time.

To illustrate: Lady Danvers takes her part in regular family prayers and then dies in the speechless eloquence of her calm face and body. Cokayne's late words (not counting his last word) are quoted verbatim three times, as if they possessed some unusual, authenticating force.[3] Donne is, of necessity, reporting, but he is choosing to give the factual details an audible reality intended to affirm the pious character of the death. At the same time, however, he is giving that death a character and style of its own. On the one hand, the progress of the death does follow a standard pattern and schedule, and in this respect may seem less individualized. Unlike Lady Danvers, Cokayne makes all the formal stops on the way. Donne emphasizes, by repetition without detail, the expressed penitence for sins—omitted from the history of Lady Danvers's death. There is a formal convocation of family and friends, followed by last words of advice and a stage clearly marked, "his Valediction to the world." The stages at the end are also clearly marked—two days, the second night, the last morning.

On the other hand, there are those differences that, both in their emphasis and in the sense of latency they create, mark this death as more highly wrought and more personal in its calculated effects upon a large congregation. For one thing, there is the deliberate art of the pulpit orator, creating interest and collecting attention by verbal flourishes:

> This City is a great Theater, and he Acted great and various parts in it; And all well. (7:274)

> He was served with the Processe here in the City, but his cause was heard in the Country; Here he sickened, There he languished, and dyed there. (7:275)

> To returne to him in his sicknesse; He had but one days labour, and all the rest were Sabbaths, one day in his sicknesse he converted to businesse. (7:276)

In the deathbed scene the witnesses are as usual anonymous forms in the background, but the preacher's art chooses to bring them forward, obscurely, to lend what happened an indirectly dramatized specificity:

> And his last and dying words were the repetition of the name of Jesus; And when he had not strength to utter that name distinctly and perfectly, they might heare it from within him, as from a man a far off; even then, when his hollow and remote naming of Jesus, was rather a certifying of them, that he was with his Jesus, then a prayer that he might come to him. (7:276)

At Lady Danvers's peaceful death the imaginative tact works upon the materials of what was *not* seen, and the speaker gently guides the witnesses (and listeners, himself among them) to complete the visible form by the open inferences of personal faith ("How may we thinke"). Here, at Cokayne's death, the responsible fact of weak indistinctness of voice is put on record, and also the open figurativeness that likens the sound to the voice of "a man a far off." Then the clarity of relationships slides into the language of desire as the witnesses advance an interpretation and offer a personal *certifying* that the prayer to arrive became, "rather," an announcement of arrival. The speaker's own presence in this report is notably absent; his art is notably present.

I have already mentioned the somewhat masked reserve on the subject of Cokayne's "diligence" in doing his part for international trade. One may note a similar piece of pulpit diplomacy in a more crucial place. The man who "drove a great Trade" took his formal "Valediction to the world"; "And after this," we are told, "he seemed alwaies loath to returne to any worldly businesse" (7:276). Does this mean that he absolutely refused or that he nevertheless did return, though reluctantly? The implied admission, or even a careless ambiguity, would diminish some of the resonance of that declared "Valediction to the world." What may also emerge, however, is an emphasis of personal distinction based on familiar fact and not to be forgotten by those capable of hearing well. The man of great position whose wealth is actively engaged in the world of commerce will find it difficult to retire while possessing most of his faculties. Only during the last two days will absolutely no one ask him for necessary advice or for a decision. A related point, emphasizing the prominence of the individual as well as the Christian character that leads to a good death, may be recognized in the report of his one official day of business during the last sickness. At that time he recommends some charitable additions to his will. A secondary meaning here would show how the great man's last wishes are effective beyond death and beyond the written instrument of the law: his recommendations, "according to his purpose, have beene all taken into consideration" (7:276).[4]

And one last item, not, I am sure within the scope of Donne's intentions, but the kind of inadvertent disclosure that truthtelling in art, when the truth is restless and under pressure, finds it difficult to avoid. I have in mind that sudden turn of criticism directed toward the education of "our narrow and contracted times, in which every man determines himselfe in himselfe, and scarce looks farther" (7:274). The praise through contrast, convenient in one place, may transmit resemblances one would not wish to consider in another place—as in the narrow and constricted state that may be felt in a fully reported death. The preacher enlarges the stage and fills out the extended relationships, but the public presentation, its vivid details and concentrated focus, while emphasizing the rightness of the dying man's actions, also portrays the human solitude of dying.

Donne is, of course, doing his own part, "diligently, at least, if not vehemently, if not passionately." To be sure, a funeral eulogy, even though God is called to witness, requires no oath concerning the preacher's exposition of truth. The formal part of the sermon engages the subject of imperfection and is directed toward mortification; after that, the occasion of a funeral makes the proper subjects praise and consolation. The potential stains of greatness and prosperity are quietly subordinated; the commendable actions of public life are clearly commended. All of the spiritual hazards of deep engagement in worldly activities are by inference purged by penitential discipline and countervailed by public duty to the state, private duty to family, and personal devotion to God. Cokayne makes a welcome case, one that the rich may hope to emulate in all ways, one that may encourage the not-so-rich in whatever ways are applicable to their own circumstances. All will have to turn away from their own claims on life and try to die well.[5]

Donne's last recorded statement on the subject, delivered against a background that listeners interpreted as that of his own imminent death, is perhaps of all his many essays in prose the most rigorous and sustained account of the conditions governing death. And yet the sermon called "Death's Duel" is not in any satisfactory sense a personal statement. Donne has obligations to the text, to his choice of it, and to the congregation. He gives the text as verse 20 of Psalm 68: "In fine. And unto God the Lord belongs the issues of death. i.e. from death." In emphasizing proper human responses to the issues of death, he reminds his listeners that "Our *criticall* day is *not* the *very day* of our *death:* but the whole course of our life" (10:241). That sounds like traditional religious wisdom and advice. It is a message of encouragement, offering time to those who may think their own day of death not yet close. Besides, a preacher may then charge the *now* of this moment in church with the decisiveness of the *"very day"* of our *death"*—a public opportunity that Donne does not himself neglect in private. The argument also allows Protestants to be glad they are not members of a benighted church still gambling on the erroneous doctrine that one can be saved by last-minute, last-gasp confession. A conscientious preacher will use that self-congratulating impulse to move his congregation to the strenuous work of private spiritual initiative.

These are developments Donne often makes in the pulpit, but now he is about to attach a radical condition to the message most listeners would find hopeful, since it allows them to transfer their immediate anxiety over a fixed moment to the more familiar indefiniteness of personal time—"the whole course of our life." Donne's point is that from the evidence that accompanies a dying man we cannot draw reliable conclusions. Man moves toward understanding by examples: "But God governs not by *examples,* but by *rules*" (10:241). Physicians, we are told, observe symptoms and give "*presagitions . . .* out of the grounds and the *rules of their art*" (10:240). But *we* have no "rule or art" to predict damnation by what we observe in a dying man. Indeed, "wee may bee deceived both wayes: wee use to comfort our selves in the death of *a friend,* if it be testified that he went away like a *Lambe,* that is, without any *reluctation*" (10:240). We may well misread the evidence, and to limit dying well to "an easie, a quiet death" (10:241) is to set a higher value on such comfort than is borne out by the example of Christ and the history of devout Christians.

As for witnesses, to whom I have given repeated close attention because they were clearly important for Donne's purposes and, presumably, for his larger concerns—they are not now, it would seem. God's mercies, he avers, work in subtler dimensions of time than the attunement of observers can record. Nor is time the only obstacle: the mercies work "*momentarily* in minutes, and many times *insensibly* to bystanders or any other then the party departing" (10:240).

To take a half-step backward: as we follow Donne, each death is an example; to speak in general is to invoke rules, and the rules governing the issues of death belong to God. Listeners are drawn into the example as participants and witnesses; they reflect the conditions of our social interdependence to the end. As witnesses their testimony is desired by others and by themselves; they will receive spiritual instruction, whatever they learn. While befriending *moriens* they will have before them an example of their own death, and they may see, Donne suggests, a dying man observed by others but wholly intent upon another source of communication. To take a full step backward: we, the witnesses three and a half centuries later, may observe that the exclusion from exact knowledge of "any other" but the dying man does not account for the voice now assuming authority—declaring the limits of what bystanders may see and declaring a "rule" governing the private communication between God and the dying.

In what Donne's pronouncement denies, the ability of witnesses to judge the evidence and report the truth, the voice is that of alert human reasoning that exposes to doubt the positions of those who may imagine themselves to be certain but have not considered the grounds of uncertainty. Yet the affirming voice neither identifies itself nor acknowledges any special powers in casually asserting the unquestionable assurance of "the party departing." Donne is himself speaking. He does not speak as when he said of Lady Danvers's death, "How may we thinke"—speaking then for others who were, like himself, between grief and consolation. If identified and held for questioning, Donne's affirming voice cannot escape some relationship to the voice that undertook the artful reporting of what the bystanders concluded as they listened to Cokayne's last naming of Jesus. One might say of the voice assuming authority in "Death's Duel" that Donne slips into a contradiction and indicates no awareness of so doing—at least not the awareness that being artful would suggest. One could also say that he is rational and humane in applying doubt and that he observes limits: he does not take up the question of whether the subtle intimations of an adverse judgment may also be received by "the party departing." In speaking of a merciful God and of a dying man, he freely speaks an old and simple language of faith into which no freak of doubt could enter. He speaks from the pulpit and to those who are present, who need guidance in the practice of restraint and in the practice of hope.[6]

Writing about One's Own Death

For often when there are reasons which force death upon a creature,
Nature turns away in horror, but the will accepts it.
BOETHIUS, *Consolation of Philosophy*

By my troth, cousin, methinketh that the death which men call
commonly natural is a violent death to every man whom it fetcheth
hence by force against his will. And that is every man which when he
dieth is loath to die and fain would yet live longer if he might.
Howbeit, how small the pain is in the natural death, cousin, fain
would I wit who hath told you.
SIR THOMAS MORE, *Dialogue of Comfort against Tribulation*

Part Two title page illustration:
from an engraving by Martin Droeshout of John Donne in his shroud,
frontispiece to *Deaths Duell,* 1632

CHAPTER FOUR

Respice Finem

The brief sampling that follows will indicate something of the established ways of thinking about personal death in verse. Most of these poems were written in a manner that soon would become outdated, but we may still get some glimpses of why these repeated ways of thinking about death did not become boring. We shall come to strong and sensitive poems that do not abandon everything shown here but are able to apprehend subtleties as well as simplicities with a convincing mastery of personal application.

"I loathe that I did love." Thus the "aged lover" begins his renunciation of love and the things of youth. Thomas Vaux's poem,[1] a popular favorite in Tottel's *Songs and Sonnets* (1557), set to music, misquoted by the First Gravedigger in *Hamlet,* touches all the right notes to please its listeners. The customary joys of life, the customary facts of change and loss, the retrospective thoughts that meet the familiar anticipations of listeners who are not yet old enough for renunciation—all express the appropriate things and deliver trusted advice but do not turn and grind into objects of loathing the present memory of past delights. In spite of his emphatic opening declaration, the speaker seems not quite certain of his actual position; at least he is old enough to renounce what has left him. Then reason quietly ages him further, and he notes the convincing symptoms of "The cough, the cold, the gasping breath." His thoughts move him to the digging of his grave, and then, "Me thinks I hear the clerk / That knolls the careful knell." But the bell is only one more reminder, for he turns to younger others and passes them his "wanton cup." Youth and life will carry on, as he did. Even when he speaks as if from beyond the grave, the elegiac voice mingles touches of celebration and mystery into the cycle of beginning and end:

> For beauty, with her band
> These crooked cares hath wrought,
> And shipped me into the land
> From whence I first was brought.

The epilogue is in the voice of an old and popular subgenre, that of warning advice to the living from one who has returned, licensed, as it were, by literary convention and charitable purpose:

> And ye that bide behind,
> Have ye none other trust;
> As ye of clay were cast by kind,
> So shall ye waste to dust.

The effectiveness and appeal of the poem are not difficult to recognize. One assumes that for contemporaries the looseness of the writing had its own charms, and that the somewhat uneven naivety strengthened the evidence that the report was a true one. No single item was new or at the time seemed too old, but to poets who would soon appear almost everything must have seemed hopelessly old-fashioned. From the point of view I shall be taking up later, let me emphasize these matters: that the poet vacillates between writing of his own imminent death and turning away to subjects of opportunity; that there is no coherent engagement with time and no effective ordering of scene.

Another poem that contemplates death, but with a single-mindedness appropriate to actual imminence, is attributed to Anne Boleyn's brother George, perhaps while awaiting execution.[2] It begins, "O death, O death, rock me asleep, / Bring me to quiet rest." He addresses the "passing bell," which "will tell" others. He must die; "There is no remedy." His pains are said to be inexpressible, and alone in prison he laments his "destiny." Each of these is the subject of a stanza, and each is followed by the refrain addressing the bell. A bare farewell is then addressed to "my pleasures past," and an increase of present pain is welcomed as a sign "That life can not remain." Then the passing bell is ordered to stop and the "doleful knoll" announcing his actual death to begin. "Lord, pity thou my soul!" But the concluding lines prolong the moment of death and begin with a half step backward:

> Death doth draw nigh
> Sound dolefully!
> For now I die,
> I die, I die!

For the most part the declared situation and simple references express the pathos—these and the slight development provided by the manipulation of time. This latter seems to be an effort to represent the literal record of his feelings and their progression rather than the passage of actual time; he clearly lacks the power of imagination and art to coordinate the two. There is no overt didacticism, but it goes without saying that the pathos will remind witnesses of their own life and death. The limited range of topics, and these hardly more than mentioned, is like the person of the anguished speaker himself: a kind of exchangeable anonymity prevails, for anyone may fit himself into the basic part, for all must die.

John Harington the Elder's "Elegy Wrote in the Tower, 1554"[3] begins and ends in praise of death. First it is the relief from a life "that loathsomely doth last." The pace of time is painfully slow, and grief is ever "green"; therefore, "The death is sweet that short'neth such a life." The second stanza itemizes the previous life of pleasure under diminishing segments of time: the "pleasant years," "merry days," "joyful nights," "happy hours." They are all gone quickly, "And death makes end of all that life begun." The third stanza draws up a balance sheet of comparisons: death is a port of joy, life a lake that drowns all painfully; the sweetness of death ends "all annoy," "Life is so lewd it yieldeth all in vain"; as life brought bondage, "by death was freedom wrought." The speaker portrays himself as perhaps less anguished than bored, and the death he meditates on lacks all particularity or imminence. The meditation might have been written anywhere under various conditions, and the manner is almost as appropriate as the subject to furnish a prison exercise. The observations and the wit, the conventions and the organization—all were part of a general store of expression.

A fuller meditation in the form of an undeviating inventory is Thomas Proctor's "*Respice finem*,"[4] which begins, "Lo here the state of every mortall wight, / See here, the fine, of all their gallant ioyes." The steady inclusiveness has only two variations: it begins by listing the certainty awaiting representative examples "of every mortall wight," and after thirteen lines turns to cataloguing the uncertainties that corroborate the moral. Another variation is a kind of sermon in pronouns. It begins with the third person plural, *their, they*, which turns to the singular, *himself, he, his*. At the transition from certainty to uncertainty the pronouns shorten the reader's negotiable distance and become *we, our, us*. The last six lines are all *you* and *your*.

If the poem is dull and often crude, we cannot blame its defects on the materials themselves. Forty years later an anonymous poem, far better written, surveys the sepulchers in Westminster Abbey as "A Memento for Mortality."[5] It opens with the basic message, "Mortality, behold and fear!" The instruction evolves from tested examples of proved worth, expertly chosen, interpreted, and described. The momentum is a deliberate part of the general effect as examples radiate out from the commands: "Think how many . . . How . . . That," "Know . . . How," later simplified to "For here . . . Here . . .

Here . . . Here . . . Here." At the end the lessons are concentrated entirely in a few standard examples:

> Think then, this scythe, that mows down kings,
> Exempts no meaner mortal things.
> Then bid the wanton lady tread
> Amid these mazes of the dead;
> And these, truly understood
> More shall cool and quench the blood
> Than her many sports a-day,
> And her nightly wanton play:
> Bid her paint till day of doom,
> To this favour she must come.
> Bid the merchant gather wealth,
> The usurer exact by stealth,
> The proud mar beat it from his thought—
> To this shape all must be brought.

Nothing is new but the quality of the writing, which demonstrates how effectively the old thoughts and attitudes can still speak in a living voice. All the deceptions of the world and flesh can be reduced to an old unanswerable irony:

> Here are sands, ignoble things,
> Dropped from the ruined sides of Kings;
> With whom the poor man's earth being shown,
> The difference is not easily known.

And the contrast between palace and coffin repeats details and a final image centuries old but in a syntax, diction, and rhythm that admirers of Jonson might relish:

> Hence removed from beds of ease,
> Dainty fare, and what might please,
> Fretted roofs, and costly shows,
> To a roof that flats the nose.[6]

My last example is Nashe's "Adieu! farewell earth's bliss!"[7] The refrain at the end of each stanza declares, "I am sick, I must die. / *Lord, have mercy on us!*" The plague is referred to, "the bells do cry," and the speaker seems to be making his own farewell. Yet, the inventory that begins in the second line would fit a meditation preparing for the speaker's last day whenever it might come. "Earth's bliss," which might express the feelings of imminent loss, takes on the possibility of a longer view when the second line reminds us, "This world uncertain is." We soon hear that death is inescapable and proves that life's pleasures are trivial. Rich men are enjoined not to trust in the gold that "cannot buy you health." We are further reminded that "All things to end are made."

The famous third stanza begins on the same track but takes a different turn:

> Beauty is but a flower
> Which wrinkles will devour:
> Brightness falls from the air;
> Queens have died young and fair;
> Dust hath closed Helen's eye:
> I am sick, I must die.
>   *Lord, have mercy on us!*

Beauty as but a perishable flower represents the shining brevity of human desire, its objects and what they will become. The clusters of meaning acquired by insistent usage allow the emblematic flower to suggest a floral deathshead and also a process by which the flower of attractive youth becomes withered, corrugated, and "devoured." This last is taken from the open, imagistic exchange where gluttonous death and time have their attributes available for borrowing. The three lines that follow are three distinct lyric cries, parallel and without overt connections but still felt as a series. The brightness falling from the air is something that is declared to happen *now*, but the falling is not characterized by any objective reference or by suggestions concerning the nature of the brightness or the relative velocity of change. We know what the observer feels; the import of his response is that, as fact or feeling, the time of death is descending on the world. Then the nameless young queens of many stories are invoked. They have fallen from time, but their stories are part of the sense of ultimate loss as ever present. The third cry invokes a single story, ancient and enduring, one that makes Helen's beauty remembered. Her beauty, the cause of the vast, tragic story, is represented by her eye. The imagination of how the eye looked, and its power, is evoked after it has been closed, and after it has been identified as Helen's. The order produces an aftershock as the mind works back from the eye to Helen to Troy and forward again from "dust" as euphemistic agent to actual state.

But the unusual moment lapses and the standard inventory begins again. That "Worms feed on Hector brave" is not much more than a particular instance of what must happen to all strength. Then wit receives its full stanza and is thus ranged in importance beside beauty and strength:

> Wit with his wantonness
> Tasteth death's bitterness:
> Hell's executioner
> Hath no ears for to hear
> What vain art can reply.

This would include writers like the poet himself, who think so well of their calling that they now deserve special notice along with their betters who have been providing such examples for centuries. Finally, the coda includes everybody and urges every social rank

> To welcome destiny:
> Heaven is our heritage,
> Earth but a player's stage:
> Mount we unto the sky.

In spite of a thrilling broken moment, the poem is an old-fashioned meditative exhortation and dirge to remind the writer and all others that death is certain and that one must turn thoughts from the world to heaven. In the context, even "I am sick, I must die" hovers among a state of actual urgency, a poetic use of refrain, and the application of an effective device for giving meditative exercises a concrete point of departure. Only one strand of lyric feeling seems to speak momentarily for itself.

The discrimination made in the preceding sentence is recognizably modern, and I might perhaps think it too obvious to mention if it were not for the personal sense of wonder I wish to express. My chief purpose in these introductory pages has been to prepare the reader for what, though now antiquated, was once looked for and expected. My purpose does not, however, include making exquisite discriminations in the realm of the musty. The general subject in hand, particularly when the materials are composed in verse, requires the writer as well as the reader to keep improving his responses to the expected. This will surely affect one's recognition of and response to the unexpected.

CHAPTER FIVE

Death in Earnest: "Tichborne's Elegy"

It is the heaviest stone that melancholy can throw at a man, to tell him
he is at the end of his nature; or that there is no further state to come,
unto which this seemes progressionall, and otherwise made in vaine.
BROWNE, *Urne Burial*

Over *a long period* the philosophical and religious arguments on the
subject of death had been worked out with an irresistible clarity. By the
end of the sixteenth century these arguments had been supplemented
by a body of bold alternative arguments and briefly flourishing variations—all programmed for exemplary self-destruction. For whatever
the length of rope to be played out by subversive counterarguments, the
rope was real, fixed, unfrayable, and always ready for abrupt recall.
Many of the authoritative ways of understanding death could be reduced to rule and aphorism illustrated by some reliably familiar pregnant images. These conditions did not, of course, eliminate all free
room and energy for conflict. In taking up the task of presenting wrong
arguments, conscientious writers, well motivated but inspired by the
desire to make the bad look as tempting as possible, could produce
deviant arguments and their supporting images, which, however wise-
ly contained at the last, might still retain an uncertain incandescence and
be perhaps too well remembered. This danger latent in images has
always worried the teachers of right thinking as they have weighed the
obvious benefits and the partly unpredictable risks.

But the great historical enemy of right thinking was the restless
crowd of affections within, those passionate desires that could generate
a power and display capable of sweeping the individual toward good or
plunging him into ill. Nor did the affections lack their own forms of
reasoning—products of chaos, no doubt, but stubbornly determined,
elusive in changing their apparent shapes, and not without a cunning
apparatus for selective hearing, vision, and memory. Though every
instructed person knew the right way to think about the passions, the
methods appeared to work best in the absence of strong opposition.

In writing on the subject of death, I repeat, poets addressed their thoughts along the ways known to them. They needed to speak in the language they had, which belonged, by the history of use, both to right thinking, as that was understood, and to the passions. Their language was also in part a special one, endowed with the privileges and restrictions of poetry as these had been granted by custom or acquired by the history of successful accomplishment. These privileges and restrictions included the traditional materials, methods, and rules of expression. To these may be added the uses of commonplaces, conventions, and other punctuating assurances that a discourse licensed to imagine nevertheless resembled truth. Everything was to be ordered by the poet's wit (which included his power to invent) and by his "learned discretion," as a means of satisfying both the particular and the more comprehensive laws of decorum while figuring forth the chosen subject and, as not a few believed, the author by the style.

I begin by considering poems that can illustrate, but may also test and perhaps offer some qualifying views of the general conditions I have been describing. Poems written under the anticipation of imminent death—as on the eve of the author's execution—present a category so convincing that few readers will want to resist believing in the literal truth of the circumstances and the timing. What the poet writes in his "last words" will easily command a special attention. Indeed, belief may be disposed to anticipate matters by some willing initiative, and not a few poems were circulated and received as Sir Walter Raleigh's last literary testament. We shall come to him next, after looking at "Tichborne's Elegy":

> My prime of youth is but a frost of cares;
>   My feast of joy is but a dish of pain;
> My crop of corn is but a field of tares;
>   And all my good is but vain hope of gain:
> The day is past, and yet I saw no sun;
> And now I live, and now my life is done.
>
> My tale was heard, and yet it was not told;
>   My fruit is fall'n, and yet my leaves are green;
> My youth is spent, and yet I am not old;
>   I saw the world, and yet I was not seen:
> My thread is cut, and yet it is not spun;
> And now I live, and now my life is done.
>
> I sought my death, and found it in my womb;
>   I looked for life, and saw it was a shade;

I trod the earth, and knew it was my tomb;
   And now I die, and now I was but made:
My glass is full, and now my glass is run;
   And now I live, and now my life is done.[1]

If the title had been lost (not likely), or never been assigned (almost as unlikely), one might just possibly be reading a meditative exercise. Nor would the verses be out of place as the formal speech of a character in an early drama (or a later one cultivating an old-fashioned scene and style)—a character who has just heard bad news or felt some premonition that moves him at once to a set speech taking an inventory of life from the perspective of death and across the passage of time. The actual imminence of death may be the point of leverage but does not obtrude itself, and the fact of death, not any particular form, swings its weight more like a pendulum than an axe.

We may observe that rejection of the values of life, like many rejections of love, will be supported by traditional reasoning but also by the resources of the passions and their dubious but insistent forms of reasoning. Under some circumstances a kind of opportune, if temporary and informal, partnership can be arranged, by which the passions are available for trying to hate what cannot be possessed or loved. In order to achieve a willed and honorable acceptance of necessity, and to do so by means of a difficult transition that cannot be memorized or reduced to habit, if a man finds himself rejected he may need to answer by a reciprocal action that also rejects. Toward life the comprehensive religious answer was acceptance of its loss, but that answer has traditionally accommodated itself to human weakness, including a transitional middle ground of rejecting the values of life by summoning up the rhetoric of contempt or hatred, after which the expendable instrument of hatred can simply disappear into the true form of the highest love for the divine.

These matters will occupy us further, but let me touch briefly upon another habit of thought which may be observed in Tichborne's poem. Some of the qualities of stiffness make claims on our attention. Men had written similarly for a long time. Eyes, ears, and expectations had been thoroughly trained, and the normal reading, we may well think, would have responded, not to the peculiar and the individual, but to the aesthetic satisfactions of recognizing the expected and its ordered appropriateness. The manner is deliberately artificial, in the old sense of the word, and is made by art to express a formality proper to a serious address. Every age enjoys, as a privileged courtesy, the experience of recognizing the particular right kind of skillful expression of shared taste—and also enjoys, when the timing and the skill are right, the special opportunities for making that taste the occasion for artistic games. In the 1580s, through long familiarity and respect, the formal manner provided pleasure on its own, and a capable poet would know how to impose apparent solemnity upon slight fictions as well. Sidney had the gifts and the refined sensibility to make poems out of the exploitation of what he was rejecting.

A decade later the style could be mocked and usefully parodied by writers moving toward a different outlook and trying out new skills widely available but not yet fully exploited. By then the old taste had lost much of its appeal and authority. The deliberately stiffened address and some of the very limitations that once were anticipated and desired, and must then have struck the right chords of response, had become predictable in many of the wrong ways. Stories of this kind are well known, and it always requires an imaginative effort to acknowledge what may no longer be experienced as it was. Every outmoded style, once valid, raises many problems. Even when the style may have been discarded chiefly because newer manners opened more and apparently better possibilities, there will always be losses, often not inconsiderable ones, which other improvements will not be able to replace in kind.

Occasionally the charm of a famous gesture may owe something to the fact that the manner went out of date before the gesture, which became prominently fixed in a style that could not be revived. I am thinking of Dyer's best-known poem, "My mind to me a kingdom is," but I mention it for other purposes. The basic form is that of the inventory, which is, however, less tightly organized than in Tichborne's poem. But the address and the manner do not neglect the reliable properties of formal seriousness. Contrasting pairs are frequently yoked in service and the linkage of consonants and of syntactic units makes certain that the pairings are not marred by any unwanted shadows or muting:

> No wily wit to salve a sore.
>
> . . . .
> They get with toil, they keep with fear.
>
> . . . .
> I fear no foe, I fawn no friend.
>
> . . . .
> Their treasure is their only trust,
> A cloaked craft their store of skill.

The climax of one stanza collects the sober march of antitheses with an extravagant exhibition of virtuoso compressions:

Some have too much, yet still do crave;
　I little have, and seek no more.
They are but poor, though much they have,
　And I am rich with little store:
They poor, I rich; they beg, I give;
They lack, I leave; they pine, I live.

(Ault, p. 124)

A flourish of sententious fireworks like this may signal the end of a long, once thriving line. Still, better poets like Sidney or Raleigh could continue to dazzle without abandoning all the old ways, while producing more strenuous inventions gracefully carried through.

The taste for certain formal rigidities may be difficult to recover once it has been lost, but such basic devices of expression as refrain, ironic antithesis, inventory, and the summing up at a time of crisis could hardly go out of poetic use, whatever modifications might be made from time to time. We may feel confident that we have not lost touch with these devices.

If Tichborne is writing in anticipation of certain death on the morrow, he is nevertheless doing so while following one set of established rules for the regular meditating on death by arraigning the deceptions of life. Whatever the actual circumstances and the actual time schedule, he fixes the *tempus dramatis* of personal death in a special dimension of time, an intensely imagined present. The declared "now" of the poem is an imagined present in which the mind methodically reviews and judges a past that deceived or disappointed in every respect, in which the inventoried past confesses the faults of illusions and false promises—an imagined present in which past life, present life, and future death exist together, now.

The inventory is drawn up in double columns as the paired items begin to march by, one pair to a line and every line end-stopped. When the first stanza comes to a close with no evident progress and is apparently summed up by its last line, the second stanza turns back as if to begin a similar series. But the antitheses do not again begin by juxtaposing the hopefulness of then and the wretchedness of now. The dominant copular unit "is but" becomes "and yet" in stanza two, and the second term of each pair does not now complete any absolute contrasts like those in which spring "is but" winter; joy, pain; harvest, weeds. Instead, in all but the first and fourth lines the first term presents the now (fallen fruit, youth spent, thread cut), and the second term, in all the lines, unfolds a potential dissipation or anomaly of the first term. The effect is to ring out changes on the unfulfillment of time and to emphasize an abnormal arrested state, "And now I live, and now my life is done."

Looking back, one can see that though stanza one makes no evident progress and has to start again, a shift probably begins at line four ("And all my good is but vain hope of gain") and is clearly evident in the following line ("The day is past, and yet I saw no sun"). But it is the kind of transition that is more likely to be noticed in retrospect—after the repetitions of the second stanza have confirmed the change. Stanza two comes to a close, having made its repeated and varied point, circling without apparent progress. The last line announces itself as a refrain, which promises that it sums up more than the single stanza and that we shall hear it again, with further meaning possible and further feeling certain in its renewed vibrations. When we look back, the refrain seems to confirm the state of standstill, in which the illusions of the past have been brought up to date, and in which present illusion includes the baffling sense of living and concluding life in the same arrested moment of time.

The third stanza immediately begins a progressive development. The paired antitheses occur in a syntax again slightly altered, but the verbs are now active and purposive. The speaker is himself the agent, and what the antitheses represent is expressed with a charged intensity and concreteness:

> I sought my death, and found it in my womb;
> I looked for life, and saw it was a shade;
> I trod the earth, and knew it was my tomb.

The pointed succinctness of the first three lines offers a review that makes the previous reviews seem leisurely by contrast, with ample time to arraign and lament betrayals and losses and the loss of time. Death is now first named directly, and the contrasting term declares an identity at the source before personally experienced time and its metaphorical representations began. Everything points toward a deepening quality of knowledge by a responsible agent who sought, found, saw, knew. It did not, somehow, happen to the man; he made it happen, was actively present in the process of discovery, and established, one is led to think, some purposeful relationship with what he came to understand. The knowledge is not at all original but reflects philosophical and religious traditions of thought and imagery. The knowledge feels, or is made to feel, new to him, however, and comes in a new way, breaking the old rhythm of exposition. For one thing, the sense of time is different, no mingling of past and present but all put in the past tense. Yet the past invoked is a special one that exists in a state and a relationship that assert unquestionable authority. Though this past is never explained, it is made to feel different and separate from the past of the previous itemizations. The summary effect is also different—like a past action brought to mind with a present clarity that suggests the imminence of a further action, or resolution, of the mind. A parallel effect is that such a firm and focused grasp of traditional thought would lead those familiar with the issues, and with their history in human crises, to expect a further step available to religious belief and resolution.

Instead, the episode turns out to have been a climactic recapitulation that finds in active, urgent knowledge only a deeper level of illusion in the nature of life itself. No further step occurs, and the old rhythm begins to assert itself again. "And now I die," he writes, as if to counter the refrain from a new perspective of time and knowledge gained from the past. But he concludes the line with an antithesis that fuses past and present in a powerfully imagined abbreviation: "and now I was but made." The sense of personal wonder and dismay is directed toward the illusion of time as a fact that cannot be suppressed. It simply is, and does not yield itself to moral or intellectual rearrangements—to established patterns by which rejection becomes transformation and enters an order leading toward comfort and hope. The second half of the line that comes after the climax ("and now I was but made") suggests a muted cry of anguished bewilderment, articulated as a kind of semiobjective wonder but felt within as a stir of recognition protesting the blank brevity between death and birth. The expression is also in effect a nonverbal refrain that heightens the self-directed movement in those brief, undeveloped, unconnected statements of unfulfilled personal history: "My tale was heard, and yet it was not told . . . I saw the world, and yet I was not seen."

The penultimate line seems to return to the style of the first two stanzas: "My glass is full, and now my glass is run." But the opposition, only this once, imitates the form of the refrain. The fullness of life comes first and is present, while time has run out. In effect, the illusion is like that of the preceding line but does not repeat the sense of pained immediacy which comes in part from acknowledging an interval, however short and meaningless, between birth and death. The refrain then finishes the closing up—of the poem, and of the speaker's relationship to the poem—which expresses the speaker's relationship to life, imagined in a moment occupied by past, present, and future and wholly dominated by a future implicit in the past but explicit only in the present.

The reader who anticipated the disclosure of a further stage of meaning in the refrain was partly mistaken. Like the forward movement in the first three lines of the last stanza, the promise latent in a refrain serves only to confirm the turning back. All that is new is that the old meaning was and is final. The imagined present and the methodical review have stated their evidence against the illusions of life and time, but the poet, by what he says and by what he will not say, refuses to move beyond the determined shape of his vision.

Life can be, and is, rejected by the mind here expressing itself in naming and characterizing externals while describing itself very little, and that indirectly. Death is not, and cannot be, rejected. It is not, however, here accepted by the mind, though the human records demonstrate that it can be accepted, and some of the ways to do so are well known. In the poem death is not dealt with as an illusion but was there from the beginning and could be *known,* as a future implicit in the past. All of the history of death's having been *felt,* however, is contracted into the imagined present of eighteen lines of poetry which create the sense of an arrested moment of composite time, in which all parts freely move and interchange—except the future, which is death and the unmoved mover of the poem.

Life looked for was seen to be "a shade"—a summary judgment of the world and of everything in it. "My tale was heard, and yet it was not told." Is that only a single item in the inventory of illusion or a special protest in his own case, one not adequately covered by the definitive judgment against life? Is he referring to the foregone conclusion of early death recognized when the "end" of his personal story (his "life," the testimony he gave at his "hearing") was known in advance to the listeners, and perhaps to the dispirited teller? Does he refer uniquely to a peremptory hearing, *pro forma,* in which his own giving of evidence was blocked and confined routinely and was telling only in its failure to be taken into account? In an older sense of the word, "told" could mean "reckoned," "esteemed." If he is entering a personal protest, the disabling unreality of life would make the desire to *tell* one's tale so that it would be *heard* a joint venture in idiocy. If life is altogether illusory, his own case is trivial and repetitious. What is he trying to tell now so that it will be heard? Not that "all must die," though that was an inexhaustible sweeping theme into which every item he adduces could be made to fit, even if not in the poem as he composed it. The judgment against life, if true, would extend to his own feelings. They may be absurd but they are not registered as unreal; nor is that dominant, unjudged urge to persevere in writing the poem unreal.

Except perhaps for the tale heard but not told—and that chiefly if interpreted as a personal reference, disguised and muted but smoldering with disruptive potency—there are no thoughts, images, or rhythms that may pass as original. Yet the poem is moving, beautiful, and original in its deployment of the familiar. If we fail to respond unreservedly to the formal parade of meditative rediscoveries, arranged and costumed in accord with a prevailing code of intellectual and aesthetic propriety, we may still give respectful attention to the tale and to the values represented by once-current ways of thinking, though these are dressed out in a style that has been antique for centuries. Our critical habits of thought, insofar as they are habits, must be different from Tichborne's and from those of the first readers of his poem. But one may not unreasonably imagine that any "judicious sharp spectator" (Raleigh's phrase), or Raleigh himself, would have heard the part of the tale that was not told. That it would have been heard with differences we cannot doubt; nor can we enter fully into a superior, living sixteenth-century response.

What I have tried to hear and describe is a lyric that expresses both in its subject and in its composition a commanding sense of the urgent pressure of time. The lyric is unflinching in its meticulously orthodox use of the passions to produce the arguments of illusion in the service of the established ends of reason. But the poet refuses to discard the passions when they have done their appointed work and to move beyond them to a further path. He does not move beyond the one mystery discovered and adhered to, the personal reality of the arrested moment that contains all of his own past, present, and future.[2]

CHAPTER SIX

Dying in Jest and Earnest: Raleigh

As if when after Phebus is dessended
And leves a light mich like the past dayes dawninge,
And every toyle and labor wholy ended
Each livinge creature drawth to his restinge

Wee should beginn by such a partinge light
To write the story of all ages past
And end the same before th' approchinge night.
. . . .
Thus home I draw, as deaths longe night drawes onn.

RALEIGH, *The 11th: and last booke of the Ocean to Scinthia*

Raleigh *inherited the* same basic ways of thinking about death as his younger contemporary, Tichborne. He was, however, not an obscure youth remembered for a poem about a personal crisis. The great courtier, captain, exile, and prisoner inhabited a world in which other people, friends and enemies, were real and not to be thought of as secondary images in the general shadow of existence. His own actions and words were reported and studied at home and in centers of power throughout Europe. His sense of himself as private and public person was not subject to disabling thoughts about illusion and reality. In response to conflict he acted with a certainty that commanded imagination and excluded any reflexes not to his purpose. So if there is a tale to be told, he will make it heard.

The poem written in his Bible and left in the Gatehouse the morning of his execution I shall consider last and approach from the discussion of three poems that present views of death. The first is "The Life of Man," which jests at the methodical order of play that comes to an appointed end:

What is our life? a play of passion,
Our mirth the musicke of division,
Our mothers wombes the tyring houses be,

Where we are drest for this short Comedy,
Heaven the Iudicious sharpe spectator is,
That sits and markes still who doth act amisse,
Our graves that hide us from the searching Sun,
Are like drawne curtaynes when the play is done,
Thus march we playing to our latest rest,
Onely we dye in earnest, that's no Iest.[1]

Until the radical coda, the relish of the wit lies in discovering and placing the few right points of comparison that will give a figurative answer the look and feeling of truth. The answer offers a selection of metaphorical equivalents and does so with casual precision, as if these were drawn from a comprehensive inventory that a more solemn writer would have delivered with unsparing completeness. The last line, however, the extrinsic point upon which the fiction turns, would seem to strip the fiction with one rending gesture that mocks the whole enterprise—which includes the self-conscious art that conceals its grim determination and acts out the neatly turned and fitted nature of a well-made play, the precision of marching parallels that do not sense the end of the game they are playing. Yet something is not included and persists beyond the final answer that seems to dismiss the figurative answer. For the image of "our life" is not itself retracted. The answer is a figurative one, and both the initial choice and the selected comparisons contain a critical view that does not neglect the element of illusion—from womb to the grave that stops all searching inquiry; from the dressing rooms, where the illusion is made ready in advance, to the drawn curtain that finally divides the spectators from the actors. The one simile of the poem likens grave and curtain; we are left to imagine ourselves on either side of that full stop. Everything in the imagined play must be directed toward the satisfactions and regrets that mark the success of a final curtain; at the same time the comedy must maintain, among its other illusions, that until the very end the end has no part in the action. What is not included in the mockery, or pointed to as an answering moral to cap the fiction and the last gesture that seems to destroy it, is any discernible suggestion that the existence of "earnest" death should make us revise the acting of our lives, or should lead to the closing of the theaters or to an act of abolishing the basic validity of the comparison between life and the stage. The heavenly Spectator takes critical notes on individual performance in the spectacle; we may note that the Judge seems to take excellence for granted and records only "who doth act amisse." We may also note that the Judge seems to side with the figurative answer, that life is a play and the standards are those of the stage.

Indeed, for the play that is an image of "our life" there is no distinct audience except God.

A human audience is nevertheless implied. The poem takes up the familiar message that "all must die" and makes the jesting communal and symbolic, like the experience of spectators. The "earnest" part is actual and individual. No competent reader of the poem needs to be told that we die separately, one at a time, and that we may treat life like a play, and it is, until the end. The ultimate wit of the poem is in its not saying more than it does. It presents a truly elegant *memento mori* without a shred of applicable advice.

"The Lie" begins:

> Goe soule the bodies guest
> Upon a thankelesse arrant,
> Feare not to touch the best
> The truth shall be thy warrant:
> Goe since I needs must die,
> And give the world the lie.
>
> (p. 45)

After an inventory of the world's ills, the poem concludes with one reference to a rule of social custom (that giving the lie "Deserves no lesse then stabbing") and one reference to higher law:

> Stab at thee he that will;
> No stab thy soule can kill.

"Since I needs must die" would suggest that the truth-telling is occasioned by some calculated imminence of death. By the end of the poem we must revise our sense of the calculation.

The central method is encyclopedic. That is, the coverage is extensive but selective in the length of the entries, the omissions, and the choice of detail. The warrant for truth and full coverage is also a license that permits some latitude (not unprecedented in encyclopedic practice) for afterthoughts and items not quite in order but self-justifying and a shame to leave out. The survey begins with two brief, well-placed demolitions—of court and church—and then moves with more leisure to the analysis of "potentates," executives in high position, and wealthy free-spenders. These are real figures in any Renaissance polity; nor were their names unknown in England. Then comes a list of particular abstractions that men serve or seek or possess ignorantly—each pricked off in a single line. "Wit" and "wisdom" conclude this stage of an evolving list, each honored by requiring two lines to set them down properly. Then certain learned institutions and their ways are lined up, and also charity, fortune, nature, friendship, and so on. What is told to each of these is concentrated into one line; seeming to conclude this group, "arts" and "schools" both receive the relative amplitude of two lines of exposure. Finally, there is a kind of addendum of four items which have thus far gone unmentioned. The last two items read like rough notes from an unending list not yet put into grammatical form:

> Tell manhood shakes off pittie,
> Tell virtue least preferreth.

The force is cumulative and the point of view single in its direction, though the wit adjusts itself skillfully to the accepted challenge of revealing an essential falsehood in every object brought under attention. Part of the warrant would seem to be that of a *contemptus mundi*, though the illusions of life are not the standard ones for man contemplating the world and the state of his soul; the illusions are, rather, more special ones—those that belong to the institutions and preferred values that run the world.

Instruction to the soul is a motivating device—like "Say, Muse," or the later instructions to a painter, or the still current allegorical processions. As we begin with the leading figures of power in the state we seem to be invited to view a procession. But the apparent order changes, and by the tempo and bulk of its inclusions a parade becomes a crowded show, as the undeviating purpose quickly applies to each representative subject (literal or figurative) a comment that exposes the limiting or disabling fault underneath its name.

The telling suggests a last testament, a compendium long in the making and, as it were, under the compacting pressure of extended time and enforced silence, a final telling, now with no time to waste. An anonymous man, ready to die, reads from his prophetic scrip and tells the devastating truth to a world that lives by a code requiring rebuttal in the brief and punctual form of stabbing. The initial cause of the poem, the soul's errand ("since I needs must die"), is transposed, with a silent omission of process, into effect. And while the soul tells mortal truth, a comprehensive story of the world's body, the soul's own tale is not told. Its authorized compulsiveness is borrowed without due payment except for the brief, bare, defiant reference to the known immortality of the soul. There is no mention of higher values; nor is there even the suggestion of a hierarchy of falsehood which might imply some positive guide leading toward a central fault such as pride, self-love, avarice, or lack of charity. Instead, we are treated to a whole world of appearances, all different, all the same, and the many lies are without a master lie.

But the inventory of accusation pointedly ignores the standard inherited illusions man has repeatedly found in life. For all of the crowded room is preempted by the display of man-made illusions crafted out of the opportunities of position and privilege. The death briefly and vaguely referred to at the beginning is a feigned death, a jest that is the occasion for a long, earnest comedy, mocking what man has made out of life. One unmistakable effect flowering from no acknowledged cause is that the poet takes exceptional pleasure (certain to infuriate contemporaries) in the act and display of his marksmanship. Everything is exactly aimed, and there is a flowing wealth of targets. Toward each there is an appropriate concentration of economy—one or two shafts, though potentates merit three. The soul celebrates its expected enfranchisement from the body by producing the remarkable flourish of many acts of ostentatiously spare precision.

Time is pretended, not seriously engaged or imagined time, the occasion of the jest but not part of the subject. For all of the itemization is concurrent and exists in a kind of corrupt eternal present from which the immortal soul is taking its own sweet ceremonial departure. No private revenge upon his body will be able to match his public arraignment of the false souls that animate the world. And to judge from the record, the master jest of a master poet can safely anticipate the angrily inept poetic replies provoked by his individual condemnations and his general imputation, always carefully repeated, that all ventured answers will be falsehoods in defense of falsehood.

"The Passionate Man's Pilgrimage" does not use the point of death as a platform from which to deliver an oration that gives the world the lie. The point of death has a literal basis, which makes its use as a pretext a more powerful and flexible conceptual device for writing the story of one's own death. The poem mingles abruptness and leisureliness, earnestness and jest, in unprecedented ways. We are at first introduced to objects and attitudes that belong to thoughts of death as the entrance into the desired second life. The traditional enemy of life, time and its circus of treacherous illusions, is quite ignored. The poem will weave together an open, unrationalized schedule of time in the hereafter, and then the calculated placements of past, present, and future in a skillful deployment of narrative time. The standard illusionary aspects of life are not taken up directly. Our bodies, for instance, have simply been shaken off as "gownes of clay" somewhere or other on the path of travel. The opening vision acts as if it is too happy contemplating its new life to waste time and attention by considering, in order to disparage or belatedly reject, the flawed materials of earthly life. Everything necessary is expressed by the implied contrasts between life and the eternal rewards of peace, faith, joy, and glory in the bliss and beauty of a heaven where the fulfilled soul no longer thirsts. As an ecstatic vision, the early part of the poem differs from what might be expected, chiefly in the matter-of-fact tone with which the soul settles down among the standard wonders that can only be dreamed of in the different landscape of earthly life. It is also remarkable how easily the rapt courtier slips into a homely pilgrim style of seeing and saying, as he names the activities and the accouterments of his journey. The one assertive abruptness that momentarily disturbs the landscape and anticipates the central scene of heaven's court and trial is the powerful

> Blood must be my bodies balmer,
> No other balme will there be given.

He begins alone, not praying exactly, and speaking in the grammar of the imperative mood but neither demanding, quite, nor entreating, nor exhorting. "Give me," he says, as if to some invisible quartermaster, the following standard equipment for my pilgrimage:

> Give me my Scallop shell of quiet,
> My staffe of Faith to walke upon,
> My Scrip of Ioy, Immortall diet,
> My bottle of salvation:
> My Gowne of Glory, hopes true gage,
> And thus Ile take my Pilgrimage.
>
> (p. 49)

He speaks from a willed threshold of imagined time, present to the mind and hence graduating to a distinct mental future, a freely moving modality of time, as if autonomous, but still anticipating in the narrative an ordinary future that is on the schedule but has not yet arrived.

Then comes the abrupt, punctuating reference to blood, anticipating the plea of Christ's blood—past and eternally present, to be invoked, but not yet—to coincide exactly with that near-future moment when the executioner's axe will release his own blood. The poem takes its own good time in the leisurely travel of visionary exploration in the new world of heaven. Soon the speaker enjoys the society of similar happy souls, and he shares the knowledge of his (unexplained) visionary priority, showing them where to drink and fill their pilgrim bottles with "immortality." Then they travel, as one, to their destination, the high court of heaven. The earnest, naive manner of pilgrim vision drops away without the slightest trace of anticipation, or any token of narrative rationalization, or later renewal by touch or echo, as the descriptive account begins in a new voice to insist on the explicit contrast between heaven and earth:

From thence to heavens Bribeles hall
Where no corrupted voyces brall,
No Conscience molten into gold,
Nor forg'd accusers bought and sold,
No cause deferd, nor vaine spent Iorney,
For there Christ is the Kings Atturney:
Who pleades for all without degrees,
And he hath Angells, but no fees.

The jury then evoked, however it may resemble the terrible ones constituted on earth, is nevertheless made up truly "Of our sinnes and
sinfull fury," and the verdicts against our souls are just, but Christ
pleads his own death, "and then we live."

All companions drop silently away, and he returns from the imagined future to the imagined point of death.

And this is my eternall plea,
To him that made Heaven, Earth, and Sea,
Seeing my flesh must die so soone,
And want a head to dine next noone,
Iust at the stroke when my vaines start and spred
Set on my soule an everlasting head.
Then am I readie like a palmer fit,
To tread those blest paths which before I writ.

The conclusion begins in the high rhetoric of public oratorical prayer,
the first member of a proposition that characterizes itself as an "eternall
plea" and implicitly claims a place in the community of prayer by
including a basic ritual of praise to the Creator. At the same time, the
syntactic form of the prayer is clearly indicated: that of a suspended
sentence, the closing of which lies within the control of the speaker,
within his choice of the degree and kind of intervening detail and its
termination. He first moves from the "eternall" to a nonvisual "seeing,"
the death of the flesh, "so soone." He then constructs a detached and
humorous visual scene of his personal death—presenting a gracefully
indifferent close view of the violence of the severing as if it were merely
a natural act of description. When the "everlasting head" closes the
period of his prayer, it does so with a dazzling virtuosity of exact
temporal coincidence—executional, syntactic, and devotional. The jest
is consciously one that may have to be made good in earnest, before the
eyes of friends and foes, which this dress rehearsal anticipates in calm,
clear defiance—so perfectly poised that it can afford a generous measure
of delight in the performance.

The last couplet brings time back to the present moment of contemplation. "Then am I readie," for all has been brought up to date—the past of narrative vision, the episode of heavenly judgment, the future ("so soone") imagined as present, and the formal last word of the "eternall plea." To which is added a further last word, as epilogue. The emphasis of the poem is left where intended by the casual brusqueness and air of finished business, the vision already on record, and no further inclination to repeat or vary or amplify it. One assumes that the manners of the speaker's piety were not intended to please all. Participants in Raleigh's own trial would feel themselves aspersed, defamed, traduced; and even dispassionate participants, or friendly readers, would nevertheless be reminded uncomfortably of their own acquired religious wisdom concerning the proper frame of mind and spirit for accepting death. Raleigh's taste and tone are quite out of the ordinary at a time when nothing but the ordinary can be thought right, and the poem should trouble many decent practitioners of piety—not less because the speaker, in those matters he regards as the essential ones, is aggressively orthodox. He takes the limited phase of earthly existence quite for granted; he indulges in no angry dismantling of illusions he can no longer enjoy. All the weight of his emphasis falls on the mercy and fidelity of the Christian promise and its absolute difference from the practice of power and justice on earth. Therefore, the part of the message he proclaims does not lead to being dutiful and docile—least of all to those who run the world. He is himself, however briefly, acknowledged to be a sinner who nevertheless claims the due of his faith in Christ's sacrifice. The acknowledgment is hardly a penitential confession, but it does resemble his prayer from the scaffold, inviting all witnesses to join in his prayer for forgiveness and salvation as he rejects the sinful state of having lived in a sinful world—of having lived as a man "full of vanity . . . a sinful life in all sinful callings." In the poem he is briefer and more general, acknowledging "the grand twelve million Iury, / Of our sinnes and sinfull fury." That is a good round number that seems to take sin seriously but is an obstacle to any penitential consideration of one's own particular sins. He is less brief and general in contrasting chosen aspects of Christ's exemplary life with earthly departures from that model.

The *manner of* his leaving the world, for which the poem offers itself as testament, has indeed made parts of his challenge to the world and its lies extremely difficult for his Christian enemies to forgive—though that, properly, is their problem and not his. Friends and dispassionate, "judicious" spectators will observe that (except for neglecting to forgive his enemies) he does not act "amiss" in the difficult last scene, which he plays through as a comedy for which he has already written the happy ending. It is one's own death, individual and center stage, but with something of the free, eccentric, venerable hilarity that the old oracular message, "all must die," could liberate from strange recesses of the human mind. As for the absence of any trace of humble acceptance and resignation, or of the humanizing tact of discernible hesitancy or reluctance, what he has to offer instead is the demonstration of un-cowed, clear-eyed contempt for the human agents of his death, and the demonstration of a simple, untroubled Christian faith.

Finally, there was a last night and morning and the verses he left at the Gatehouse before his execution:

> Even such is tyme which takes in trust
> Our yowth, our Ioyes, and all we have,
> And payes us butt with age and dust:
> Who in the darke and silent grave
> When we have wandred all our wayes
> Shutts up the storye of our dayes.
> And from which earth and grave and dust
> The Lord shall rayse me up I trust.

(p. 72)

The first six lines are borrowed, with one change, from the sixth and last stanza of an earlier poem, "Nature that washt her hands in milke." "Oh cruell Time" becomes "Even such is tyme," and without a preceding fable and its kind of ironic detail and development, the one stanza now gains in stark concentration. The cruelty of time belongs to love's story and its well-known plots. The barest summary of the one essential story now tells all. Besides, a coda has been added, the Christian answer to time. We may well be uncertain: the tone is not at all triumphant, as ordinary expectations would have preferred, and the last line may be, one cannot tell, more or less muted. I read the ending as nevertheless firm, quiet, and humble, Raleigh speaking to himself in solitary earnest. All are included in the public fate presided over by time (we—our—all). But the release from each death is a private negotiation between God and the self for which the only pledges and warrants are personal hope and trust.

Preparing for death, he sums up his life and character. Without the bold wit, the character here is the same as that which displayed itself in "The Passionate Man's Pilgrimage," and will play out the public scene on the scaffold, where wit is necessary to validate the truth of character.

What seems clear in the main statement of the poem is that, like Tichborne's elegy and like none of Raleigh's other poems on death, these few lines respond entirely to a vision of time and to those bare actions and consequences that, when contemplated, present the one knowable face of death. The poem speaks from a point clearly and personally chosen, one that lies beyond the possibility of seeking any relief by naming or abusing the illusions produced and fostered by time. Time takes in trust all that we have and leaves us in a state that only another trust may remedy. As in the play that represents the mirth and passion of our life, there is no suggestion that all is a mistake or dream, which we could deny and so escape acting out the illusions of life.

In this poem he does not deign to argue with the conditions of human fate. He is making no discoveries, and he is not appealing the judgment, which he can see as clearly as others who have cast up accounts on the point of death. The flourish of joys is repaid, and the all of our story shut up, the whole business conducted in a kind of encompassing present. The courtesy toward God is brief and in basic form, a summary statement without personality or fervor. The future lies in God's action, the present in the condemned man's trust. Elsewhere he is the master of an art that takes upon itself the high privilege of taunting with splendid incivility man-made illusions and their custodians and beneficiaries. In writing of his own death in earnest he is the master of an intellectual courtesy that will not rail against or lament over the illusions of life which he as others accepted in youth and joy and hope.

In other themes and other actions Raleigh can sail with the wind. He would flatter the Queen and others in passion and mirth. Time has a painful but less absolute face in the vicarious death of exile, when joys expire "Like truthles dreames"; when the story is that of a wanderer "in unknowne waies," and the worst of time is that "Of all which past, the sorrow onely staies" (p. 12). In the epitaph nothing stays, but the summary at hand is an act not altogether without some force of resistance. For the poem is an effort to complete the story himself before time "Shutts up the storye of our dayes." To name the silence is to have the last word possible, which, given the conditions described, is not a negligible accomplishment.

CHAPTER SEVEN

Imagined Dyings: John Donne

A *famous metaphor,* well liked in the Renaissance, can ring changes on the ways human life and death resemble a theatrical performance. So Herrick ends *"The Plaudite, or end of life"* with an airy amusement:

> The first Act's doubtful, (but we say)
> It is the last commends the Play.

That cheerful comic pose, which will turn apparent triviality into something else, lies outside the rule of Donne's "else Almighty" wit. His fictional deaths to furnish scenes of life are to be understood as provisional metaphors, nimbly contingent and affecting thought and passion in various ways that stir and direct the imagination. But in fictional deaths that illustrate death the metaphors are drawn within tighter lines. As for his use of the theatrical analogy, it is further constrained by the apparent absence of any expected audience other than that of the poet himself and, if He deigns to hear, God. The liberties Donne permits himself are the extraordinary ones of a special theater in which the actor-author-spectator performs.

So Donne will test the soundness of the imagined action of life by stopping it and imposing a radical revision. The last act will be ordered to begin at once: "Oh my blacke Soule! now thou art summoned" (Sonnet 4). "This is my playes last scene . . . my minutes latest point, / And gluttonous death, will instantly unjoynt / My body, and soule" (Sonnet 6). Or the personal last act may be enlarged and coordinated with the final day of judgment: "What if this present were the worlds last night?" (Sonnet 13). "At the round earths imagin'd corners, blow / Your trumpets, Angells, and arise, arise" (Sonnet 7).[1]

These examples represent one kind of arbitrary extreme by means of which the imagined moment of death makes room for a conclusion that may, it is hoped, release the anticipated benefits of beginning with the end. It is arbitrary, of course, to interpret these poems as only exemplifying dramatic analogy. *Respice finem* was a household word and spiritual preventive medicine. These poems also resemble the established procedures of Ignatian meditation. I single out the dramatic analogy both because I think it is operative and because it will help illustrate some matters still to come.

In "Goodfriday, 1613. Riding Westward," there is no peremptory beginning near the end. The elaborate pretext of the situation—the peculiarities of time and motion, stellar and human, the great event that Donne's back is turned toward as he reports what he would otherwise have seen—all is meticulously carried forward and suspended until enough time, weight, and momentum have been collected. All the details have in truth been present:

> They'are present yet unto my memory,
> For that looks towards them; and thou look'st towards mee,
> O Saviour, as thou hang'st upon the tree.
>
> (34–36)

The *looking towards* that reveals unity of countermovements breaks through the arbitrary fiction and all traditional ideas of ruling motions and transcends the laws of space and time. The speaker's casual act of perverseness becomes the opportunity for progressive meeting and turning, and these presuppose an ultimate conjunction, for "Who sees Gods face, that is selfe life, must dye."

Many good poets cannot manage their voice in speaking directly to God. Here Donne's voice is not elevated or humble or sifted through the appropriate language of Scripture but is passionate, insistent, complex, mingling strong penitential desires directed toward the self and devout reverence for God's power and goodness:

> I turne my backe to thee, but to receive
> Corrections, till thy mercies bid thee leave.
> O thinke mee worth thine anger, punish mee,
> Burne off my rusts, and my deformity,
> Restore thine Image, so much, by thy grace,
> That thou may'st know mee, and I'll turne my face.
>
> (37–42)

The strength of personal desire approaches the style of command, employing as due to the human exigency the grammar of the imperative mood, but punctuating that mood by sure, brief observances of who commands the needed mercy and grace; and further, the tacit presence of a clear intention directs the human assertiveness toward conditions that express the known ways and ends of God's will. Although the arbitrary initial fiction seems to be used up once the vision of memory and the mysterious "looking" of Christ on the cross meet and are locked together, the fiction then renews itself in a further development.

For the poet speaks as if he is privileged to name his own conditions and as if it lies within his own power to turn his face. And yet the privilege he asserts is that of prayer, and the sanctioned desire he names as the essential condition is that he be *known* in the restored image that Christ desires to see. Among other understood matters that are unnamed are these: a vast pivotal *if,* and all the progressive degrees of *knowing,* and all the degrees of turning the face which come short of the perfect meeting of divine and human desire. Insofar as his own will participates in the issue of death, and counts, he will turn his face and die a true death only when, by grace, the original image of Adam has been restored "so much . . . That thou may'st know mee." The last sentence of the poem, harsh with the passionate urgency and strain of human effort to assert desire inside and outside the territory of the will, is a marvel of religious grammar and syntax.

To repeat my limited point, not easily extractable without some lingering over the dense contexture: the crisis represents an imagined dying, a turning away from past considerations and toward the last act conceived and felt as immediately present. Such a crisis and such an occasion involve a certain violence, here expressed by physical actions to accompany and corroborate the mental ones. We may recognize the condition as a familiar one, that of the sinner's desiring purgative afflic-tion. But violence may be conveyed by another extreme, such as the strain of a near-exhaustion under which a great agony can barely speak, but what is spoken will strive toward the naked utterance of simple truth, the last words that will be validated by the last act. Either instance might represent a death of the personal will, which is felt as a terrible obstruction that cannot be mastered by the efforts of reason and will. Yet the efforts are necessary.

In the sonnet that begins "Batter my heart, three-person'd God," though the violence is most prominent, and famous, there are de-pressed moments drained of energy. The abrupt opening pressure lets up momentarily while the poet converts the familiar language of grati-tude and praise into a strange lament addressed to God who "As yet but knocke, breathe, shine, and seeke to mend." Then the violence returns as the poet asks for the divine gifts of breaking, blowing, burning. This is followed by six lines that describe and explain, with some show of weariness, the hopeless personal situation. Though he states, in a muted way, as if helpless, that he loves God dearly "and would be loved faine," he is, nevertheless, "betroth'd unto your enemie." The manner of ex-pression is reserved—as in some oblique replies reporting the existence of another engagement, or as in the polite embarrassment of proffering a self-explanatory reason, such as the simple fact of a terminal disease.

But the image itself, centered on love, is charged with the historical power of continuous, passionate, and effective religious usage. When the level of energy rises again, the violence that concludes is both mental and physical, praying to be possessed by God—in images that seek valid ends of religious desire while destroying the traditional frames in which valid concepts of free will and chastity are held:

> Divorce mee,' untie, or break that knot againe,
> Take mee to you, imprison mee, for I
> Except you' enthrall mee, never shall be free,
> Nor ever chast, except you ravish mee.

In his love poems Donne everywhere establishes himself in the full and varied character of the masculine lover. When he makes love to God, however, the sense of absolute need dominates, that of a helplessness which must be mastered from without. He offers the radical transformation of his nature to the traditionally feminine, invoking and assuming the mental attributes of utter subordination and dependence and the brutal psychic condition of ravishability. In part, at least, what he seems to be willing here is a sacrifice represented by a death of the masculine will.

In the great penitential sonnet beginning "Thou hast made me," the direct appeal to God is confined to the opening statement. The body of the poem acts out the full, brief argument of an indirect appeal, and the tense conclusion comes back only some of the way toward the direct appeal of the opening. The prospect of death is but the emergent occasion and not the subject. "Decay" does not refer to the physical condition, and "Repaire," which may also awaken the etymological sense of "return home" (*repatriare*), is a near-equivalent to the "Restore thine Image" of "Goodfriday, 1613." But the prospect of death is the moment of time and action and is the essential element that releases the attributes that are acted out to demonstrate and support the appeal.

> Thou hast made me, And shall thy worke decay?
> Repaire me now, for now mine end doth haste,
> I runne to death, and death meets me as fast,
> And all my pleasures are like yesterday,
> I dare not move my dimme eyes any way,
> Despaire behind, and death before doth cast
> Such terrour, and my feebled flesh doth waste
> By sinne in it, which it t'wards hell doth weigh;
> Onely thou art above, and when towards thee
> By thy leave I can looke, I rise againe;

> But our old subtle foe so tempteth me,
> That not one houre I can my selfe sustaine;
> Thy Grace may wing me to prevent his art
> And thou like Adamant draw mine iron heart.

The horizontal movements toward each other of death and the protagonist create so intense a pressure that the will is paralyzed. A great line of poetry expresses, with inspired art and dreadful conviction, the inside and outside of that state: "I dare not move my dimme eyes any way." The domination of present-future and the sense of the past as impotent open the way for the master sin of despair and its ruthless power to multiply itself. Now the movements become vertical, the steady weighing down and the intermittent rising. That stage of paralysis followed by despair is crucial: it leads to the downward movement, the nadir of hell, which sums up all movements to this point. Only then, with everything else closed in, is the "Thou" of the opening address returned to. The timing, incidence, and distance kept are delicately precise. So too is that conjunction of horizontal and vertical movements which may be a tactful, emblematic reference to the cross.

The speaker has participated, whatever the apparent helplessness, in the weighing down, for there was a bewildered freak of the voluntary in his running toward death, and there is a perverse reciprocity implied in the pleasures that are "like yesterday." He has lost the past and with it the art of memory which, as Donne taught, was a key to the art of salvation. All his yesterdays are therefore like shallow, forgettable pleasures. Only the rising, which he looks for and which, when had, is easily available, lies wholly outside his will as he brings his personal history up to date. As for the answers: God's grace "may wing me," and the loadstone of the universe may "draw mine iron heart." And so the last item names, as barely as possible, the source of residual stubbornness and self-will, the heart that has changed its nature almost beyond imaginable help.

In the pulpit Donne is a learned expert on the nature of good and bad religious hearts. He rests his case here on the worst in himself. The poem creates an image of complete helplessness and terrified need. The deepest fear is that of dying unregarded by God, and the penitential strain is extreme, but it is not directed toward one of the standard goals, such as that of "emptying" one's nature of itself by the rituals of "inanition," which make room for God to enter and which "melt" the heart resisting God.[2] Instead he prays once briefly, acts out the demonstration of his need, and leaves the issue to God, resting his case—not without the wise skill of a courtly advocate experienced in pleading before the highest court. Below there is an "iron heart" turning itself into what it is, drawn to death and despair, adding a certain grim ponderability and gravitation to the wasting flesh and capable only of presenting its predicament and naming its imaginable hope.

"A Hymne to Christ, at the Authors Last Going into Germany" possesses a strange and haunting verbal music. Each stanza is open and declarative, like an anthem of praise, but the materials and their development (including the musical "argument") do not openly and directly sing the praises of God. Within each stanza what is said of God and of the self creates an implicit dialogue in which penitential matters participate, but not in any customary way; they are brought forward, but not as the main subject. The feelings of the speaker resemble those of penitence, but only up to a point, and the voice of the speaker seems closer to that of Job than to that of David. For the voice and the implicit dialogue one may take as cue the beautiful sentence Donne wrote in the *Devotions upon Emergent Occasions:* "I have not the *righteousnesse of Job,* but I have the desire of *Job, I would speake to the Almighty, and I would reason with God"* (p. 21). Donne's Hymn begins:

> In what torne ship soever I embarke,
> That ship shall be my embleme of thy Arke;
> What sea soever swallow mee, that flood
> Shall be to mee an embleme of thy blood;
> Though thou with clouds of anger do disguise
> Thy face; yet through that maske I know those eyes,
>   Which, though they turne away sometimes,
>   They never will despise.

Embarking or drowning, these are the casual chances of sea travel, and all uncertainties are presented as the occasion for true certainties, the emblems that faith declares and is ready to embrace. The leverage of grammatical concession ("though . . . though") introduces further emblems: the angry and the hidden God known to human history and personal memory. These emblems expressing divine action, God's response to human action, do not lend themselves to declarations fixed in a time and place. What Donne declares is the human knowledge of God's regard for man, God's love and mercy. What is fixed is the known relationship between God and man which is evoked by the affirmation, "never will despise." The quotation comes from Psalm 51: "The sacrifices of God are a broken spirit; a broken and a contrite heart, O God, Thou wilt not despise." One would not expect Donne to echo such a momentous passage from one of the great penitential psalms and intend only a passing allusion, one that does not define the position of the speaker and will not begin to enter into the spirit of the psalm. The next stanza introduces the subject of sacrifice:

> I sacrifice this Iland unto thee,
> And all whom I lov'd there, and who lov'd mee;
> When I have put our seas twixt them and mee,
> Put thou thy sea betwixt my sinnes and thee.
> As the trees sap doth seeke the root below
> In winter, in my winter now I goe,
>   Where none but thee, th'Eternall root
>   Of true love I may know.

As an act of contrition the sacrifice is indirect and figurative. His sacrifice is not the "broken spirit" itself but is represented by an offering; the indirectness of the sacrifice which surrenders to God all human feelings toward place and fellow human beings is followed by the directness of a proposed exchange to obtain forgiveness for his sins. The absoluteness of the line leading from Psalm 51 does not carry through, and we must seek other connections. This is puzzling, for one does not expect Donne to refer to a resonant expression from such a context, much pondered by him and others, and to neglect the implications of the context. To begin again: we can observe that he has moved from images of outward journey to inward, from affirmed acceptance of whatsoever ship or drowning to purposive seeking, from emblems to a different kind of figure applied to himself. The tree, the sap, and the root provide a natural analogy to his present state of being, "in my winter" (which overrides the temporal fact, the sailing date in May). He declares that he is returning to the root "Of true Love," and he states the going as a simple fact or act; the direction is both fact and figure, a seeking and choosing of one love only. What is tentative or problematic in the "may" and the "know" it is perhaps better to let pass unchallenged, and to swallow one's own uncertainty.

The speaker, now a declared lover, has made a sacrifice and proposed an exchange concerning sins. The seeking and knowing do not touch upon any questions about reciprocity. But in the next stanza the speaker who has already pledged the concentrated intensity of his seeking "none but thee" remembers that his God is a jealous God, and responds, "so I am jealous now":

> Nor thou nor thy religion dost controule,
> The amorousnesse of an harmonious Soule,
> But thou would'st have that love thy selfe: As thou

> Art jealous, Lord, so I am jealous now,
> Thou lov'st not, till from loving more, thou free
> My soule: Who ever gives, takes libertie:
>   O, if thou car'st not whom I love
>   Alas, thou lov'st not mee.

The transaction remains dubious and is not helped enough by the quali-
fication of the first two lines. If the precedent and strict standards of
Psalm 51 do not apply, a suitor who knows that a loving God "never
will despise," and who renounces all love but the love of God, has put
himself in a position to remember God's jealousy by anticipating it in
his own feelings.

The last stanza revises the image of sacrifice to that of divorce and
remarriage and extends the list from those who loved and were loved to
include the youthful objects of his affection:

> Seale then this bill of my Divorce to All
> On whom those fainter beames of love did fall;
> Marry those loves, which in youth scattered bee
> On Fame, Wit, Hopes (false mistresses) to thee.
> Churches are best for Prayer, that have least light:
> To see God only, I goe out of sight:
>   And to scape stormy dayes, I chuse
>   An Everlasting night.

The divorce is well illustrated by a bill of particulars; the remarriage is
only stated. Is it an act of penitence to remember the abandoned and
"scattered" loves of youth and to excavate them so that nothing in the
past or present has been withheld from the sacrifice? Or is it a proof of
his true jealousy, rejecting all, rededicating all? The "stormy dayes"
escaped by an act of choice would remove the "clouds of anger" of the
first stanza; nothing in kind replaces the felt knowledge of "those eyes."
The drive toward the conclusion of the hymn has no leisure to mark or
mention any further progress made in the knowing of (or the being
known by) "true Love."

In the declaration of love at the end of the first stanza, the very
incompleteness of the realization helps form the emotional intensity,
and the clear notes of yearning may be heard through the resolution that
concludes the stanza with a statement of faith. That love is the love truly
expressed in courtship. But the marriage is a contract published with
one signature. Its authorization depends upon the speaker's inferring —
in spite of his training in law and higher law—that if he "despises"
everything but God, the God who "never will despise" will abrogate,

not only all normal conditions of love as courtship, but also the general provisions of a God who does not limit "The amorousnesse of an harmonious Soule." Whether the contract of marriage would limit God's other objects of love lies outside the present question—though it may be part of an unheard but felt dissonance, a common one, all too familiar, made by those who plead their own case with a fixed determination that ignores due sensitivity. If the model of Psalm 51 were operative, we should also have to remember that David concludes by praying for Jerusalem—or the whole church, according to the general understanding.[3]

Darkness aids prayer, as it aids the concentration of memory. These are items of commonplace knowledge that serve chiefly to make a transition. A sense of urgency prevails, but the closing down and shutting out are not located in time or place, and the movement at the end seems to forget everything else in the poem and to express far more anger and rawness of grief than love of God. That he was ill and depressed we know, and the third stanza treats materials that find their way with greater dignity in the sonnet on his dead wife. Imagining the valedictory preparation for death seems burdened by overresolute fictions and turns the formal choice of an accepted assignment on a diplomatic mission with practical, hopeful business to do—turns that accepted assignment, which will be enjoyed, into a stillborn choosing to reject the world expressed in a movement that comes close to identifying God's love with death itself.[4]

The sins disposed of in one line of the hymn I have been discussing are inventoried as the basic material for the simple plot of "A Hymne to God the Father." Each of the first two stanzas lists two sins: in the first, the one derived from Adam and the sin regretted but never overcome; in the second, the sin augmented by influencing others and the sin avoided for a while but "wallowed in" during long relapses. Only one more remains to be mentioned in the last stanza, for the list is not long and matters are not intensified as they are elsewhere. The sins are invincible and carry on, but once confessed they appear to have no aftereffects. Their sting is that of humor and detachment, cast in a cheerful rhythm. The refrain used as transition might renew itself indefinitely and still be serviceable to the posthumous continuation by another hand, but it is not ominous. Forgiveness granted, or at least apparently accepted, is followed by the promise of a further task for mercy, and no indications of anxiety are directed toward any accounts other than those that have not yet been brought forward:

> When thou hast done, thou hast not done,
> For, I have more.

The sins are general, shared by all men, not better or worse for the fact, but spared the passionate singling out that Donne turns on the sense of sin that threatens the heart of his existence. What is individual is the play on his name, for God continues to have His work to do. In a far simpler way the conditions are those of "Goodfriday, 1613": the sinner will not be satisfied, will not dare to turn his face until God acknowledges that the image has been restored enough to satisfy Him.

But the sinner has mercy on God's patience and curbs his imposing gift for encyclopedic thoroughness. After only four listed items he comes to the master sin of all, his fear of the last, unknowable moment. The good cheer of the exercise in penitence is wholly explained by what has preceded and accompanied the recital—the sense of Christ's shining presence "now" and the memory of the same comfort "heretofore." All that is needed to sweep away every hesitation is God's assurance that the future will correspond with past and present:

> I have a sinne of feare, that when I have spunne
>   My last thred, I shall perish on the shore;
> Sweare by thy selfe, that at my death thy Sunne
>   Shall shine as it shines now, and heretofore;
>   And, having done that, Thou hast done,
>   I have no more.

The calm and relaxed good humor are themselves a grace and an achievement of grace. There has been previous hard work, we know; how necessary we cannot know. The achievement looks easy and it is easy, but we may think it is not available to art or will, and Donne would not have thought it a gift for the indolent or the timid.

Finally we come to the master poem, the "Hymne to God my God, in my sicknesse." From the beginning the stage is past fear. Penitence has no work to do. A sense of leisure prevails, a mysterious enjoyment of the objects of both time and space. A departure is imminent, but it will not be marked by any rejection at all. The spirit of valediction is open and generous and admits as a kindred spirit that of holiday. To some extent Donne is reflecting the atmosphere of the Old Testament deaths he admired, characterized by "peaceful hearts and cheerful countenances," with no need of a "foil of depression" or any other comparison to set off that which is good in itself.[5] He will not, nevertheless, forget all sense that the new dispensation is founded on difficulties that must be honored. He must rise to a particular occasion and speak for himself in his own voice. I quote the poem in its entirety:

> Since I am comming to that Holy roome,
>   Where, with thy Quire of Saints for evermore,

I shall be made thy Musique; As I come
   I tune the Instrument here at the dore,
   And what I must doe then, thinke now before.

Whilst my Physitians by their love are growne
   Cosmographers, and I their Mapp, who lie
Flat on this bed, that by them may be showne
   That this is my South-west discoverie
   Per fretum febris, by these streights to die,

I joy, that in these straits, I see my West;
   For, though theire currants yeeld returne to none,
What shall my West hurt me? As West and East
   In all flatt Maps (and I am one) are one,
   So death doth touch the Resurrection.

Is the Pacifique Sea my home? Or are
   The Easterne riches? Is *Jerusalem?*
Anyan, and *Magellan,* and *Gibraltare,*
   All streights, and none but streights, are wayes to them,
   Whether where *Japhet* dwelt, or *Cham,* or *Sem.*

We thinke that *Paradise* and *Calvarie,*
   Christs Crosse, and *Adams* tree, stood in one place;
Looke Lord, and finde both *Adams* met in me;
   As the first *Adams* sweat surrounds my face,
   May the last *Adams* blood my soule embrace.

So, in his purple wrapp'd receive mee Lord,
   By these his thornes give me his other Crowne;
And as to others soules I preach'd thy word,
   Be this my Text, my Sermon to mine owne,
   Therfore that he may raise the Lord throws down.

    The beginning statement stands apart as an introduction that clear-
ly announces itself as such while establishing the basic agreement for
the harmonious relationships that will prevail. The subject is announced; it is like an elevated musical statement that stirs and fills the
mind and that seems complete in its rounded brevity but creates anticipation. The initial concord will not be broken, but neither will it be
repeated or varied as if it were part of the set thematic material. It stands
apart yet intimates the whole. The infinite is "that Holy roome," the
approach is a coming "for evermore," and the musician will join the
choir of the blessed, not to make but to "be made thy Musique." He is at
the door and still coming; the tuning is at once what he is doing and

what he is thinking. Everything is clear in itself and in its anticipations: the quiet joy at the nearness of death; the easy, imaginative relationships between the accepted obligation to act and the simple expectation of being acted upon, made to become forever what one prepares to do; the easy, imaginative relationships that convert the infinity of heaven into a familiar form of space and that separate time and eternity by a "dore" where one may pause to make a formal, respectful, decent entrance, not difficult.

Everything is clear except for one perceptible ambiguity that stands apart and intimates the whole, and yet does enter the subsequent action. "What I must doe then" seems to denote time and to contrast future action with the thinking "before." If what is to be done refers to time after he enters eternity, we shall hear no more of it than we have already heard. Donne does not usually say something to unsay it by complete silence, and it is not like him to damp the fine metaphor of *tuning* so that it will not be heard in the subsequent thinking "before." And so we may take the simple path of assuming that the "then," as time, refers to the long moment on the threshold, this side of the door, a moment preceded by the *thinking* and realized within the duration of that process. But there is a deeper side to the ambiguity. Though the rhetorical emphasis favors "then" as denoting time, the word may—I believe, must—indicate consequentiality (accordingly, consequently). Donne makes the double point quietly. His poem is not based upon or aimed toward ambiguity or paradox, and our feeling the imaginative triumph of the poem does not depend upon a hidden intellectual subtlety. But he does, however unobtrusively, imagine the issues of the poem as ones in which it is perfectly natural to identify the process of time and the process of reason. The here-now and the then-there-consequently will be bound together in the sequence of a long moment. And one further preliminary matter may be noted, less an ambiguity than a latency of thought: "what I *must* doe then" would seem to be a fixed, unquestioned obligation the content of which is to be determined by a free and voluntary obligation, "thinke now before." It is worth noting the potential difference only because the poem exhibits that there is none. Fixed and free obligation, like doing and thinking, are the same as the poem proceeds with its "tuning," the burden of which is to "thinke now before."

The thinking moves out from the literal point of here and now, in a sweep that is grand in scope and governed by its own laws and own freedom. The time scheme is that of one imagined moment. While the physicians are practicing their art, a kind of premortem that will plot the course of death, the patient simultaneously practices his own art, headed in the same direction but free to move and enjoy places on alternative routes. It is plain which art he prefers, but there is no overt comparison and no sense of judgment. From the physicians he receives the benefit of an amusing observation on the nature of their love, and a figurative suggestion that becomes the vehicle for mental voyaging and expression. His body flat in bed turns into a vast stage for the presentation of geography and time. Places are named in a valedictory voice that resonates with praise and deep affection. The poet possesses a fluent language of time which he can both expand and contract, reaching into the remote historical past to indicate present places once settled by the sons of that patriarchal mariner who surely is part of the music of heaven: "Whether where *Japhet* dwelt, or *Cham,* or *Sem.*"

When the thought returns in stanza 5 to the starting place of the here and now, the literal point is still what it was, unchanged in its essential nature but now flowering with figurative meanings. Other places and times have been brought home and are actively implied in the present. The starting point left and returned to is the same, but the here and now have gained something that the account of the experience represents. The mere capability of having such experience demonstrates a power to fill time with significant resources of mind and spirit, and the expressive response has demonstrated itself as inherent both in the capacity to have the experience and in the ability to be the master of it. If there has been no sense of the passage of time, as there has been no change of place, the effect has been produced by an extraordinary instant held suspended in the mind freely ranging over places and times. The physicians are like those "bystanders" in "Deaths Duell"—"insensibly" witnessing the fact that God's mercies work "momentarily" by imperceptible subtleties on "the party departing" (10:240). We the readers have a more privileged position. We may therefore think that the movement out and back serves as the preparation for an extension of the moment, and we may think that the preparation seems to have made the continuing present of the suspended moment more fully present. It is not more intense by any expressive tightening or other sign of urgency often characteristic of lyric immediacy. It is full and calm in its rich musical cadence. Nor is it a passive present in which one might find oneself located; we are made to feel it as an active present.

The fifth stanza comes to a point of potential crisis, one which, however unobtrusively approached, Donne must have understood was coming, and foresaw by the long practice of his own art of trying to know God, and death, and himself. The point is that part of time and place when (where) apparent opposites "touch," like west and east, death and resurrection. Now these touch: the *doing "then"* and the *thinking "now before."* Insofar as the doing "then" fuses a sense of time and a sense of thought characterized by rational progression (according-ly, consequently), the "now" contains a potential crisis. Donne imagin-ing the unknown experience at the threshold must find the heart and voice to speak for himself to God.

The voice resembles the one we hear at the end of "Goodfriday, 1613," directing human passion, assertiveness, and command into the grammar and syntax of prayer. One difference is that in the hymn penitential concentration is removed from the center and is present only in the references to sweat and thorns. The imperative mood is used but is now more gently modulated, and the general absence of strain and urgency makes way for a strange beauty in the expression—at once precise, authoritative, and gracefully at ease in its movement and in all its internal relationships. The free course of what he has been thinking "before" carries over into this address as part of the preparatory "tun-ing." Time and place, Paradise and Calvary, the cross and the forbidden tree, come together in the "We thinke," which borrows from popular legend and its unexamined passion for literal correspondences. The connections are transitional and indifferent —no more decisive than the questions in stanza 4 that ask the name of the one place where home and hope are. What is decisive is the higher history of salvation which binds Adam and Christ in a true history, one in which the dying man may identify himself:

> Looke Lord, and finde both *Adams* met in me;
> As the first *Adams* sweat surrounds my face,
> May the last *Adams* blood my soule embrace.

The imperative of "Looke" and "finde" turns toward the "May" of prayer, moving on the "As," which marks a conjunction of past and present duration and signals a rational progression of consequentiality, "then." From the literal face to the comprehensive soul; from the sweat of sickbed fact and historic curse to the blood of history and promise; from the inspired "surrounds," neutral as a fact but threatening as an imposed barrier that closes in and closes out, to the comprehensive word of faith, the taking in of "embrace": all are simply and perfectly modulated in time and thought.

In the last stanza the imperative returns briefly and marks another progression, for only the second Adam now figures, and his thorns are all promise: "By these his thornes give me his other Crowne." There is no attempt to renew the completed prayer. The poem began with a "Since" of time, which also involved causality; the last stanza begins with a "So" and the final line with "Therfore." All are emphatic in their expression of rational thought.[6] But the "So" introduces another reason for the unification of time, thought, and action, and the following "as" introduces a personal history that links in duration and causality John Donne, others, and the word of God. The "Therfore" of his own text and sermon is the grand conclusion that encompasses time and resolves personal and universal history. Donne passed through the anticipated crisis of the doing "then" swiftly and easily. In doing so he expressed the kind of infallible assurance of salvation he believed to be available to "the party departing." The coda advances the personal, but with evidence that would not be inappropriate in a funeral sermon delivered upon another. The self as another does not lie outside Donne's imagination. If we can believe Walton, with his last living breath Donne closed the eyes of the man who would be dead in the next moment, and had time to complete the gesture of his hand by returning it to its place, leaving the body perfectly composed for burial.

When he creates for the poem a general atmosphere of hope and assurance, Donne resembles the self we see in his formal, public meditations on the good death. But he is most deeply and tenaciously himself at the crux: the full submission of the will to God by an act of will, speaking up for himself directly to God. He would have the calm resignation of Lady Danvers at the end and have her imagined joy, but he requires more of himself. In his praise and consolation presented to others he makes her example an ideal of the ordinary, as she performs her regular lifelong religious duties two hours before her death. For himself, in addition to his act of participatory will, speaking to God as himself, he claims his place, in the privileged language of prayer, as one belonging to the true history of salvation (summarized by the two Adams, the sweat, blood, thorns and crown) and creates an air of the familiar and easy in an ultimate passage from "Since" to "Therfore."

The poem is remarkable for its inwardness. The outward movement is no less remarkable in its management of time and place and the coordination of these with thought and action. There are bystanders, a regular feature in his formal accounts of dying but notably absent from the other poems we have been considering. Even the direct reference to others, the souls of those to whom he has preached God's word, strikes one as an extraordinary inclusion. They are invoked as an invisible audience of those who have heard and felt his presence as a voice touching their souls, and they are witnesses that he has spoken faithfully in his own voice, of God and to God. They are not present now, but the inwardness of the preacher's work in the past has moved outward to strengthen the inwardness of their memory. If they were present, they would witness a scene like the one imagined by Donne in his prayer for the unknown benefactor of Devotion 17:

Breath inward *comforts* to his *heart,* and affoord him the power of giving such outward *testimonies* thereof, as all that are about him may derive comforts from thence, and have this *edification,* even in this *dissolution,* that though the *body* be going the way of all *flesh,* yet that *soule* is going the way of all *Saints*

As for the physicians, though they do not accompany him very far they provide an important, if amusing, external stimulus. The poet and the physicians are strange partners, bound together by honorable human obligations, both students of the same destination, but their mental journeys have almost nothing in common.

The imagination of time flows through the thirty lines as a testimony that the man enjoys an individual condition of luminous freedom. If we insist on skepticism, we may take literal note of the circumstances and the probable length of duration and remind ourselves that sensible people have denied that poetry can prove anything. And yet, to show that such a state exists in the mind and may be attained is to show, streaming with life, an image of the idea of freedom that may be realized in death. The achievement does put into different perspective the narrowing resolutions of "Batter my heart" and "A Hymne to Christ," but we may decline to pass judgment on the stresses he found, invented, and endured in the crises that are the rehearsals of dying. As for death in earnest, everything was demanded of the self, but there could be no inner certainty that did not come from without, from the God to whom all of the striving self was addressed for His receiving. Donne's rehearsals included failures and limited successes in scenes of his own choosing and staging, necessary to their moments and to his own persistent sense of the path he was traveling.

In both "A Hymne to God the Father" and "Hymne to God my God, in my sicknesse" Donne also dances naked before the ark. There is danger but he has no fear, or no fear that is not subdued by a stronger force. In "A Hymne to God the Father" he speaks, or sings, with a calm "evenness" of tempered piety which he always admired and praised but apparently seldom possessed. The joy is quiet, conveyed by the easy humor directed toward himself in confession and by the intimate disporting of himself before God in a hymn that is an advanced stage of prayer but is also a colloquy, one that weaves in a thread of self-mastery in being a dialogue of one. In "Hymne to God my God, in my sicknesse" the joy is more exuberant and varied, not neglecting the last opportunity for humor on the last subject. And the joy is expressed in a strange, sober, spontaneous *hilaritas,* celebrating, in the doing, what is to be done.

Finally, to reinforce a strong point of interpretation, I return to

Donne's act of will in submitting to God's will, the speaking up for himself in his own voice. In spite of some obvious differences, Donne shares an important trait with the Raleigh of "The Passionate Man's Pilgrimage" and "Even Such Is Time." In both men wit and will work together closely, expressing a courtesy due the self in their display of character, a clear sense of self, and self-mastery. As religious man and conscious sinner, Donne despises "Flattering speeches" that "court God," but he defends "faire language . . . when it apparels a reall curtesie":

> Harshnesse, and morosity in behaviour, rusticity, and coorse-nesse of language, are no arguments in themselves, of a plaine, and a direct meaning, and of a simple heart. (3:136–37)

Raleigh had a strong sense of his own dignity (offensive to enemies), how to maintain it and how to express it. Donne's vocation did not make him altogether different in this respect. He had his own strong and conscious sense of the dues and demands, the rights and obligations of being human and himself. Interpreting "this Dialogue between God and *David*" in Psalm 51,

> we may heare *David* reply, *Domine Me;* Nay but Lord . . . Blessed be thy Name, for having wrapped me up in thy generall Covenants, and made me a partaker of thy generall Ordinances, but yet Lord, looke more particularly upon me, and appropriate thy selfe to me, to me, not onely as thy Creature, as a man, as a Christian, but as I am I. (5:306–7)

And he concludes the sermon entirely in his own voice:

> So then, this is our Act of Recognition, we acknowledge God, and God onely to doe all; But we doe not make him Soveraigne alone, as that we leave his presence naked, and empty; Nor so make him King alone, as that we depopulate his Country, and leave him without Subjects; Nor so leave all to Grace, as that the naturall faculties of man do not become the servants, and instruments of that Grace. . . . for as Grace could not worke upon man to Salvation, if man had not a faculty of will to worke upon, because without that will man were not man; so is this Salvation wrought in the will, by conforming this will of man to the will of God, not by extinguishing the will it selfe, by any force or constraint that God imprints in it by his Grace: God saves no man without, or against his will. (5:316–17)

CHAPTER EIGHT

Entering the History of Death: George Herbert

For we both are, and know that we are, and delight in our being, and our knowledge of it.

ST. AUGUSTINE, *City of God*

Death enters many of Herbert's poems and, as one may expect from this poet, in many different ways. But only one poem, "The Forerunners," takes up as direct subject his own imagined death, and that example will not hold us long. A second poem, entitled "Death" and coming late in "The Church" among the "last things," will be his main contribution to this part of the book.

In "The Forerunners" a common observation is elevated into a moment for facing the approach of death:

> The harbingers are come. See, see their mark;
> White is their colour, and behold my head.[1]

Other external signs, if any, are ignored. White hairs are responded to as if suddenly noticed, and they are imagined as the "forerunners" who seek lodgings for the royal progress. From that peremptory start the poet develops his elected figure with a free mixture of the fantastic, the pious, and the literal. After declaring that he has been allowed to keep his "best room," the heart where God dwells, he turns to his main development, a valediction to the world. In this case it is the world of poetry, which is addressed not as life in the world, which one is ready or unready to turn away from, but as one's life's work, which one must leave unfinished. He presents matters in a little story, that of love poetry brought to the service of a higher love. The valediction mingles homely, affectionate praise, a pessimistic view of poetry relapsing into its old ways, and a lofty declaration:

> True beautie dwells on high: ours is a flame
> But borrow'd thence to light us thither.

There is no acknowledgment that the declaration goes beyond aesthetic statement and touches the religious truth governing death as well as life.

After the opening and until the end, the sense of time exerts little influence within the poem. Time is running out, but it is not time that counts, nor does death itself occupy much of his attention. If what is uppermost in his mind can afford so much space to a scolding, affectionate farewell to poetry, we may conclude that all the other standard items in the business of dying are felt to be well under control. The basic piety is clear and firm, as it is not in Raleigh or the example from Herrick to be considered later. But Herbert also does the unexpected thing and does not respond to the human crisis by repeating the standard forms of devotional wisdom. The main subject is so well in hand that he is free to change the subject, with no suspicion that it is an act of evasion, and he is conspicuously free of the grinding human compulsion to think the utterly normal thoughts that belong to the occasion.

"The Forerunners" presents the expected personal death while ignoring most of the expected parts of the subject. The poem "Death" never mentions the self at all. The pronouns of response are "we" and "our," while death (as "thou," "thee," "thy") is prominent in every stanza but the last. In effect, the poem subordinates death and its nature to a temporal sequence in which human responses may be located and shown to develop. Death does not die, as in Donne's tour de force, "Death be not proud." It persists but changes its meaning. The general atmosphere is charged with humor, some of it bizarre. Separate points of emphasis read like a sophisticated modernizing of the old theme, that "all must die," and its traditional supplies of equivocal mirth. But the initial emphasis moves steadily toward the final destination, and though the spokesman never emerges from his function of speaking for all, he is not a standard guide exercising the license of a rhetorical "we." The spokesman says nothing in the name of others that he has not fully imagined. His authority depends upon his being able to speak for others because he can speak so convincingly of what he knows.

> Death, thou wast once an uncouth hideous thing,
> Nothing but bones,
> The sad effect of sadder grones:
> Thy mouth was open, but thou couldst not sing.
>
> For we consider'd thee as at some six
> Or ten years hence,
> After the losse of life and sense,
> Flesh being turn'd to dust, and bones to sticks.
>
> We lookt on his side of thee, shooting short;
> Where we did finde

The shells of fledge souls left behinde,
Dry dust, which sheds no tears, but may extort.

But since our Saviours death did put some bloud
Into thy face;
Thou art grown fair and full of grace,
Much in request, much sought for as a good.

For we do now behold thee gay and glad,
As at dooms-day;
When souls shall wear their new aray,
And all thy bones with beautie shall be clad.

Therefore we can go die as sleep, and trust
Half that we have
Unto an honest faithfull grave;
Making our pillows either down, or dust.

The poem tells the story of death in a series of episodes, each separate but arranged in a deliberate sequence. Though the general manner resembles that of a naive history designed to make familiar truths vivid and to strengthen established beliefs, the effective simplicity of the poem invites no patronizing of the naive. Time, which had little to do in "The Forerunners," now controls and shapes the development of "Death." In the first three stanzas, the period before Christ's death, the dimensions of time have no distinct existence, and there is no definite point of orientation. Indeed, the time before Christ's death seems to be characterized as a time that is indistinct because Christ's death, actual or prophetically anticipated, is not present to give shape and meaning to time. As a result, those witnessing the stark evidence of death have no means to orient themselves properly. Against the background of vagueness the small denominations of time acquire disproportionate, momentary emphasis—such as the span of six or ten years for measuring stages of dissolution, or the grotesque apprehension that there was a time of previous groaning and singing by a head that has become a hideous skull. In the second stanza a brief projection of future time emerges from the general, unlocated past of "we consider'd," and then the third stanza criticizes that "short" view while bringing in a new image (skeletons as "shells of fledge souls"), which leads to the turning point, that of Christ's death. Then the past has become located, and its effect is realized in a progressive present that may be seen at once and extends unbroken from since then to now. In the fifth and climactic stanza, the "now" is greatly magnified and becomes vision, reaching at once to the end of time and the Resurrection. Finally, the last stanza sets its action completely in a literal present that has had its nature established and defined in relationship to what has preceded.

The temporal development begins by placing in conjunction an indefinite past and an unlocated present. When the past becomes defined it commands the future, and the result is, at least in regard to death, an easy sense of location in the last stanza, the first clearly inhabited present contemporaneous with the writing of the poem. The scheme is basic, and simple enough, though it may answer to a considerable scope of human experience. Yet the simplicity never obtrudes as if it were of value for itself, and the final achievement of the present can hardly be considered a routine gift of the scheme. Nothing would succeed if the individual effects were not worked out with such light-handed, brilliant precision. For example, the "we" traveling in time are expertly jolted and penetrated as our present capacity to respond makes us more than casual visitors in the unlocated time of the first three stanzas. It would take conscious effort to prevent the suggested time required for dissolution from transferring its measure to our own uncertain six or ten years hence. We can sing and close our mouths. The dust that cannot weep "may extort" tears only from ourselves or those like ourselves, not yet dust.

The last stanza, where all must be made good, occupies a literal present finally arrived at. Its actions, objects, and movement are those of humble, unhurried dignity. In spite of the great differences in texture and rhythm, the last line of the poem ("Making our pillows either down, or dust") recalls, with delicate modesty, the last line of the fifth stanza ("And all thy bones with beautie shall be clad"), when time itself comes to an echoing close, declaring a passionate splendor that does not conclude its imaginative opening out exactly when the stanza closes. The final line of the poem has no intimations of grandeur—quite the contrary—but it ends left slightly open, leaning forward as it were. The openness reveals, as in the fifth stanza, a last, surprising potential in a stanza notable for its epigrammatic disposition to end with a summary closure as the spare, taut line has characteristically turned inward. The poem ends with the central action, that of man in the poised condition of controlling his place in the present. That action, I infer, represents Herbert's religious and poetic sense of how to relate, in the history of death and its expectation, the crucial present to the crucial past.

Herbert's presentation of death combines the philosophical ideal of quiet calm and the Reformation concept of a strenuous episode for which there must be disciplined preparation. The strenuouness plays no part in the effect; only by looking does one recognize how much has gone into the poem and its final effect. At the end he elevates the humble and transforms into a particular Christian accomplishment the aristocratic grace of nonchalance, related to classical temperance and Renaissance *sprezzatura*. At the same time, wholly within the traditions of Christian thought, he can bring together effects that are no less astounding. His Christian enactment of the history of death presents the powerful joy of a commanding vision of the Resurrection and follows that great moment with a human action responding to personal death and the knowledge of time with holy indifference. The central part of the central matter requires establishing control of oneself in time, an actual present assisted by what can be drawn from other times. What is chosen and how, for the poet and others, tells a story that can be acted, that of a man truly inhabiting his present. The poetic solution, like the practical solutions of other human beings, may act the part of willed intensity resolutely excluding what it cannot afford to acknowledge and still be what it is. Such a solution can convince us of sincerity, faith, terror, need, or other genuine attributes, but it will not convince us that it is the rare kind of personal mastery which can be expressed by unconstrained ease. That achievement represents possession, and the possession identifies the speaking self with an action fully prepared. In Herbert the action issues forth with a marvelous poise of graceful casualness.

CHAPTER NINE

"The Plaudite, or end of life"

And what a melancholy beauty this gave to women when they were
pregnant and stood there, with their slender hands instinctively resting on their large bellies, in which there were *two* fruits: a child and a
death. Didn't the dense, almost nourishing smile on their emptied
faces come from their sometimes feeling that both were growing
inside them?

RILKE, *The Notebooks of Malte Laurids Brigge*

"Remember, God, the soul of Elya Gruner, who, as willingly as
possible and as well as he was able, and even to an intolerable point,
and even in suffocation and even as death was coming was eager, even
childishly perhaps (may I be forgiven for this), even with a certain
servility, to do what was required of him."

BELLOW, *Mr. Sammler's Planet*

If *one tries* to think of the last human act in a bare, literal, objective way,
one must also try to forget that when the moment of dying is thought of
as an *act* the subject has already been shaped by the history of thought on
the nature of death and on the nature of an act. As things are, we have
been well schooled to expect that where death is concerned both conceptual and figurative thought will be as difficult to exclude as to keep
separate from each other. Except as brute fact confirmed by a body,
someone else's, death is a fountainhead of metaphors.

I end Part 2 with a remarkable poem by Herrick, almost as exotic in
its period as the epigraphs above would be if they had been written then:

> *The Plaudite, or end of life.*
> If after rude and boystrous seas,
> My wearyed Pinnace here finds ease;
> If so it be I've gain'd the shore
> With safety of a faithful Ore:
> If having run my Barque on ground,
> Ye see the aged Vessell crown'd:
> What's to be done? but on the Sands

"The Plaudite, or end of life"

Ye dance, and sing, and now clap hands.
The first Act's doubtfull, (but we say)
It is the last commends the Play.[1]

The poem is an easy mixture of an initiating image borrowed from Ovid, some items from traditional religious allegory (seas, ship, faith, shore, salvation), and a theatrical conceit. The last item ensures the prominent contribution of a highly unusual deathbed audience, which the poet undertakes to instruct. He raises a question that moves three lightly posed "ifs" into an actual state, one that requires a definite response: "What's to be done?" And he replies to his own question as if its only purpose were to usher in with a proper ceremony, not *an* answer but the one certain truth governing such circumstances: "What's to be done but . . ."

The suggestion of a time sequence places the dancing and singing before the applause, which then follows in an ambiguous way: "and now clap hands." If we ask our own questions and seek definite answers, we are prevented from knowing the real sequence. For to express approval by bursting into dance and song would make the later hand-clapping a rather faint formality, one that would seem to separate the polite, uniform message of a theatrical audience from the uncalculated spontaneity of a communal celebration. Yet if the clapping is not separate from the festive joy, it becomes a climactic addition to the rhythm of both dance and song. One may sift these elusive parts in other ways, and Herrick may be more elusive than cunning, but we cannot tell that either.[2] The casualness that is part of the air and accomplishment permits the deft placement of theatrical jargon ("doubtfull," "commends") and impersonates the audience while the author slips into it, not acting quite, but joining (while initiating) the collective voice, which repeats the well-worn wisdom of veteran spectators ("but we say").

The audience of active joy is the most striking effect, and it comes out of a context of general good humor. The personal death is the ostensible subject, but the poem chiefly communicates the pleasure of living and a convivial sense that turns the solemn solitude of death into an occasion for inviting others to carry on the spirit of a proper ceremony. Herrick forestalls our taking him seriously. The poem is a kind of quip, a fanciful sally of light-heartedness which picks up the formidable subject and handles it as if it were an ordinary theme for an occasional poem. If we think him also light-minded, we still must acknowledge that he does not seem to have many companions for this kind of venture in expression. Here, as elsewhere, he can say wholly unexpected things easily and can disturb settled and sober habits of thought and feeling.

Like the Raleigh of "The Passionate Man's Pilgrimage," Herrick also demonstrates a simple, untroubled faith, and he too brings forth the extraordinary for an occasion when only the ordinary is expected and trusted. The liberty of his humor becomes the license to unbind workaday repressions of that old message, "all must die." But however we explain it, his way of including the spectators brings a new and surprising answer to the problem of how to write about one's own death.

"Tichborne's Elegy" and Raleigh's "Even such is time" confront personal death and time without ease or grace. They are poems that speak with power and authority of what they know. Herrick's poem resembles these only in also being *sui generis* in a field where not many competitors choose to appear. And one last point, like nothing we have seen so far: as master of the revels, Herrick not only treats himself as another, he treats others as himself. All are drawn into the celebration.

On the Death of Someone Else

Enkidu, my brother whom I loved, the end of mortality has over-taken him. I wept for him seven days and nights till the worm fas-tened on him. Because of my brother I am afraid of death; because of my brother I stray through the wilderness. His fate lies heavy upon me. How can I be silent, how can I rest? He is dust and I shall die also and be laid in the earth forever.

Epic of Gilgamesh

O my son Absalom! my son, my son Absalom! would God I had died for thee, O Absalom, my son, my son!

2 SAMUEL 18:33

My name is Constance, I was Geffrey's wife,
Young Arthur is my son, and he is lost.
I am not mad, I would to heaven I were!

. . . .

If I were mad, I should forget my son.

SHAKESPEARE, *King John*

Part Three title page illustration:
Albrecht Dürer, *St. Jerome in His Cell;* from an engraving of 1514.
243 × 187 mm.

CHAPTER TEN

Introduction

A*t the beginning* of *The Faerie Queene* Spenser takes the opportunity of relating the shape of his career to the famous Virgilian model: pastoral, eclogue, epic. In doing so Spenser quietly removes from the record some earlier apprentice work, his *Complaints,* the "Sundrie Small Poemes Of The Worlds Vanitie." "Small" in part belongs to the courteous idiom of self-deprecation but is not quite the equivalent of calling *The Faerie Queene* "this rusticke madrigale."[1] Spenser must also have had in mind as one reason for the suppression the derivative nature of his *Complaints.* They include essays in lofty elegiac lament based upon admired models, set pieces in a not quite yet "worn-out poetical fashion," the content still believed to be timeless but the manner perhaps beginning to feel dated, still looking backward and not yet ready to draw the authentically old into something new. What Spenser learned he could say in a voice more clearly his own in "November" of *The Shepheardes Calender.*

For that poem still older models, but recently renewed, provided more flexibility and flow and some new opportunities for achieving a different inner balance. In "November" the "trustlesse state of earthly things" does not overpower alternative possibilities of statement, and another set theme, the encouraging rediscovery of the earliest humanism, does not appear—the blazoned immortality (as it were) of good fame in good verses. Instead, the verse performs its aspiring work without pausing to praise itself as a human answer to time. The poet is not himself the chief mourner but speaks for others (at least one of whom is more important under his pastoral name). In a major thematic development the poet relates the occasion of grief to the human world and to the world of nature (all of which laments except the "wolves," who continue about their business and their opportunities). And when the time is right, after the brief lesson drawn from the unreliability of "earthly things," the poet brings forward the solving truth: "Dido nis dead, but into heaven hent."

The joys in prospect of those "Fayre fieldes" of the supernatural provide the concluding answer to human grief in the present and past.

The poem of mourning is over and the subject brought to a close. But when the naive auditor replies he speaks in character, for himself, and the larger audience of readers are free to measure their own responses against his. For the terms of this pastoral drama are designed to prevent any complete identification and to encourage the larger audience to remember their individual differences. They will enjoy a conscious displacement (what's "Dido" to them or they to "Dido" that they should weep or rejoice for her?), and they will relish toward the representative auditor a sense of their own superior discrimination while they also feel a submerged flow of agreement.

In addition to the formal answer to grief provided by the lament and consolation, any of the unrationalized excesses and confusions of death have been removed from the present occasion and from the subject itself, removed or at least deflected and in part transferred to the naive auditor's response:

> Ay, francke shepheard, how bene thy verses meint
> With doolful pleasaunce, so as I ne wotte
> Whether rejoyce or weepe for great constrainte!
> Thyne be the cossette, well hast thow it gotte.
> Up, Colin, up, ynough thou morned hast:
> Now gynnes to mizzle, hye we homeward fast.

"Thenot" testifies in his own way to the effectiveness of inspired art and properly has the last word, for he requested the song, though an elegy was not his first choice. The poet has mourned enough—"Thenot" can say so as an authoritative answer, which, if it were addressed to the reader, would be a tactless irritant the poet and his spokesman avoid. The opportune tears of nature's drizzle remind the man of his nearest abode. He feels better and finds the conflict in his emotions a pleasant one, a created irresolution that feels no desire for a further extended answer.

The poet who can step into a formal context and so has a position from which to perform a service for others does not have to establish his personal credentials as a mourner. The central speech of his lyric discourse then can begin without expository and other preparations and can end at the moment most advantageous to the development of his poem. Among Sidney's many verse experiments in *Arcadia*, the 1593 version assembles a group of elegies in response to the supposed death of Basilius.[2] The poems were brilliantly executed but not likely to inspire a tradition in English. On the one hand, they serve the general purposes of Sidney's romance, and he exploits his technical virtuosity as part of the normal atmosphere of Arcadia. One remarkable effect is that of imposing an extraordinary exoticism upon the familiar materials of public mourning. On the other hand, the poems remain isolated experiments. They belong in their narrative context, an unusually full one for the subject but altered and blurred by subsequent revisions.

The community of shepherds grieve, especially "the very borne *Arcadians*" (2:138); the others, though moved by human pity and a sense of their past benefits, could not "so naturally feele the lively touch of sorrowe." "Good olde *Geron*" articulates the anxieties of change in prose; then Agelastus, noted for his skill in poetry and for the austerity of his grief, produces a sestina that "seemed to despise the workes of nature." (In the 1593 version the recognized poet volunteers; in the *Old Arcadia*, after the random praise and lamentation of individuals, they all unite in desiring Agelastus "to make an universall Complaynte for them in this universall mischeef" [4:265]). Others then volunteer to follow his example, and the single lamentation quoted ("as well as might bee") is a formal pastoral elegy. Nature is enlisted, urged, and drawn upon for lamentable comparisons. After a hundred lines in which (so the claim of more sincerity than art declares) "One word of woe another after traineth" (2:142), the scope of "detestation" is enlarged briefly and then focused upon the loss of the leader and the consequent losses of the community. The modest personal merits of Basilius impose no limitations on the general or poetic grief. He is dead (supposedly), and therefore "favoure and pitty drew all thinges nowe to the highest poynte" (4:264) The resolution of a Christian answer is not available to their pagan mourning, and only when the "Muse hath swarved" from the true subject to the bereaved subjects does the poet anticipate obliquely, as conclusion, topics that might be an evolving part of traditional Christian arguments with death: "Death is our home, life is but a delusion. . . . His death our death" (2:142–43). Finally, "one of great account among them" is allowed to contribute a rhyming sestina. This poem serves to fix the universal complaint even more strictly:

> Let teares for him therefore be all our treasure,
> And in our wailfull naming him our pleasure:
> Let hating of our selves be our affection,
> And unto death bend still our thoughts' direction.
> Let us against our selves employ our might,
> And putting out our eyes seeke we our light.
>
> (2:144)

In revision Sidney's purpose of illustrating the implications of social and political behavior at the death of a prince is considerably narrowed and muted when a brilliant passage of description and authorial comment is omitted. (I shall quote this in a moment.) The poems as they stand clearly do not memorialize the truth of Basilius' life; they do, however, put into highly formalized order the griefs and worries released by his death. Sidney would seem to be well aware of the artistic privilege he is exercising. The poems are wildly extreme in feeling and rigorously mannered in form. A modern prince might expect to receive poems that were better coordinated, harmonious and believable, more befitting an enlightened age. In them the feelings might perhaps appear to be mannered, but only as they struggled visibly under their civilized restraints. Avoiding extremes, the poesy in all its expressive aspects would aim at a gracefully rigorous sincerity, and any hesitation or lapse would clearly show itself as tutored by honest grief. In Sidney's original prose comment the mob of mourners, and the objects and motives of their grief, are brought under some cool, ironic attention. Their frenzy may tell too many stories and may initiate a dangerous raid on the sacred treasury of grief, but the original comment described their behavior as "a true testimony, that Men are Loving Creatures when Injuryes putt them not from their naturall course" (4:265)—a testimony that a prince might well consider when alive. In any case, the poems are highly ordered, marvelous productions of pagan spontaneity. No doubt they tempered the impulses of the listening mob, if only by repeating and concentrating them. At least the mob was turned into an audience by listening.

The excesses and confusions of death are extravagantly disported, compressed into rigid attitudes, and left without connections to other known attitudes. The incompleteness may be no less deliberate than that of Spenser's "November," but Spenser's incompleteness belongs to the poem and its relations to an immediate and a larger audience. The larger audience of Sidney's poems could acknowledge little relationship to the fictional audience of the *Arcadia,* and the poems themselves acknowledge no incompleteness. They are severely ordered to present views complete in themselves. The omissions are obvious, and savage perhaps, but they are overshadowed by the triumphs of virtuoso specialization. What is omitted is outside the poems—to be thought of, no doubt, but assisted by no bridges of feeling.

Colin will not sing on any subject, but he is quite ready to express the burden of grief he carries. The mourning for Basilius does not suffer from a lack of volunteers, and whatever the usefulness to the audience the relief to the speaker may be taken for granted. It was a well-known truth that the best medicine for a sad heart is to lament aloud. Or as Malcolm responds to the silence of Macduff at the news that his family has been massacred:

> Give sorrow words. The grief that does not speak
> Whispers the o'er-fraught heart, and bids it break.
>
> (*Macbeth*, 4.3.209–10)

As a first channel of release, though not only that, words were essential to human beings. Donne turns an old example to enlarge the point. If one cannot pray, one can at least confess that one cannot pray: "For, as in bodily, so in spirituall diseases, it is a desperate state, to be speachlesse" (5:233).

But words were notoriously subject to secret partnerships between the passions and the will. The traditional tripartite soul was understood as characteristically transferring certain surpluses from one part of the soul to another, a difficult economy to manage in spite of the wide agreement concerning means and ends. For instance, the everyday asceticism practiced in forms of self-denial could be rationalized as disciplined restraint of the "sensitive" faculty in order to strengthen the "intellectual" faculty.[3] A more complicated exchange moved the fear of death along charted paths toward the love of God and the promised good of immortality. But there were imponderables. Bacon puts his fundamental trust in the evident force of custom as "the principal magistrate of man's life," for we commonly "hear men profess, protest, engage, give great words, and then do just as they have done before; as if they were dead images, and engines moved only by the wheels of custom." So Bacon could observe, relishing the wit, "A single life doth well with churchmen; for charity will hardly water the ground where it must first fill a pool." Furthermore, the greatest public contributions are likely to be made by childless men who "have sought to express the images of their minds, where those of their bodies have failed."[4] These are standard examples of transfers from one part of the soul to another, and easier to observe and apply to illustrate particular aspects of life than to encompass in a general theory. Besides, there were often intricate exchanges and counterbalances governed by particular conditions. When there was a crisis of passion, as in the death of another, the settled customs of explanatory wisdom might encounter some unexpected observations: "Silence augmenteth grief, writing encreaseth rage."[5]

"Man is a stranger to himself," Henry King writes in a meditation on the ills of life reviewed from a sickbed.[6] In a sunny letter of old age Petrarch congratulates himself on having conquered his passions and their power (either directly or by insidious imagination) to disturb his mind. He feels at home with himself and free of that "perpetual civil war" in youth between "the different parts of my mind" (p. 256). Even the wrench of grief at the death of dear friends must be kept in bounds:

"I shall stand upright if I can; if not, fortune will lay me low dry-eyed and silent" (p. 223). Montaigne reports being "amid ladies and games" when struck with the remembrance of one who died suddenly, "on leaving a similar feast, his head full of idleness, love, and a good time, like myself" (1.20.60–61). Montaigne thinks of himself and how his own end may be the same at any time. His account is unmorbid and cultivates indifference, the purpose being to counter egoistical extravagances and to lay out casually the materials for acquiring a rational attitude toward death. Be that as it may, the dead man remembered by Montaigne is not remembered as a friend but as some one, "I don't remember whom"; and the self of the writer, in spite of a sprinkling of token intimacies, remains aloof, like some one or other writing on the subject of how to regard death. There are many ways and many degrees of being a stranger to oneself, and the steep climbing toward a state of no feeling may do as much as the abrupt plummeting of excess.

CHAPTER ELEVEN

Lament, Praise, Consolation:
Pain/Difficulty, Ease

I *saw him dead,"* Marvell wrote in his elegy for Oliver Cromwell, "A Poem upon the Death of O. C." The poem is a large ceremony and does many things, but only when the dead body is viewed does Marvell insist on his own direct presence:

> I saw him dead, a leaden slumber lyes,
> And mortal sleep over those wakefull eyes:
> Those gentle rays under the lids were fled,
> Which through his looks that piercing sweetnesse shed;
> That port which so majestique was and strong,
> Loose and depriv'd of vigour, stretch'd along:
> All wither'd, all discolour'd, pale and wan,
> How much another thing, no more that man?
> Oh! humane glory, vaine, oh! death, oh! wings,
> Oh! worthlesse world! oh transitory things!
> Yet dwelt that greatnesse in his shape decay'd,
> That still though dead, greater than death he lay'd;
> And in his alter'd face you something faigne
> That threatens death, he yet will live again.
>
> (247–60)[1]

The closed eyes are most wondered at as the poet's attention first centers on the remembered effects that those eyes made. The gentler side of a strong public figure is a normal subject for personal praise in a funeral eulogy. But the wise and accomplished orator, like the poet, will draw upon his own resources of feeling, and Marvell's art does present him as speaking for himself and to himself with minimal regard for others and the public occasion. The temporal relations of past and present are clear and fixed in a literal way, yet the life that the eyes gave the countenance dominates the description vividly. For the poet is imagining Cromwell alive, and the fact of deadness only frames the picture.

What follows, the memory of the carriage of the body, is not, however, shielded from the contrast of present appearance as Cromwell's eyes were. The fact of deadness now shocks and moves from the frame to the center of attention. Though the particularities of description are registered as they are, they are intensified by the pained response of feeling, which receives, as it were, the report of the senses with, so it seems, minimal participation in the act of recording. (The epithets themselves are almost clinical in their objectivity, though not as they ring in the verse, and not the "all" repeated.) Finally, a powerful climax in the plainest of language, the delayed recognition of the deadness as otherness: "How much another thing, no more that man?" At this point the disciplined order shatters, and the viewer responds with a cry, the expression of an ancient impulse turning against the worth of life, rediscovering life as a hated illusion convincingly revealed by death. Fragmentary phrases, key words, and the punctuating "oh's" evoke in a single, framed moment the whole literature of lament for the vanity of human purpose. The outburst says all, in a *contemptus mundi* of record brevity, but it is an outburst, not so much a climax of emotion as a necessary purge of unexpressed feelings. For when the dead body is looked at again, the facts of alteration and otherness no longer shock but now permit the access to second thoughts, a renewal of long-practiced human ways of perceiving images of necessity. Something composed of memory and imagination can reconstitute the indwelling presence of greatness. Then the poet's eye returns where it began, to the face. He speaks to himself in a customary otherness of the poet as maker (feigning and forming, handling and shaping by touch, *fingere*), and the dimension of time is now future:

> And in his alter'd face you something faigne
> That threatens death, he yet will live again.

Belief in life dies hard and not all at once. Marvell finds the way to admit an awkward stubbornness in the honest feelings of a rational viewer, the perseverance in himself of human stirrings that make and keep the legends and myths. And so the otherness in death becomes altered, becomes a not-quite-admitted personified abstraction, less material than aura or wraith, but a figurative otherness not unlike the indwelling presence of "greatnesse" in the dead body—a figurative otherness that seems to take the place of the factual otherness of the dead body. If "no more that man," then still "another thing"; Marvell apprehends him still living in another way, which does not oppose death as fact and alteration but death as annihilation. When he draws back from this moment of strange testifying in the personal shadows, Marvell's imagination resumes its work under the steady and familiar illumination of practical reason. Cromwell's future life, that of "praise," will renew itself when truth emerges from the obscurities of present partisanship and envy. As for the superior form of living again, that of the soul in bliss, which derives from no expression left on the face, the topic receives a separate celebration, entirely expected but by no means routine in its individualizing appropriateness.

For the poet, as if he were a naive semi-literalist, faithfully follows the main road and applies the traditional principle of imagining immortality as crowning mortality by banishing all the impediments of former ill and by heightening to the fullest all previous acquaintance with good. The otherness the poet saw in the dead man, and felt with dismay, achieves its final identity as Marvell himself presides over an imagined dialogue, in heaven and without words, between Cromwell's "great" soul and a "thee" who in his regard for space and purity seems to have an unbroken connection with Cromwell's former self:

> There thy great soule at once a world does see,
> Spacious enough, and pure enough for thee.
> How soon thou Moses hast, and Joshua found,
> And David, for the sword and harpe renown'd.
>
> (291–94)

After their separate, but evolving, heroic destinies, Moses, Joshua, and David consort timelessly in divine retirement, and Cromwell joins that select company. The materials for praising the great man as he lived are too intractably assertive to accommodate themselves to the mythmaking, and they obtrude. An insuperable obstacle was that Cromwell had to be represented as himself in a story too individual to fit the old supports and their fictional authority. He could not, like Spenser's shepherdess "Dido," act for someone else in a perfected story and thus represent the general conditions of human grief and consolation.

But my chief purpose in dwelling upon the poem, and its episode of viewing the dead body, concerns that intense confrontation of the otherness in death, the poet's using the immediacies of his personal experience, and his imaginative efforts to transfer and reconcile the brute fact of otherness.

In writing about the execution of Charles in his great "An Horatian Ode," Marvell does not testify directly. He is writing history in which the episode of a crucial death occurs, one that is presented vividly as "that memorable Scene," "that memorable Hour." He takes for himself the inconspicuous place of an eyewitness, which he fills with the power and advantage of a poet:

> That thence the *Royal Actor* born
> The *Tragick Scaffold* might adorn:

> While round the armed Bands
> Did clap their bloody hands.
> *He* nothing common did or mean
> Upon that memorable Scene:
>   But with his keener Eye
>   The Axes edge did try:
> Nor call'd the *Gods* with vulgar spight
> To vindicate his helpless Right,
>   But bow'd his comely Head,
>   Down as upon a Bed.
> This was that memorable Hour
> Which first assur'd the forced Pow'r.
>   So when they did design
>   The *Capitols* first line,
> A bleeding Head where they begun,
> Did fright the Architects to run;
>   And yet in that the *State*
>   Foresaw it's happy Fate.

(53–72)

We view the living body and the present circumstances framed by pregnant suggestions placed there by the poet. The past is implied in that rich introductory reference to the life of acting and the acting of life. Marvell does not need to mention that the scaffold has been raised outside Whitehall. The future is implied in the analogy of an ancient "bleeding Head," and the axe does not fall in the scene, for the death happens off stage, as it were, though the governing proprieties do not seem to be those of classical tragedy. The otherness of Charles is that of a man not dead but getting ready to be dead. He is another man than the king has been, and in more than one way opening to ironic reflections. But the otherness is not as extreme as that recognized in a friend's dead body, to be dealt with as best one may but with no access to the intellectual help of irony. The otherness is a more familiar kind, that of a tragic actor true to a role that has the established purpose of creating terror among its emotions and opening the mind to images of death— mysterious enough in the power to draw and hold an audience while allowing individual lines of partial withdrawal. But the death to take place on that stage is in earnest, and the acting is, if not unrehearsed, still not to be performed again. Facing death Charles acts admirably, suppressing all that is "common" to human nature and rising to meet, as by choice, the full height of the role that is forced upon him—in accordance with his image of himself in his last royal appearance, while living up to the ideals of the gentleman's manly code and exemplifying, more briefly, the spirit of religious teaching on the acceptance of death.

As for customary otherness of the poet as maker caught up in his concentrated imagining of the scene, we all admire that and the memorable dignity created by the sympathetic detachment of Marvell's art. But the poet does make his personal presence felt, though not by using and developing the immediacies of his own experience as in confronting the otherness of the dead Cromwell.

The introductory reference to "the *Royal Actor* born" is no eyewitness report but a complex imaginative summary; if it does not extrude like reverberations of an authorial voice, it nevertheless derives from an individual intelligence imposing itself on the materials of history and giving them a distinctive verbal shape. The "armed Bands" applauding are presented as reported fact—but with shocking differences. Their hands are "bloody"—a metaphor so close to fact that the narrow margin is filled with calculated violence. For the solitary actor is surrounded by expectant hatred applauding in advance as if to disrupt the noble illusion of a stage performance. And the author quietly separates himself from that part of the audience, which takes on a "common," "mean," brutal, hateful otherness against which the self-contained otherness of the tragic actor shines like an elevated emblem of human virtue. (That audience applauding blood is an organized mob, and the savagery stimulated by a spectacle ambiguously resembling art may bear comparison with Sidney's mob of mourners in the intervals between their listening to poetic laments.) The description of Charles's actions which follows is a highly selective mingling of metaphor and almost literal report. The first and third alternating statements, presented as if they were mere report, say what he did *not* do. The second statement, describing the eye "keener" than the axe, is an action produced by the poet's imagining eye, the same eye that would detect the signs of "greatnesse" in Cromwell's dead body, and "something" in the face that "threatens death," etc. Similarly, the fourth statement describes a voluntary action of humility, a graceful bowing of "his comely Head," accepting death as sleep.

Then the author "appears" most forwardly, though in the coolest voice imaginable, summarizing the events like an official release or like the consensual report of a conference of historians belonging to the same school. This is followed by the explanatory "So" of a neutral-sounding analogy drawn from ancient Roman history. But the personal intelligence directing this operation has assumed an intellectual separateness colder in its digestion of violence and more the master of brutality than the otherness of the simple-minded "armed Bands." The

"So" of historical analogy wanders into the charm of a well-told story, an example as parable, suitable for any handbook of revolution, illustrating the principle that political power is founded on blood—not gentility of blood but the power to shed it, and not neglecting the political force collected by the commitment of having shed it, the Rubicon of the "forced Pow'r." The hired "Architects" are frightened, as we might be in the bodies of our common humanity, but a more mysterious body, "the *State*"—reassured by whatever dark consultations it listens to—"Foresaw it's happy Fate."

This last episode distantly recalls the (later) moment, in writing on Cromwell, when Marvell stubbornly struggles in that darkness where the deepest human desires cannot accept the thought of annihilation as a fact:

> And in his alter'd face you something faigne
> That threatens death, he yet will live again.

There he is personal, immediate, and openly tentative, professional artist and stricken amateur man doing the best he can under heavy obligations, trying to reconcile the brute fact of otherness in death. Here he is utterly professional, towering in his detachment, a stranger to himself and not a little frightening. Nor should we retreat from such a sense of the man as artist if we intuit some violence against himself in that voluntary alliance he makes with the "armed Bands," transferring as in a succession of symbolic objects their "bloody hands" to the portentous, not bloody but "bleeding Head," which *he* has introduced from the neutral pages of ancient history, and introduced to take the place of the head of Charles, which the recent history omits in reporting the scene. That head was, at that time, really bleeding. The analogy transfers the dignified person of Charles to the absolute otherness of an object from history which is transformed into an emblem, a guiding light out of the darkness—not a kindly or cheerful light, and illuminating itself like some magic mirror vision of necessity, a strange mirror that seems to be held by no hands.

These are poems and exercise their due privileges. Poets are also known to be readers of their own words, and a day-by-day life may continue for many years along with the existence of the manuscript of a stunning unpublished poem. If, incredible, Marvell never reread the poem, he would have remembered it, and if he suppressed in the writing, or was not aware at the time, he would have learned that Charles's noble resignation—a truly "good" death in the eyes of many laymen and churchmen—produced some legal ambiguities in the matter of succession. Was it a legal as well as a religious resignation? Marvell could not have forgotten that Charles's bleeding head refused to be converted altogether or for long into an omen of "happy Fate." The head and the body would continue their own existence in the history of men's thoughts and feelings—Marvell's too.[2]

But to withdraw a little from the counterinvasion of art by life: Marvell tried hard and gave shape to a rare kind of personal truth communicable to others in the justly less famous poem on the death of Cromwell. He falters and loses, but the best of what he manages to say deserves to be remembered, though the key passage is not in any usual sense beautiful; not, like the "memorable Scene," a moment that can fill and haunt the imagination for centuries, as affecting in the quiet of the solitary reader as in the recitation by Winston Churchill (the heroic lines only) in a rousing wartime speech—incomparable in its depth and intricacy of glow, the sympathetic, enchanting resonances, and the disturbing sharpness and finish. One does not need to add to the chorus of praise for his verses on the death of Charles, but it may be worth adding that the power of the piece would have been unattainable if Marvell had not worked by inspired and calculated omissions. And a final remark in the same vein: in at least one respect the passage resembles the complex, bravura primitivism of Sidney's elegiac poets, who in their artistic concentration bring forth highly ordered, fluent, and limited views of experience.

"Man is a stranger to himself." "Silence augmenteth grief, writing encreaseth rage." Trusting the immediacies of personal experience in confronting the death of another is filled with uncharted risks. One may need the advice of another voice to resist the inner voice—preferably the authoritative voice of the other who has not died yet and may justly worry about such influence on random chance. Don't have bad dreams, the departing Donne counsels his mistress. Do not, especially, have this particular one:

> crying out, oh, oh,
> Nurse, oh my love is slaine; I saw him goe
> Ore the white Alpes, alone; I saw him, I,
> Assayld, fight, taken, stabb'd, bleede, fall, and dye.[3]

In the same poem, arguing in another mood against her accompanying him disguised as a page, he praises her true identity and urges: "bee not strange/To thy selfe onely." Donne himself became a learned expert and adventurer in the possibilities of being strange to oneself. Not all of the ways are deep or perilous, or incapable of supporting subdivisions and the healthful exercise of good humor which others might enjoy as their own. Thus he turns around the passionate human cry, Why to me, why not to someone else?

> How many men that stand at an *execution,* if they would aske, for what dies that Man, should heare their owne faults condemned, and see themselves executed, by *Atturney?* We scarce heare of any man *preferred,* but wee thinke of our selves, that wee might very well have beene that *Man;* Why might not I have beene that *Man,* that is carried to his *grave* now? Could I fit my selfe, to *stand,* or *sit* in any Mans *place,* and not to lie in any mans *grave?* I may lacke much of the *good parts* of the meanest, but I lacke nothing of the *mortality* of the weakest; They may have acquired better *abilities* than I, but I was borne to as many *infirmities* as they. To be an *incumbent* by lying down in a *grave,* to be a *Doctor* by teaching *Mortification,* by *Example,* by *dying,* though I may have *seniors,* others may be *elder* than I, yet I have proceeded apace in a good *University,* and gone a great way in a little time, by the furtherance of a vehement *fever;* and whomsoever these *Bells* bring to the ground today, if hee and I had beene compared yesterday, perchance I should have been thought likelier to come to this preferment, then, than he.[4]

Like gallows humor at its best, the performance is playing to the audience that will be there to savor the precarious relish. The author is speaking in his own person, but that person is responding to the special constrictions and liberties of one who is ready to leave and is practicing his farewells to life while enjoying (as author-actor) the unique privilege of saying what only one in his position can say with such convincing and unsettling authority. Even the predictability of some of the wit, uncharacteristic of Donne, exploits with a sure hand what a public audience will most want; and while the moment of drama lasts, even those individuals of refined taste and judgment will accept their feeling, as members of the strange, brief community of an audience, what their unseen neighbors feel. The author is speaking in his own person, but his mind is playing and is like the appointed persona of an evolving drama, a persona that shows no signs of understanding its real intention, that of preparing to leave this interlude and all the prominently displayed opportunities of the position and its moment. In the following Devotion Donne will welcome the answer from without (reality untainted by any suspicion of his own mental collaboration), and in responding to his own condition in another man's he spontaneously turns from himself to pray for the soul of his unknown dying neighbor for whom the bell tolls. In the act he is indeed loving his neighbor as himself, and the self is reduced to a minimal state beyond which it could not recognizably love someone as distinctly other than the self—or so Donne might have said with a characteristic turn of thought.

The self I am trying to describe is not consciously indifferent, as in the example of Montaigne's thinking of someone recently dead, like himself, but "I don't remember whom"; nor like the rigorous, active, uniquely mixed detachment of Marvell writing on the death of Charles; nor like the "holy indifference" of the "we" in the last stanza of Herbert's "Death." These are distinctions that may be recognized but do not lend themselves to simple categorizing or defining. It may be better to say that when Donne prays for his unknown dying neighbor his own self is less reduced than transformed.

The sustained context of Donne's *Devotions* is one in which pain and difficulty are made convincingly real. Without the power, weight, and endurance of the whole preceding course of introspection, the turning outward would be different in quality; its nature is, if not defined, at least corroborated by what it turns away from with inspired spontaneity. The ease of the turning acts as a validation of itself; the pain and difficulty experienced are both indirect proof of and a direct connection to the ease.

I am not prepared to announce a fixed principle that will not require some adjustments for differing circumstances, but the relationship of pain/difficulty and ease occurs often in my subject and has already occurred, though not singled out for separate attention. I now present some reminders and a brief review. The underlying plot of Spenser's "November" is the transformation of pain and difficulty to ease (a kind of "doolful pleasaunce"); the basic plot is a sure model for Milton's "Lycidas." In contrast, Montaigne and others will seem conspicuous in resolving difficulty and stressing ease. In their context Sidney's laments suggest an unbridged interval between the savage pain and the fluent ease of expression.

As for Marvell, whose ease makes the expositor sweat: the scene of Charles's execution is a long moment preceded by no pain or difficulty and dominated by a strongly willed ease, that of an extraordinary collaboration between the control of the artist and the control of the tragic protagonist who is being presented. It is a moment in which mind and spirit exercise their privilege within a space of scenic time outside of which the impending violence waits. The following scene is utterly different, and especially its kind of contrived ease by which an exchanged "bleeding Head" will be produced as the solving moral of the historical tragedy. In the great scene that leads to the point of execution and then allows historical fact and narrative convention to complete the undescribed event, we may feel, as many readers do, a kind of undercurrent of pain, of difficulty, in the deliberately constrained suggestiveness of the language: as in the gross violence of the applauding spectators, and in the thoughtful calm at the center of the scene, the irony, the sympathy about which accredited interpreters argue well and without resolution. If we do not find open pain under the ease, we do find some shifting difficulty and may believe that it is not all of our own making.

On the other hand, the clarity of Marvell's painful struggle in the presence of Cromwell's dead body registers itself as an authentication of *his* experience. There he presents the materials and order of his responses in the form of a personal story, but that story, however immediate and spontaneous, is also representative, the vehicle of expected and time-honored elements of elegy: lament, praise, and consolation. The consolation is freely wrought, woven into and out of the praise, and yet the consolation separates itself with troubled difficulty, and therefore not altogether, from the lingering resonances of lament. The consolation resembles in part the "doolful pleasaunce" of Spenser's "November," the mixed pleasures of art and assurance taming the wild grief of loss. Yet, since Cromwell in his own person could not be assimilated to a general myth, Marvell's efforts are not capable of disappearing into the story. Throughout the poem, as in the discussed episode of Cromwell's entrance into immortality, Marvell's efforts are strenuous and individual in adapting and modernizing, sometimes well, sometimes too well, many of the commonplaces and tropes of consolation. The expected credentials of personal pain as the mourner tells his own story are, however, too individual to be contained in the embrace of old forms. In the cumulative sense of ordering, which has the purpose of tempering grief with consolation, his personal shock at the brute otherness of the dead was too strong and unforgettable to be turned into general consolation and hope. Although where the course and resolution of pain are familiar and expected what is old conveys a kind of ease, in Marvell it is an unsettled ease in which a truth of personal feeling once expressed will not be denied and cannot be changed into something else—at least this master of feeling and expression does not do so. If we do not encounter other examples quite like this one, we may believe that other poets did not see what Marvell saw, or did not let themselves both see and say the irredeemable thing.

CHAPTER TWELVE

The Death of a Loved One: Personal and Public Expressions

What I propose doing now takes as one point of departure the example of Donne's turning from introspection to a liberating love for his dying neighbor. Instances of love for the person dead or dying introduce the wedge of a vast subject, love, into the vast subject of death. That the relations of the two open still another great territory is well known and much written on. I shall try not to stray from the older beaten path, which is not dull, both here and when I return to the subject in Part 4. Besides, the term "loved" as I have used it in the title above will also include, in the "public expressions," persons for whom the engaged feelings of esteem and admiration are to be understood as a kind of love.

Among the fitful dreams and incoherent debates of the insomniac soul, the longing for death may be stimulated by the death of a beloved. The dead is, one is urged to believe, now in the embrace of immortality. All of the excesses of consolation imprint that message deeply and cannot avoid the implications, or the occasional direct candor of a problematic acknowledgment, that part of the surplus of grief is directed toward the self:

> But live thou there, still happie, happie spirit,
> And give us leave thee here thus to lament:
> Not thee that doest thy heavens joy inherit,
> But our owne selves that here in dole are drent.
> Thus do we weep and waile, and wear our eies,
> Mourning in others our owne miseries.[1]

Sidney's "pagan" laments carry the essential message, both personal and social. Many in the crowd of mourners vow to kill themselves at Basilius' funeral (4:265). Such extremes of feeling in grief are a familiar part of the human record, and they are not usually submitted to a formal judgment. One does not expect anyone to isolate and hold up for literal questioning the line from Ben Jonson's sober "Epitaph on Master Vincent Corbet": "I feele, I'm rather dead then he!"[2] What is most rare is to find the extreme of feeling and the longing for death presented in a form of neutral, even antiseptic, objectivity, as in Henry Wotton's epigram "Upon the Death of Sir Albert Morton's Wife":

> He first deceased; she for a little tried
> To live without him, lik'd it not, and died.[3]

(This deserves its niche in rooms containing modern statistics on the survival of widows and widowers.)

Henry King, Donne's friend and executor, man of letters, accomplished poet, Bishop of Chichester, wrote "The Exequy" in retrospective lament for the death of his young wife, whom he was trying to live without. His longing for her passes into and mingles with his expectation of death, and the remarrying of "my body to that dust/It so much loves." The time of his thoughts goes "Backward and most preposterous," but his heart does not entirely follow and remains apologetically divided. For though his "Pulse like a soft Drum/Beats my approach, tells Thee I come," his heart is also "content to live," to "go on,/And wait my dissolution." Nothing in the letter (construed as poetry) is "irreligious"; in the spirit, the most one could say is that the poem is not religious in its orientation. As for the tempered ending, its declaration of patient waiting in an equipoise of hope and comfort, it is Christian in form, but the turning toward death is Christian only so far as "we shall meet and never part." The "crime" that asks to be forgiven is against her, his willingness to live at all, though "Divided, with but half a heart." Christ is mentioned but once, a punctuating reference in the midst of a grotesque, relaxing flight of fancy, a lecturing oration to "earth." And in the expected death that will remarry their dust, Providence remains neutral, as it were, but the Day of Judgment is celebrated as a cataclysm favorable to lovers:

> our bodies shall aspire
> To our soules blisse: then we shall rise,
> And view our selves with cleerer eyes
> In that calm Region, where no night
> Can hide us from each others sight.

If any audience is imagined, other than self and the spirit of his dead wife, it is a literary audience of peers who will admire the writing, the quality of feeling, and the graceful inventions that develop the theme. King knew what he was doing: not wrestling with himself under the rules of belief, but entertaining a half-fiction to relieve the pain of longing. Though pain motivates the poem, it is not often an immediate subject or a difficulty that will be overcome in any way other than by hearing matters out until the desired feelings of comfort, hope, and patience appear. When they do they are welcomed, not as a vision rising out of intense personal struggle, but as an everyday, livable mood of calm remaining after the stored-up moods of grief and longing have been drawn out of their silence. The equipoise reached is a humble one and welcomed with seemly modesty for what it is, more the signal of a place to end than the kind of ending from which one can see with astonishment the inevitable rightness of every searching movement from the beginning. Whatever "rage" is increased lies in a relaxed inclination to identify love of the dead with despising, not life and the world, but the disposition of one's own life, and to give a poetic rationality to a limited affair with death.

Donne lost a beloved wife. He had his own practiced ways of considering death (of which the *Anniversaries* was but one unusual monument) and could not have been very susceptible to the stimulations King finds in his theme. "My good is dead," Donne wrote in the second line of his sonnet:

> Since she whome I lovd, hath payd her last debt
> To Nature, and to hers, and my good is dead,
> And her soule early into heaven ravished,
> Wholy in heavenly things my mind is sett.
> Here the admyring her my mind did whett
> To seeke thee God; so streames do shew the head,
> But though I have found thee, and thou my thirst hast fed,
> A holy thirsty dropsy melts mee yett.
> But why should I begg more love, when as thou
> Dost wooe my soule for hers; offring all thine:
> And dost not only feare least I allow
> My love to saints and Angels, things divine,
> But in thy tender jealosy dost doubt
> Least the World, fleshe, yea Devill putt thee out.

"Hers" is the nature she inherited from Adam (and Eve), including the debt of death which nonhuman nature incidentally acquired at the same time. That other nature is politely mentioned as if separate, as if an agency administering a world in which bodies naturally wear out and women are worn out or die in childbearing. The good that is dead is the soul of everything in the natural world.[4] Her soul "early" has been "ravished" into heaven, and his mind follows without ravishment, turning by its own motivating force on the bare pivots of a *since* and a concluded episode of time: "Since she whome I lovd. . . ." "Admyring her," he had sought God and found Him. Still, he yearns for "more love" from God, and asks, "But why should I begg?" We do not hear him begging. That lies among other silences in the poem, like the felt grief allowed no immediacy of expression but allowed only a bare, absolute declaration and a few taut signs. God, who was unmentioned in the death supervised by nature, has anticipated the increased desire and the "begging": "when as thou/Dost wooe my soule for hers; off-ring all thine."[5]

The speech of the poem is unique and mysterious—its music and movement, its ways of expressing the self to the self and to God, by firm, brief affirmations ("my mind is sett") and by almost inaudible undertones. It is not a kind of speech one can characterize or translate into a message without risking travesty. Ann Donne is only spoken *of*, kept in a careful third person. No human audience is intimated. One may feel the greatest difficulty in trying to distinguish among the re-strained, the repressed, and the simplest urgency of passion. But the main issues are probably clear enough, and what by one view represents a severe repression of natural feeling and continued love for the dead other, by a different view represents an exaltation of past love in present love, disciplined by an ironic acting against the self. In the soul's exercise of strangeness to itself, it produces the stricture against loving lesser "things divine," as saints and angels. Donne acknowledges the wisdom of God's "feare," with no more than a side glance, if that much, to the normal practices of his Roman Catholic youth or to the hyperbolical diction of his amorous poetry. The world of nature and the flesh of love have not yet been "ravished" from him, though he affirms that "my good is dead." He does not seem anxious himself, but there is no point in telling God of His "feare," "tender jealosy," and "doubt" except that of repeating the elementary lessons to himself as confirmation. In doing so he is acknowledging the general human record as personal confession and as pledge of his own alert determination not to feel "secure." Yet he can himself make no pledge about the devil without and within. The devil, "yea Devill," represents a master spirit lurking in all human exchanges and altering shapes in ways visible only to God. And the devil's classic maneuver is to convert love into *the* infidelity to God.

Nothing could be easier and readier for use than the basic religious model. Death teaches the unreliability of human things and turns the soul to God. Donne turns the ease into honest difficulty. For nothing could be tougher and more individual than Donne's expression of the religious truth he accepts. In the world of nature the otherness of his dead "good," of "she whome I lovd," cannot be translated in any way; it is fixed and denies relationship. (There can be no recourse to the kind of imaginative aid Marvell applied to the otherness of the dead Crom-well.) But since her soul is not dead and not other, it does not deny relationship. When he admired the woman, his mind turned toward the origin of her soul in God, and that action is further advanced when God translates her soul into a new relationship—a present courtship in which God fully participates, as He did not in her death, presided over by "Nature." God woos Donne's soul for the sake of Ann's and offers all His three-personed love in anticipation of the final marriage.[6]

This is the climax of the sonnet and includes a third-person celebration, as brief as great, of the woman he loved, whose soul by the action attributed to God participates in Donne's compelled increase of "holy" desire. Though his personal grief is allowed no direct expression, and the poem is as remote as possible from a love sonnet, under the rigor he imposes on his feelings there is a most rare kind of tenderness which may be felt and deduced. The personal memory is transferred to God's memory and refused first-person articulation. There is not the slightest suggestion that his dead "good" is or will be a sacrifice, or that the ravishment of her soul, "early," is a fatherly affliction for his greater good, though these would have been easy and familiar transfers for Donne to have made. His feelings are, we may think, too deep and singular and precious for such intermediate handling. He moves directly to the ultimate marriage in heaven. He returns from his exalted glimpse of infinite love, where there are no others, to the prudence of religious man in the natural world. That his "good" is indeed dead requires of him an absolute return of all his feelings to their source. Yet, neither the moment of exaltation nor any random high spirits released by "setting" his mind in absoluteness can make him forget to recite the homely lessons of human weakness.

The irony of the recital, though retrospective in its implied moral movement, and though in form a colloquy with God, represents a return to the common time of an everyday present in which he must live with the problems and promises of past and future. Some easing of the tension is expressed in the wry humor, and a degree of detachment signals its presence in the restrained but suddenly new sense of personal relish displayed in his language. This is not ease but an easing, and hard-won.

So Donne accepts the otherness of his dead wife, accepts as completely finished that intimate mingling and mysterious touching of lives which the common word "lovd" expresses, and identifies himself with a reaching for the immortal source of that love which he seeks while feeling himself sought. Most of the doctrine is familiar; the history of advice, exhortation, and methodical exposition is long and full. If we were to take the sonnet as our touchstone, as the one answer to all questions, there might be nothing more to say. But there is always something else to say about death, as about God's "feare," "doubt," "tender jealosy," and "this worlds sweet":

> From being anxious, or secure,
> Dead clods of sadnesse, or light squibs of mirth,
>   From thinking, that great courts immure
> All, or no happinesse, or that this earth
>   Is only for our prison fram'd,
>   Or that thou art covetous
> To them whom thou lov'st, or that they are maim'd
> From reaching this worlds sweet, who seek thee thus,
> With all their might, Good Lord deliver us.
>
>   ("A Litanie," lines 127–35)

The sonnet is, however, one kind of reliable touchstone. For though its basic doctrine evokes a standard response, that of surrendering the dead to the life of eternity and rededicating one's own hope to that life, Donne's poem could never serve as a textbook model of what to think or say. In its severity the statement echoes a Reformation emphasis but is distinctly his own. The transfer of love is austerely bare, reduced to an essential, the image of marriage in heaven. Personal feelings not expressed in response to the death are, one may conjecture, transferred in part, with no admission that any subject is in mind but the marriage in heaven, to considerations of the problems of how to live as a survivor. In any case, one is not likely to doubt the presence of a living person responding to a common human grief in some customary and in some unquestionably individual ways.

To illustrate a difference I quote from a letter that I shall refer to again. It is a personal letter of consolation to a friend by the Christian Platonist Ficino; its warmth is chiefly that of exhortation, and the engagement of the self of the writer is dominated by his loyalty to the doctrine he expresses. Granted, the resemblance between that doctrine and Donne's is encumbered by divergences, and there is an unbridgeable difference between advising a mourner and writing a true poem on the death of one's beloved wife. Still, the fluency of Ficino is (at least to me) dismaying, while on the contrary what Donne does not say is a strong part of what he says. But enough; here is the quotation from Ficino:

> You will only cease to weep, Gismondo, when you cease looking for your Albiera degli Albizzi in her dark shadow and begin to follow her by her own clear light. For the further she is from that misshapen shadow the more beautiful will you find her, past all you have ever known. Withdraw into your

soul, I beg you, where you will possess her soul which is so beautiful and dear to you; or rather, from your soul withdraw to God. There you will contemplate the beautiful idea through which the Divine Creator fashioned your Albiera; and as she is far more lovely in her Creator's form than in her own, so you will embrace her there with far more joy.[7]

W*here doctrine, or* the relationship of self to the dead other, is less exacting, the subject remains more open and flexible—as in poems memorializing the death of public or private figures, or even friends. The necessary claims of lament, praise, and consolation must all be satisfied, but except in poems modeled on the pastoral elegy, lament and consolation tend to be subordinated to the memorializing by praise. Often, as in the example of Marvell in the presence of Cromwell's dead body, ways are found to make the eulogistic assimilate and indirectly express the dues of grief and comfort. Such poems have their own problems, and their successes are usually relative to the expectations of their subgenre and to their occasion, which not many of them outlast very long or very well.

The chief problem was that over the centuries everything on the subject had been said, or so it seemed when the occasion was public. Though variations were always available, in emphasis and disposition, in the development or not of oblique suggestions, no major discoveries were likely to have been overlooked. Furthermore, some of the basic materials had achieved a kind of inevitability, and to have ignored them on certain appointed occasions would have seemed like an act of violence against the tried and true. For public occasions the indispensable topics were praise for the departed, lament for the loss, and consolation for the survivors gathered together and about to disperse to resume their individual schedules of dying.

For a different audience, not physically present but an audience of readers, an audience who will read in isolation as individuals but who may need to be imagined as gathered together, some of the potential divergences between oration and poetry were freer to develop. Like the orator and priest, the poet has a function to perform, that of presenting and representing to others what they will want to think and feel about the death. But in his role the poet is a volunteer, and self-appointed even when invited or expected to perform. He nevertheless assumes a public function, and he becomes answerable to the unwritten rules governing the particular occasion, and answerable to the traditional proprieties for discourses on death and to the general rules governing poetry and the specific genre he has undertaken. The impersonal aspects of the priest's function are not available in the same ways to the poet, who must establish his motivations for thus appearing. To whatever is old in the repeated messages of death he will usually feel obliged to bring forward something new, immediate, and personal to justify his speaking presence. If the death is that of a monarch, or a prince, or a prince of poets, or even that of an Edward King, the elegist will know in advance that his poem will be one contribution among many. The other contributors will surely look at what he has written, as will strangers and friends; and the approval of some of these probable readers will be desired for its own sake, an honorable value that does not preclude lesser and perhaps more tangible values. Thoughts of such may be dispersed in dark corners and blanketed with serviceable cobwebs by the mind composing in grief. Finally, the voluntariness of his act brings the poet into a personal but publicly shared conjunction with the otherness of the dead, and into a related but different conjunction with the otherness of the audience. Since the poet's connections are not strictly defined by office, they are therefore less constrained but more subject to pressures from without and from within. These problems do not apply in the same ways to personal elegies.

Donne's public elegies are among his less memorable work, but he does address the problems in hand with a professional skill that is worth observing. He makes very sparing use of the "I," and thus with a single stroke avoids the standard awkwardness of having to establish his presence and relationships in the poem. Instead, he assumes the function of a meditative "we" honoring the occasion with an elevated discourse in which praise of the dead is partly personal but more symbolic—chiefly drawn in images and imagistic arguments that express what that life meant and means. The sense of grief and the consolation are also characteristically turned toward indirect expression; their presentation is reduced and their representative aspects developed. In the elegy on Prince Henry the last sixteen lines are spoken by a passionate "I" who is the poet testifying, though less as a person than as an inspired voice that speaks for others. In that poem, while extravagantly praising a worthy young prince (whose death ruined many hopes and plans), Donne does not forget to praise the father in the son. But otherwise the audience apparently consists of those for whom the poet may be thought to speak and of those unseen admirers of wit before whom a virtuoso performance has been presented. His best elegy of this kind, in my view, is the "Obsequies to the Lord Harrington, Brother to the Lady Lucy, Countess of Bedford." The "I," consistently used here, is that of a courteous friend and admirer—not a rapt, inspired convert to mourning, but a serious volunteer composing at his best a meditative essay worthy of Lucy's young brother and of herself. Both poet and audience compliment each other by the warm impersonality of the discourse and by its intellectual dignity.

While fulfilling the general purpose of memorializing a death, Donne's approach and method tend to be meditative and essayistic— further from the methods of oration, for instance, than in sermons that guide listeners to the consideration of a good death. At his best he makes his own path between epicedium and monody, speaking not quite *to* or *for* an audience consisting of one reader at a time, each of whom will find familiar and unfamiliar thoughts expressed in a voice and manner no reader could simply feel as his own or assent to without the conscious awareness of doing so. The restrictions placed upon the poet's full personal presence are paralleled by the kind of attention directed toward the dead. Personal touches are consistently drawn toward an abstract representation signifying intellectual, moral, and spiritual qualities.

Ben Jonson, who seems to me the best poet in English when it comes to writing direct personal praise, seldom masters all the difficulties inherent in the public performance of the elegy. For the most part, unlike Donne, he does not often manage the difficulties or his own best talents without occasional embarrassing lapses. In a few poems, he strives to combine his own gifts for epigrammatic compression with Donneian wit and abstract representation—as for instance the epitaphs on Cecelia Boulstred and Henry L. La-ware, and those on the Countess of Shrewsbury and the Baroness Ogle. In his "An Elegie on the Lady Jane Pawlet" (*Underwood*, 85) he gives himself more room in the general form of an oration, prefixed by a fable that hardly measures up to his standard of the fable as the soul of a poem. He tries to put himself squarely into the poem, but that trusted position does not easily fit the expansive form, and the master of plain, direct expression has to finger the trope of inexpressibility for a dozen lines. Lady Jane's reported death scene is a roseate performance, her perfection sentimentalized, though in a manly style. (Jonson works as hard as Donne does in the sermon on Alderman Cokayne, but too fast and with less reserve.) Lady Jane addressed her torturing physicians and urged them on:

> 'Tis but a body which you can torment,
> And I, into the world, all Soule, was sent!
>
> (lines 55–56)

She comforted her husband, blessed her son, cheered her "faire sisters," tempered with gladness the grief of her parents, made joys rise above the fears of her friends,

> And, in her last act, taught the Standers-by,
> With admiration, and applause to die!
>
> (61–62)

It is a poem for family and friends; out of its occasion the faults are peculiar chiefly in bearing the blurred stamp of Jonson's virtues. No one else, I think, could have written it with just those faults.

He writes a better elegy to celebrate the death of Lady Venetia Digby (*Underwood, 86*)—a full oration consisting of preface, a lament (brief and tempered), and a long consolation turning into a longer personal eulogy, which turns itself into an apotheosis. The fiction that she was his muse (a kind of feigning Jonson sometimes regards as compromising truth) authorizes the personal station he takes within the poem and works well enough in the poem and no doubt even better in the eyes of her husband, who was Jonson's friend and benefactor. The poet's "wounded mind" is free to "rage" and soar, but most of the time he can sound like himself, even if not as on subjects where he is at his best.

He is at one range of his very best in the third epitaph for the friend who died in his arms, Sir John Roe:

> Ile not offend thee with a vaine teare more,
>   Glad-mention'd *Roe:* thou art but gone before,
> Whither the world must follow. And I, now,
>   Breathe to expect my when, and make my how.
> Which if most gracious heaven grant like thine,
>   Who wets my grave, can be no friend of mine.
>
> (*Epigrammes,* 33)

There the tense relations between self and other are not mitigated by any contrived fictions, and the identification imagined imposes a touchingly unbelievable end to his own grief. Another range of his best is the ode "To the Immortall Memorie, and Friendship of that Noble Paire, Sir Lucius Cary, and Sir H. Morison" (*Underwood, 72*). There by a famous act of rhyming and timing he places himself in an unprecedented relationship with the dead other, while the old message, "all must die," is redirected into a gay dance of death between dead and living friends:

> Call, noble *Lucius,* then for Wine,
> And let thy lookes with gladnesse shine:
> Accept this garland, plant it on thy head,
> And thinke, nay know, thy *Morison's* not dead.
> Hee leap'd the present age,

Possest with holy rage,
To see that bright eternall Day:
Of which we *Priests,* and *Poets* say
Such truths, as we expect for happy men,
And there he lives with memorie; and *Ben*

Johnson, who sung this of him, e're he went
Himselfe to rest,
Or taste a part of that full joy he meant
To have exprest.

(lines 75–88)

The great poem to Shakespeare (*Uncollected,* 42) shows Jonson at his best in praising the dead; because of the subject he can bring fully to bear his great power to praise the living. Mourning and consolation are excluded; the death of the poet is a matter of history to be mentioned only for contrast with the assured life of his book and the lineage of his mind. The fact of death permits one moment of longing nostalgia, the thought of Shakespeare's appearing again, in verse, and helps conclude, on a light note, where many such poems heavily begin:

Shine forth, thou Starre of *Poets,* and with rage,
Or influence, chide, or cheere the drooping Stage;
Which, since thy flight from hence, hath mourn'd like night,
And despaires day, but for thy Volumes light.

(77–80)

In praise of living friends Jonson can love another like himself, inflecting the distinctions of gratitude, admiration, and respect into the syntax of shared values. Toward the dead who will not hear the good language his generosity reaches a little further, and the other poet becomes an image of himself, not only in the hopes expressed for the living book, but in the description of the art which makes books live:

And, that he,
Who casts to write a living line, must sweat,
(such as thine are) and strike a second heat
Upon the *Muses* anvile: turne the same,
(And himselfe with it) that he thinkes to frame;
Or for the lawrell, he may gaine a scorne,
For a good *Poet's* made, as well as borne.
And such wert thou.

(58–65)

The praise rings with sincerity and counters the popular notion of Shakespeare's natural and fluent ease, but it is pure Jonson.

Though he can praise attainments unlike his own, his free admiration gives him an honorable place in the worth of others; and though he can resourcefully despise the unworthy, or despise the world or the stage as world, and though he can mock himself or project inventive scorn that derives from the darker recesses of himself, he cannot or will not praise another by making the complimentary identification of writing like him. This last is admittedly a rare form of praise, and I mention it only because a brilliant minor poet, Thomas Carew, accomplishes the feat in one of the best elegies written for a poet, "Upon the Death of the Deane of Pauls, Dr. Iohn Donne." (He also, with effective authority, writes a poem criticizing Jonson in the voice of Jonson.)[8]

To speak in general: numerous public elegies of the time, including those for poets, were too much burdened with the necessities and manners of the occasion. Too many things had to be said and had already been said, and the poet had limited access to his own feelings while being pushed into an excessive dependence on professional will and skill. For the public occasion it seemed obligatory to say something new, if only to explain one's entrance upon the scene, but as Jonson declared (a judge who sometimes found himself rubbing elbows with the criminals), "who doth praise a person by a new, / But a fain'd way, doth rob it of the true" (*Underwood,* 85, 37–38). The unfeigned and true finds it difficult escaping from the trite but true. And therefore a small family of images gain credit as vehicles of safe conduct. Where the known facts do not embarrass it is well to hear that a good man's life is his monument and the poet's monument is his book. Such dependable figurative truths, besides their contributions to the necessities of praise and consolation, have a special value in a field where certain alternative thoughts are unthinkable, such as those of simple, blank extinction. But if in treading carefully the poet restricts his images and walls out all untested thoughts, his intellectual determination may seem to be only the other side of obtrusive fictionalizing. Or if he explains his entrance on the scene by cultivating the normal expressions of shocked disbelief and dismay at the dreadful news of ———'s death, his distraught writing and the irresistible drift toward expressing intimations of the end of time will produce the kind of beginning from which poems seldom fully recover.

The list could go on much longer. But I end by mentioning one practical matter in the management of tact. The variable distance between the writing self and the dead other must be negotiated with some careful awareness of the dues of courtesy. One cannot thrust into the intimacies of grief without some risk of offending real mourners, and the safest compliment lies in being on the periphery as a compelled witness, an organ for producing reflections suitable to the dead and for testifying to the known repeatable truths. In a word, though the occasion is one of pain and difficulty, the imaginative exchanges and transfers, however labored the writing, tend to be too easy. Yet between the self writing and the dead other, pain and difficulty are the most believable, and certainly the most prevalent, credentials offered to an audience.

It was a piece of proverbial wisdom, and praise, to say that one regarded his own physical pain as if it were another's, in the body of someone else. Denham, among the hyperboles with which he studs his poem "On the Earl of Strafford's Trial and Death," arranges a still more strenuous exchange between the victim and the audience:

> Each seemed to act that part he came to see
> And none was more a looker-on than he.[9]

The effect of the figure depends, of course, on transferring the believed fact of pain from actor to audience. Here we can recognize a basis in experience and convention which supports the possibility and may enlist admiration. But the believed facts of pain and of death are not quite the same, and in the staging of death the otherness of the principal person makes all transfers perilously figurative, for the facts related to death are difficult to keep from drifting in the wrong direction. The dead feel no pain, we believe, but the general disposition of mourners to feel pain may resist being transferred like a sum to any mourner.

Let us return to examples of private expression. In a late letter Petrarch wrote of his grief at the death of his grandson (Bishop, pp. 274–76). He cites, for the record it seems, religious and practical reasons for not mourning and then goes on to speak more personally:

> But I admit I was profoundly shaken to see the sweet promise of his life reft away at its beginning. . . . I tried then to fix my thoughts not on his age but on my own, for it is disgraceful for all men, and especially for the old, to bewail the human lot. . . . I have learned that complaints are useless, that nothing avails but patience, in the things we cannot change. . . .
>
> Now—to let you know all my weakness—I have ordered a marble tomb in Pavia for my little boy. It is inscribed with six elegiac verses. I should hardly do this for anyone else, and I should be most unwilling that anyone else should do the same

149

for me. But suppressing my tears and lamentations, I was so overcome by my emotions that, having no other recourse, I did what I could. He is in heaven, beyond all earthly cares, and I could offer him nothing but this last vain kind of tribute. It is useless to him, it is some solace to me. And so I wanted to consecrate something, not to evoke tears, as Virgil says, but to preserve his memory—not in me, who have no need of stones or of poems, but in chance passersby, that they may learn how dear he was to all, from the very beginning of his life.

The document is remarkable for its candor in expressing, along with the halfhearted efforts to touch them up, the materials of the soul in crisis; it is an instructive example of Petrarch's gift to Western civilization of what he learned from his discovery of Cicero's letters to Atticus. His pain is real, and the difficulties of proper reasoning are chiefly bypassed by the confession of weakness and the seeking of personal comfort by making "this last vain kind of tribute." He would not want anyone else to do the same for him; that would involve an act of judgment and subscribe to the vanity by directing it toward himself. Yet that involves him in denying to someone else the feelings he accepts in himself, and it exposes the ribbon edge of a smaller vanity, the distrust of other taste in the inscribing of "six elegiac verses." The little boy "was the fourth Francesco, the solace of our lives, our hope, the joy of our house. And . . . chanced to possess unusual beauty and intelligence. . . . His only fault was to resemble me so much that one who did not know his mother [Petrarch's illegitimate daughter, Francesca] would certainly have called me the father."

The passion of identification is countered by prayers that deliver his repeated embraces of the child to the care of a loving God—a remedy of first and last resort, well recommended by the records of analytical reason and instinctive piety. Having taken this clear and definitive action, Petrarch adds a more lingering and intriguing surrender, or distribution, of the self transferring its sense of past and present identity with the beloved other. The act is individual and made particular, but is grounded on blind anonymity and unknown chance, which contribute their elements of obscure desire to the exchange between self and other. The avowed aim is to preserve "his memory—not in me . . . but in chance passersby." The house of death that stands in two worlds may indeed "trouble a good man's resolution," and truth is honored, in part, by the ragged loose ends of the struggle. "I did what I could," Petrarch says—a statement of fact that stands for a summary human cry. Did his "weakness" intend to preserve nothing of himself in that pure axis between the otherness of the inscribed tomb and the otherness of future witnesses who will chance to pass by? In such matters humane discretion may be the more honorable part of judgment.

Petrarch's letter leads us to Jonson's "On My First Sonne":

> Farewell, thou child of my right hand, and joy;
>   My sinne was too much hope of thee, lov'd boy,
> Seven yeeres tho'wert lent to me, and I thee pay,
>   Exacted by thy fate, on the just day.
> O, could I loose all father now. For why
>   Will man lament the state he should envie?
> To have so soone scap'd worlds, and fleshes rage,
>   And, if no other miserie, yet age?
> Rest in soft peace, and, ask'd, say here doth lye
>   Ben. Jonson his best piece of poetrie.
> For whose sake, hence-forth, all his vowes be such,
>   As what he loves may never like too much.
>
>   (Epigrammes, 45)

The poem begins with a farewell repeated as in a formal conclusion, "Rest in soft peace," uniting Benjamin, the "child of my right hand," with "Ben. Jonson his best piece of poetrie." But an epilogue has a further word to say. In between the two farewells, the struggle to accept the painful loss observes traditional forms of counseling acceptance and of retrieving, from the familiar history of life, reasons that may afford some relief. His voice is primarily that of natural, not religious or philosophical, man speaking with an anger carefully disengaged from both self and the boy—by expressing, with overtones, a standard content of moral and religious reasoning. A definition of sin is excess, and a son is also an earthly thing toward whom hope is conditional. The debt of the sin of Adam is paid on the due and therefore the "just day"—a blend of personal history and catechistic recital delivered with an expressive tonelessness. An abrupt parenthesis marks what will not be said: the desires of grief to revoke one's fatherhood (lose), or the desires of grief to release the simple passions of a father (loose). The self then steps backward to ask questions in the name of "man," questions breathing with conflict—though we might have to revise that impression if we knew the motives of the asker. But we do not know for sure, and Jonson is not going to tell us. We think him to be lamenting for himself, holding up for view an allowable expression of longing for death not absolutely inconsistent with the appointed ends of Providence. He names in their hated otherness present and anticipated miseries of life. It is a brief contemptus mundi, a kind of rage—naming the compulsions of the flesh that make a man a stranger to himself, and the alien state of age that becomes oneself. These are held up as the human lot, and his lot, and imagined as both immediate and encompassing—in a lament not acknowledged as lament, and the boy has escaped so early.

The outburst resembles Petrarch's confessed entanglement in personal weakness. Jonson's answer to the pain and difficulty is ornamented with a slight fictional design: if anyone asks, little Benjamin's grave is authorized to answer, like an epitaph, *Hic iacet,* the "best piece of poetrie" of his father-maker. The poem is an epitaph, the child is now a poem, no longer a "thou" but a "here doth lye," and the father stopped saying "I" in line five.

His last word is less "a piece of poetrie" than a charm, one that echoes in a kind of mutter overtones audible in the poem proper. Like other elegists he steps back from that special order of time concentrating on the loss to strike an attitude adjusted to the everyday time of ordinary life. Toward an open, uncharacterized, and gray-hued future the sensibilities draw themselves tighter, adapting a stoic cloak suitable for a time of less hope, less hurt. If he had written a letter to a friend, articulate with free details of self-explanation yet stumbling in the honest bafflement of the human situation, Jonson might have said like Petrarch, "I did what I could." If the answer to the difficulties of the poem seems easy, it will not, I think, seem too easy, and the epilogue says in another voice that the answer does not fully speak to the pain.

His epitaph "On My First Daughter" (*Epigrammes,* 22) is not racked with pain or difficulty. From the beginning, voice and statement establish a quiet concord, which is an authentic but rare expression in lyrics on death. The calm ease requires no hidden fiction or open counterpoise to command belief, and the poem never strays into mere fluency. The child lived only six months, before human hope could turn the sense of divine gift into a divine debt, which, whenever called in, had to be acknowledged as "the just day." The infant remains in the third person throughout, as do the parents, and in this poem there are two parents:

> Here lyes to each her parents ruth,
> *Mary,* the daughter of their youth:
> Yet, all heavens gifts, being heavens due,
> It makes the father, lesse, to rue.

In expressing his own tenderness and moderated grief, the father acts to set a guiding example for the mother, and in the next five lines he speaks for and to her in a gently consoling dialogue of one:

> At sixe moncths end, shee parted hence
> With safetie of her innocence;
> Whose soule heavens Queene, (Whose name shee beares)
> In comfort of her mothers teares,
> Hath plac'd amongst her virgin-traine.

In the last three lines he speaks for both parents, touching on the hope of the resurrection and turning from a musically damped austerity of language to the only direct address in the poem:

> Where, while that sever'd doth remaine,
> This grave partakes the fleshly birth.
> Which cover lightly, gentle earth.

After the gracious acquiescence of heaven, presented as free and certain, the poet returns to time and place, burial, and the implied weight of human feeling that yearns to be lightened in all turning away. And it is lifted by a courteous invocation and by the delicately touched transfers between earth and parental feeling, none of which distorts the pathos.

We come now to "Lycidas," and I shall limit my brief comments to topics that have already been introduced. First, the matter of pain and difficulty is brought forward at once and both sustained and varied until the moment of sudden release. The poet brings in expressive witnesses to the grief, and it is now a commonplace of criticism that the primary source of emotion in the poem is Milton's own deep anxiety.[10] Indeed, modern recognition that Milton's own hopes, fears, and doubts make the conventions pulse with life, and that the poem is deeply imagined and felt, coincides with the flow of critical attention which has elevated the poem to a new height of reputation. I do not separate myself from that general point of view but have some partly different interests to emphasize.

The speaker of the poem wears a mask and can say everything he wants through the formal gestures of the conventions. His mannered initial reluctance is also personal expression transposed, and there is, finally, a remarkable theatrical appearance. Since the dead friend was a poet, that relationship can be stretched very far. Besides, the reluctant monodist has his own autobiographical hesitations: a sense of potential power and immature accomplishment, general unreadiness and personal doubts concerning career, massive preparations and the small, stubborn problem of beginning. Before long one can see the scope of his apprehensions, for the varied lament increases "rage" to a degree unmatched by other elegists opening the recesses of their passions. The issues deepen painfully as he calls into question the purposes of a serious life, and he does not have available the ready-made answer of rejecting in the name of spirit the world and everything in it. The stern answers that his dialogue produces come from external agents, and the answers are clarifying and accepted. Without its having to be said, however, the answers are felt to be not enough, and finally he must make his own answer, from within.

In the meantime, to narrow the focus, the dead friend appears and reappears. We never see him as he was, though we hear of him, but we do get strange glimpses, like images that flash compulsively out of a remembered dream and come in where they are not expected.

> He knew
> Himself to sing, and build the lofty rhyme.
> He must not float upon his watery bier
> Unwept, and welter to the parching wind,
> Without the meed of some melodious tear.
>
> (lines 10–14)

Floating upon a "watery bier/Unwept" satisfies a ceremonious expectation and is one elegant way of saying it, no more intended to be directly visualized than "the meed of some melodious tear" is to be heard. But in between, for a moment, is that brief image that commands a different attention: "and welter to the parching wind." Similarly, the dead friend going under in the very act of drowning is not quite disguised by the venerable routine of questioning the nymphs, or by the ornate and bookish diction of "remorseless," in the etymology of which the violent metaphor crouches:

> Where were ye nymphs when the remorseless deep
> Closed o'er the head of your loved Lycidas?
>
> (50–51)

Finally, the unrecovered body as it now is, dead and other to the imagination searching now:

> Ay me! Whilst thee the shores, and sounding seas
> Wash far away, where'er thy bones are hurled,
> Whether beyond the stormy Hebrides
> Where thou perhaps under the whelming tide
> Visit'st the bottom of the monstrous world.
>
> (154–58)

One could not have anticipated that this would be the decisive searching of the poem. However different everything else may be, this, the moment leading to release, comes as it did in Donne's Devotion 17, when he turned toward the man for whom the bell was tolling and prayed for him. All the other mourning of the poem, like the strong answers from without, left the poet with one thing more to do. But the answer begins to come when he turns toward the imagined body and invokes aid for it in his own voice.

> Look homeward angel now, and melt with ruth.
> And, O ye dolphins, waft the hapless youth.

The answer comes more easily than Spenser's "Dido nis dead, but into heaven hent." It begins to come within a line, in a change of rhythm brought about by a simple repetition:

> Weep no more, woeful shepherds, weep no more.

Here I borrow an observation made long ago by John Crowe Ransom—that the line is resolutely iambic and to be read so without inflicting upon it a dramatic speech rhythm.[11] If we restrain our sophistication and hear "Weep nó more, wóeful shépherds," we hear all the resounding dolor of the poem recapitulated and cannot tell whether the reason to be offered will really counter the woe still expressed. But then the last three words will be caught in a meter that forces them to depart from the music of woe. The words are repeated but the stresses are different ("weép no móre"), and it would, I believe, require a peculiar recalcitrance to keep the tempo from quickening in step. The technical device is radically simple, but so is the personal discovery of prayer in a poem of great artistic elaboration.

What the shepherds see and hear is a vision of Christian consolation, splendid and tender:

> So Lycidas sunk low, but mounted high,
> Through the dear might of him that walked the waves;
> Where other groves, and other streams along,
> With nectar pure his oozy locks he laves,
> And hears the unexpressive nuptial song,
> In the blest kingdoms meek of joy and love,
> There entertain him all the saints above,
> In solemn troops, and sweet societies
> That sing, and singing in their glory move,
> And wipe the tears for ever from his eyes.
>
> (172–81)

It is a vision flowering with promise, without saying so or adding advice or invitation. Lycidas is no longer a dead other; that hateful image has been obliterated by the vision (like the sea-bottom stain from his hair).

"Thus sang the uncouth swain. . . ." The poem begins to end with yet another scenic ceremony in which the poet himself now appears. He is not "speaking" now but is spoken of, in a third-person role and by a new voice that is a part of the scene it warmly describes but is neither located nor identified. The new voice speaks with a quality of calm, relaxed ease free of all the agitated searching and the exaltation as well. That voice disengages itself from the person and voice of the mono-dist—like a singer from the song he has sung, or an actor from the role he has been playing, or an actor dismissing his double, or anyone terminating the services of a vicarious self, *Doppelgänger,* etc. The "un-couth swain" has learned to sing from all the literary shepherds since Theocritus. And so, as if nothing unusual were happening, the new voice attributes the poem to the other voice, which sorted out and ordered the experience in that imagined interval of time and created what was not there before, new other, new self.

"Thus sang the uncouth swain," and ordinary time overtakes the song during the interval in which the music—at once the song of "eager thought" and the metaphoric instrument, at once retrospective and concurrent—comes to a real ending:

> And now the sun had stretched out all the hills,
> And now the sun was dropped into the western bay:
> At last he rose, and twitched his mantle blue:
> Tomorrow to fresh woods, and pastures new.

In the last line of the epilogue there may be a coincidence of person and persona, or the two voices may be singing a replication in different octaves that signify different woods and pastures. What is entirely cer-tain is that the last line names the radical word "Tomorrow." The poem ends opening out into ordinary time, as in elegies that are otherwise various and different, such as Spenser's "November," King's "The Exe-quy," Donne's sonnet on his dead wife, Jonson's two poems on his children, and, though I did not follow it through, Marvell's elegy on Cromwell.

Belief in life dies hard. The thought of "no more" tries to reject itself. The otherness in death becomes more endurable when it can be imagined as a figurative otherness—as living on, still in this world, in human memory, and better still if that life is renewed and altered by recognition and praise of the good or the many. So Lycidas is granted, in addition to bliss, and perhaps as direct compensation in kind for that time in the poem when he was seen perforce as a disturbing image of dead otherness, the "life" of a tutelary "Genius of the shore," one whose "large recompense" includes the privileged service of being "good/To all that wander in that perilous flood." Milton is individual and surprising when he adds the figurative change directed toward a continued spiritual existence in this world *after* he has presented the great vision of faith, Lycidas at home in the life of immortality in the world of heaven. Marvell follows the same pattern in saying farewell to "O. C." But he is more traditional than Milton in his making the vision of immortality the last word in the process of transformation. The heaven he presents, however, is novel, an Elysium of Old Testament heroes. And Marvell is aggressively realistic and rational in the evidence he deploys, both "modern" and "primitive" when he avers the renewed life of praise for Cromwell in this world after partisan envy subsides, and the service of his name to intimidate the enemy and to "inflame" the English soldier "ere he charge" (lines 276–80).

The facts of death are more consolable if they conform to the idea of a "good" death. But when that which we think difficult is presented as easy, we may acquire some retrospective doubts concerning the genuineness of professed pain and difficulty. When Jonson constructs a domestic scene for the death of Lady Jane Pawlett, he willfully strays into the bad taste of domestic idealization. The dying woman is too good in her performance, as busy as a perfect hostess as she comforts and cheers, and like a successful tragic actress as she wins admiring applause. She dies too much in earnest for any audience, except perhaps that of the first night, to read in earnest. In contrast, when Petrarch's Laura responds to the monster Death, "Do thou unto me as thou doest to all men,"[12] the triumph of time has had no effect on that answer. But strict idealization, especially when based upon the physical facts it intends to elevate, works for the desired appearance of ease but seldom conceals the evidence of strain.

The poet will not lack difficulties while seeking to reconcile the otherness of the dead to his own heightened sense of self, under the same sentence, and grieving for the loss while occupying an obligatory and privileged space of time from which the poem may need to make a decorous return to ordinary time. Another set of difficulties, those of addressing the search for reconciliation to an audience of others, can also be answered by diminishing the sense of self and its direct engagement with the otherness of the dead. In his public elegies when Donne strenuously substituted something other than his own feeling self, his professional judgment was good and the poems are not bad. They simply avoid difficulties he could avoid; other poets did not always have his talents to spare, or his prudence. But the feeling self, however handicapped by the general difficulties of the genre and special circum-

stances, was by no means incapable of making a worthy place for itself
in the expression of a public elegy. There are admirable examples, but
they are the exceptions, and I have chosen to dwell on the greater
achievements of the personal poems. Poems that wrestle in earnest with
the angel of grief, or intimate anxieties, or lesser "things divine," or
perhaps the devil in disguise, show how indispensable the deeply engaged self is to the imaginative achievement of the work. Donne's
sonnet "Since she whome I lovd" was not written to an audience; one
cannot imagine the poem, or an adapted version of it, written to memorialize the death of someone else, or imagine the poem written for
someone else to speak in order to express the spirit of an appropriate
occasion. "Lycidas" is a public poem written to be printed in a volume
of elegies for Edward King. If the search and the reconciliation move
others and they feel addressed by the poem, they are part of a large,
continuous audience that the first audience only represented. That first
audience cast no shadow between the poet and his personal engagement.

Without a heightened sense of the self engaged, both the otherness
of the dead and death itself easily become abstract ideas moved about by
the leverage of tested precepts and ready images. Indeed, grief may be
thought philosophically embarrassing and consolation insulting to intelligence and good taste. Or, if the discourse deals in solemn advice, it
may be as fanciful as poetry but does not know that and therefore
cannot hear its own words very well, and may naively interpolate when
it meant only to interpret and pronounce. I am thinking of the letter by
Ficino quoted as a postscript to the discussion of Donne's sonnet on his
dead wife. One of the peculiarities of Ficino's design for consolation is
that it exists cut off from any sense of time—intended as a transcen-
dence, no doubt, but not unlike the forgetful disregard to which an
excited, serious mind may be subject. In his idealization time does not
exist, and death as a fact receives no attention, assigned as it is to the
body, and the discourse is of the soul addressed to the soul.

Such abstractness is not limited to idealization, as we shall see in the
following chapter. I turn now to the last example of the present discussion, Milton's sonnet on a dead wife.

Sonnet XXIII

Methought I saw my late espoused saint
   Brought to me like Alcestis from the grave,
   Whom Jove's great son to her glad husband gave,
   Rescued from death by force, though pale and faint.
Mine, as whom washed from spot of child-bed taint
   Purification in the old Law did save,

And such as yet once more I trust to have
Full sight of her in heaven without restraint,
Came vested all in white, pure as her mind.
    Her face was veiled, yet to my fancied sight
    Love, sweetness, goodness in her person shined
So clear as in no face with more delight.
    But O as to embrace me she inclined,
    I waked, she fled, and day brought back my night.

Greek myth, Old Testament law, and the Christian promise unroll with
an ease that masters the great sweep of time. The ages have no leave to
assert their separateness. And though there may be no resistance to the
appearing of a vision, if it appears, there are, nevertheless, other intimations of strain—Alcestis, Hercules, "force," and the "pale and faint,"
which belongs to Alcestis, an affecting touch. But "pale and faint" may
slip—no less easily than the ages of time into each other—into the
beginning recognition by a blind poet of a "purified" wife he has never
seen. (I believe her to be Katherine Woodcock.) "Full sight" he will
hope to have; the face continues to be "veiled," and in the meantime the
veil answers a specific, unspoken, courteous, domestic arrangement
between wife and husband. Yet her virtues are so clear and shining to his
"fancied sight" that he "sees" her "in her person." No face can give or
has given or would have given more delight than what he "sees." Pathos, delicacy, and the coded indirectness of a masterly diplomatic
syntax express the private reciprocities between the dead other returning as a vision and the narrating self who tells what the mind's eye sees.
Out of respect for himself and for her he will not imagine a face he has
not seen. He can see or feel, but does not tell us how, when she leans to
embrace him, and we learn only then that he has been asleep and is
telling a dream—though it emerges like a vision that moves forward
from a stately background that seems itself to move. The dream is one
in which the imagined presence of the dead brought calm joy, but the
return to ordinary time and light brought a double loss, for they replace
the light of vision and the sweep and intensity of imagined time in
which the seeking and the being sought of love enjoyed a heightened
sense of nearness. "My night" returns the particular pain of the blind
man; the bare words say enough, and they are the last words. And yet,
though dreams impose their special kind of passivity, and though the
dreamer here receives the visit and almost receives the embrace of the
other, the Miltonic self is hardly passive. We do not doubt the dream,
and for most readers there is probably little incentive to make and
search crevices between the dream and its telling. Its telling makes the
dignity of the pain equal the dignity of the joy.

CHAPTER THIRTEEN

Episodes in the Progress of Death

But he that sinneth against me [Wisdom] wrongeth his own soul: all they that hate me love death.
PROVERBS 8:36

For the living know that they shall die: but the dead know not any thing, neither have they any more a reward, for the memory of them is forgotten.
ECCLESIASTES 9:5

In his history of death in Western civilization Philippe Ariès identifies a period of heightened, searching interest in the form and circumstances of the individual death. Most of my materials in Part 2 and Part 3 thus far have illustrated various ways in which literature concentrated on the individual death. I have also pointed out the occasional reappearance of earlier attitudes, some of them with a long history of existence.

One point of departure for what follows is that my examples indicate a kind of movement away from the concentration on personal death. The examples suggest patterns and relationships that resemble certain social and historical developments, but it is more accurate to say that what I present is an alternative way of writing on death, expressing an emphasis not generally available earlier but not itself a demonstration of historical development. Literature has its own history, and in partial compensation I shall try to show, in the case of Henry King's *"Sic Vita,"* one kind of history which that poem illustrates in its particular combination of the old and the new.

To clarify a little further: the examples do not establish their psychological distance by treating death as if it were someone else's concern. They do not correspond to, though they may anticipate, the excesses, deficiencies, and evasions that characterize modern attitudes. One motive may perhaps be that of a reaction against the highly rationalized drama of the individual death; these poems impose a kind of rationality different in emphasis and purpose. (I shall return to these matters in another context in Part 4.) The attitudes toward death which these poems exemplify are those of indifference and abstractness, and they offer some aggressive exhibitions of intellectual domination, between jest and earnest. Death as a personified abstraction is part of an old story always capable of revival; death as a mere abstraction may be related to other abstractions (such as time) and can take on something of the stark otherness of a dead body, an anonymous force in opposition to life and knowable chiefly by what it is not—as "vanity" in its inherited and extended usage is a force opposed to meaning in life.

My second point of departure will serve as a continuously available reference throughout the following discourse. In St. Paul's compelling pronouncement, "The last enemy that shall be destroyed is death" (1 Cor. 15:26), the image of death as the last enemy is part of a compressed narrative, and the otherness of death is contained and subject to relationship because its absoluteness exists in time and will be abrogated by a deliberate act of eternity. There is no refuge for this image of death in thoughts of a primordial abyss of nothingness. St. Paul's image, to state the bare facts of its influence, could authorize the felt realities of human fear and still subordinate fear to hope. The promise of death's ultimate destruction could support faith and the strenuous efforts of reason to explain and systematize all contingencies, not omitting the predictable character of all resistance, faltering, and lapse, or the unique exaltation of reason clarified by effective faith. There could be no treaties with such an enemy whose alien nature could not be subverted or seriously compromised. Instead, the enemy had to be submitted to, but in particular ways and, as well as possible, in accordance with the reasoning that governed these ways, as the natural resistance and conflict were turned inward, transforming fear into hope. But I mention these familiar matters chiefly to indicate differences. For in the examples that follow, most of the traditional force in the image of death as the last enemy is, with interesting effects and side effects, reduced or diverted.

When Donne wrote his famous sonnet beginning:

> Death be not proud, though some have called thee
> Mighty and dreadfull, for, thou art not soe,

he rehearsed some familiar images of death, shrewdly observed a few apparent limitations of death's power, and ended with a restatement of the promise which alone could validate his argument:

> One short sleepe past, wee wake eternally,
> And death shall be no more, Death thou shalt die.

The bravura of his rhetoric is impressive, and the more so because it is paired with a kind of cunning intimacy that reduces the size and remoteness of the foe. The sleep is called "short" because it will *seem* so by contrast when "wee wake eternally." Death will simply not be there or anywhere, and the fact is not observed but announced in advance.

In effect, the otherness of death is whittled down small, by means of an oratorical position taken and the argument of a poetic brief based on sacred promise and rhetorical skills. On the one hand, death is externalized, examined in selective ways but held fixed and kept mute. Materials that elsewhere could create a spreading network of rooted connections felt within are made brusquely categorical. As part of the externalization, the evidence of illustrative proof is lined up to show death as an inferior agent of sleep and as the factor of pleasure. In addition, the status of death can be known by the wretched company it keeps—"poyson, warre, and sicknesse." Whatever apparent power it may have is further limited by noting that it must wait upon the whims of "Fate, chance, kings, and desperate men." On the other hand, death externalized is treated with familiar intimacy, of attitude and phrase. The manner is entirely condescending, like the *ad hominem* reasoning; the purpose is to separate death from any claim to direct and actual power, and to leave it as an abstract idea that is on the way out.

Within the sonnet death is cleverly attenuated and its otherness distributed. Death as an agent becomes a grotesquely hybrid idea, and is deprived both of its mystery and of its power to attract the mind. At the beginning of *The Second Anniversary*[1] death is also an agent, now a groom that "must usher, and unlock the door." The act of dying does, however, hold the attention, even when the phenomena are but described and rationally explained:

> Or as sometimes in a beheaded man,
> Though at those two Red seas, which freely ran,
> One from the Trunke, another from the Head,
> His soule he saild, to her eternall bed,
> His eies will twinckle, and his tongue will roll,
> As though he beckned, and cal'd backe his Soul,
> He graspes his hands, and he puls up his feet,
> And seemes to reach, and to step forth to meet
> His soule; when all these motions which we saw,
> Are but as Ice, which crackles at a thaw:
> Or as a Lute, which in moist weather, rings
> Her knell alone, by cracking at her strings.
>
> (9–20)

Then Donne adopts a meditative mode to imagine a full scene of his own dying:

> Thinke then, my soule, that death is but a Groome,
> Which brings a Taper to the outward roome,
> Whence thou spiest first a little glimmering light,
> And after brings it nearer to thy sight:
> For such approches doth Heaven make in death.
>
> (85–89)

The soul is instructed to think of the body as "laboring now with broken breath," and the interpretation easily transfers the phenomena to their assigned significance, that of representing "thy happiest Harmonee." The body laid conveniently on the deathbed "loose and slacke" has its provident function; it facilitates the "unpacking" of the soul, and the parching fever is "Physicke," recognized as such and promptly chided for its slow pace. "Thinke that thou hearst thy knell," and that it is the call of "the Triumphant Church" in heaven.

> Thinke Satans Sergeants round about thee bee,
> And thinke that but for Legacies they thrust.

The advice includes the interpretation. Give them back the sins they gave, "And trust th'immaculate blood, to wash thy score."

> Thinke thy frinds weeping round, and thinke that thay
> Weepe but because they goe not yet thy way.
> Thinke that they close thine eyes, and thinke in this,
> That they confesse much in the world, amisse,
> Who dare not trust a dead mans eye with that,
> Which they from God, and Angels cover not.
> Thinke that they shroud thee up, and thinke from thence
> They reinvest thee in white innocence.
> Thinke that thy body rots, and (if so lowe,
> Thy soule exalted so, thy thoughts can goe,)
> Thinke thee a Prince, who of themselves create
> Wormes which insensibly devoure their state.
> Thinke that they bury thee, and thinke that rite
> Laies thee to sleepe but a saint Lucies night.
> Thinke these things cheerefully.
>
> (107–21)

The injunction to "Thinke these things cheerefully" is either not quite obeyed or is a dramatic, or perhaps ironic, proposition; in any case, the governing purpose remains elusive or becomes blurred. The heaven to which these "approches" are attributed seems to answer a paradoxical and personal vision, reflecting such opportune images as that of the "happiest Harmonee" and authorizing a strong appetite for vivid detail—hardly in accord with a prefatory declaration that this world is "fragmentary rubbidge" and "not worth a thought." The life being left is almost without character, a meaningless waste of time— witness the weeping friends, "a dead mans eye," and the rotting body that looks back toward the "state" of kingdoms. Once the eyes are closed in death, the soul extends its license and initiates personal interpretations, and some of these have the effect of punishing the body's natural hatred of death by transferring all enmity to life, as if life itself were the last enemy. Though the timing is eccentric and highly individual, the imaginative behavior does have the warrant of being a classic maneuver in the traditions of practical wisdom on how to die well. The purpose, which overrides other considerations, at least pre-mortem ones, can be understood as promoting the concentration necessary to get through a difficult moment that must exclude whatever thoughts may distract. Such concentration would also imply that the claims of life, now ignored, have had their extended opportunities and are now at once impotent to help and dangerous to remember. We shall not need to hear the old news that these claims are powerful.

In Donne, however, wit is allowed some remissions. The post-mortem joke on the dead man's eye and the true state of the world is clearly an extravagant witticism—whether it is responded to as part of the set scene or felt as the extrinsic fingering of the narrator stretching his privilege, lecturing to his dead body as if it were still alive and dangerous, and lecturing over the heads of the weeping witnesses to attentive readers. His other witticism is more subtle, even when prefaced by a little apology—that of the politic worms which the prince, by the very nature of government, creates more easily than he can control. Both jokes contribute to the scene of departure by mocking the absurd deceptions in worthless life. But as in many enthusiastic detestations of the world, vividness and wit may blur the main point; as in the description of the beheaded man, the wit shows a vital interest in that old haunt, the worthless world.

In any case, death personified as a groom presents a serviceable other, one with impeccable credentials. We are told that he ushers, that he unlocks the door; like the perfect servant, he does not obtrude in his own person. He is known by the first "glimmering light" of the taper that appears in "the outward roome." But then, tacitly as it were, the light is increased and held up to selected details of the death scene, so that their true meanings may be read out. A free element in the description is the poet's evident pleasure in his performance, but we are not likely to find that his zest improves the credibility of the scene itself. On the one hand, there would seem to be no place for making separations between poet and poem, or poem and reader, in that first apprehension of death moving with its "glimmering light" in "the outward roome." The familiar simplicity of the image—transferred as it is to a context in which bare report may command instant belief and sweep away improbabilities—gains still further power from the capacity of the image to expand until it fills the mind of the reader. Can it, does it, will it come so? There is no leisure to determine our own positioning among the intentness of the viewer and his intuitive recognition, the light that implies a bearer, and the shadows that all may apprehend without any learned assistance of the author.

On the other hand, the death scene is an oratorical narration regulated by doctrine and illustrated by images intended to be striking. Both the desired effect and similar imagistic materials were familiar and available in the traditional repertories of the literature on death. To twentieth-century perceptions the fierceness of the scene exposes unresolved antagonisms, but they are ones that religious doctrine would have little trouble explaining, given time and space. These are not, however, given. By the end of the scene the fierceness has been distributed, transferred, expressed; it has not, however, been diminished or transformed into some new integrity. Whether seventeenth-century doctrine would nevertheless be satisfied is a question hard to prepare oneself to answer clearly. One can hesitate less in being disappointed by the artistic performance as a whole. But if "Death be not proud" is better poetry, we may still want to puzzle over the conviction that the sonnet skillfully risks less and reveals less.

The precognition of death in an image of light—that sudden beginning—remains, I believe, the great moment of the whole passage. "Thinke then, my soule, that. . . ." Imagine it thus: an outward image to bear the inward message. The directions come from the mind and to the mind, as an instant act that omits all sense of process, or the history of personal thought on the subject, or the memory of bodily sensations, as the skip or stumble of organic rhythms that may follow or precede, the timing perhaps indistinct, something like an apparition, and which may have contributed to the mental formation of the image now assigned a recognizable shape and purpose. Death as "but a Groome" is indeed a serviceable other; the mystery is like something familiar, and the figure is also reduced as in "Death be not proud," but without the direct address and the ingenious elaborations of contempt. Once he has been noticed, death as a groom disappears from attention. His duties of ushering and unlocking (which might have drawn deep and minute imagining) are displaced by the soul acting as master of ceremonies and official exegete. The light of attention is transferred to the body on its deathbed; there the body serves, like the world, as an object from which a busy, meditative soul collects instructive meanings.

In this episode the soul of a witness outside the scene may detect signals which produce messages that are not altogether consonant in register. (For obvious reasons I do not include this passage among the examples in Part 2 where Donne writes with his own death in mind.) This is no account of a good death in which a formal valediction to the world might be made, not without regard for the last duties to family and friends. Other witnesses in Donne are permitted a more generous range of human feeling and religious dignity. But here the soul is merciless in its instruction to the end and beyond—a witty, conscious indecorum that takes advantage of its opportunity, though at some expense to the imaginative integrity of the scene.

If we adopt a seventeenth-century view, however, what seems to be the indulged pleasure of the soul, inspired to comment "cheerefully," may be defended (with some sense of strain appropriate to the passage) as a dramatic response to the soul's own imminent emancipation. For this episode will soon be followed by an injunction, "Thinke further of thy selfe, my Soule" (157). The thoughts then take the form of a reasoned catalogue of the soul's indignities from the first onslaught of life in the body. In the deathbed scene, therefore, it is possible to find in the soul's behavior a comic reprisal in advance. A similar device may be taken into account, that earlier illustrative image of the "beheaded man." The point of connection would be Donne's comment, "For there is motion in corruption" (22). The "beheaded man" is like "this dead world," which has struggled through another year, and the poet says of himself, "Thou seest me strive for life" (31) by the act of writing his poem of praise. But this would make the soul's striving a strange mimesis of the body in its throes. For the soul pauses to mock body and world after the eyelids have been closed, and outdoes the beheaded body's performance by lingering, much longer, to pass a comment on one lesson of decay (the politic worms).

I do not think that these interpretations would rescue much worth saving; they make the conflict between body and soul even more dubious. In poetry one learns to expect the death of another to be felt by another, and the range of intricate feelings will often include some of the perplexities of fellow feeling. But in the imagined death of the self— at least here—fellow feeling takes the strenuous course of exulting in the otherness of the body exhibited for the soul's delivery. Even those punctuating references to the "Triumphant Church" and the "immaculate blood" and the shroud that will "reinvest thee in white innocence" are made to seem nominal, something much less than the main purpose of the discourse. To be sure, the traditional privileges of advice on how to die—authorized by the vast perils and the particular difficulties of individual circumstances—are not easily confined to normal standards and the discriminations of decorum. Nor is any excess discovered as late as the seventeenth century likely to prove unprecedented. And yet, after acknowledging that this is but one exuberant episode in a very long poem, one may still ask whether death looked at so, both under-developed and overdeveloped, does not resemble the subject of an imaginative game, not quite real and not quite felt. As in the sonnet, death becomes a kind of grotesquely hybrid idea, but its otherness is not reduced and put in place to the same degree, for it shares too much ambiguous attention both with the body and the world.

Hating oneself as another admits rigors and latitudes not always hard to come by but hard to sustain well. The body and the world are no doubt useful enemies to practice on, but they are at best substitutes that provide practitioners of mortality with favorable occasions for active training while waiting patiently until a force, to which they can pre-sume to contribute nothing, gets ready to decide when "The last en-emy . . . shall be destroyed."

I turn now to a poem that contemplates a different figure for the otherness of death. In Edward Herbert's "To his Watch, when he could not sleep," we may recognize a formal conclusion that closely resembles that of Donne's "Death be not proud," but the method is radically different, and the otherness of death-as-time takes on the character of cold indifference.

> Uncessant Minutes, whil'st you move you tell
>   The time that tells our life, which though it run
>   Never so fast or farr, you'r new begun
> Short steps shall overtake; for though life well
>
> May scape his own Account, it shall not yours,
>   You are Death's Auditors, that both divide
> And summ what ere that life inspir'd endures
>   Past a beginning, and through you we bide
>
> The doom of Fate, whose unrecall'd Decree
>   You date, bring, execute; making what's new
>   Ill and good, old, for as we die in you,
> You die in Time, Time in Eternity.[2]

The poem sets and analyzes its problems as if its art of expression preferred to serve the present rule of insomnia rather than the tradi-tional laws of eloquence. The detachment of the analysis makes no claims on the assent of human feelings, which are treated like unimportant spectators of the demonstration. As the argument evolves, it turns on the nature of necessity. Since life may avoid its "own Account" (the self-knowledge of philosophical and religious tradition), then real necessity must exist in what cannot be avoided, and man has had no influence in the making of, or the subscribing to, those laws. The nature of time is that of a neutral force within an appointed function. Only the minutes receive direct address: "You are Death's Auditors" and "divide/And summ"; "You date, bring, execute"; "you tell/The time that tells our life." "You" are the dying agents of third-person time, which dies in eternity—whether as agent or not is unexpressed. And fate is a briefly personified force of individual "doom," a small but necessary motion in a vast operation.

The poem stands against the traditions of eloquence and against the many heartfelt responses to time and mutability as the messengers of general and personal death. Death has no questionable shape in this poem and cannot be thought proud or an enemy. It is neither diminished nor enlarged in its recorded practice upon life and time. Though one may infer death to be a servant of eternity, details are lacking. But in regard to human life, death operates at one remove through the otherness of time, and here the appropriate human dimension is the moving minute. In comparison, my examples from Donne seem still to belong to an older age when one might reasonably strive to handle one's own feelings and to move those of another.

In his "Nox nocti indicat scientiam," William Habington also meditates on time. Unlike Herbert, he deploys time (and space) only in large dimensions. But Habington, in spite of an ancient message and a didactic purpose, resembles Herbert in the effects produced by transferring poetic attention from death to time. From the firmament his soul discerns "as in some holy book" the "heavenly knowledge" available to man's spiritual education. The contemplative stance is not inspired by the new astronomy; looking down on the world from above affords the traditional perspective for discovering the primary law of impermanence, "The fallacy of our desires," and the ruinous "pride of life." All have the true ring of an old-fashioned meditation on sin and death. But the vision of time as an impersonal force doing its blind, repeated work presents the world with an image of itself that is deliberately modernized, like the cold elegance of the diction and rhythm. I quote, beginning with the fifth stanza:

> But if we stedfast looke,
> We shall discerne

In it as in some holy booke,
How man may heavenly knowledge learne.

It tells the Conqueror
   That farre-stretcht powre
Which his proud dangers traffique for,
Is but the triumph of an houre.

That from the farthest North
   Some Nation may,
Yet undiscovered issue forth,
and ore his new got conquest sway.

Some Nation yet shut in
   With hils of ice
May be let out to scourge his sinne
'Till they shall equall him in vice.

And then they likewise shall
   Their ruine have,
For as your selves your Empires fall,
And every Kingdome hath a grave.

Thus those Coelestiall fires,
   Though seeming mute
The fallacie of our desires
And all the pride of life confute.

For they have watcht since first
   The World had birth:
And found sinne in itself accurst,
And nothing permanent on earth.[3]

The austerity of the poem is a remarkable fusion of old and new, charged with a didactic purpose that nevertheless touches no possibility of individual human action. Nations are man writ large, but there is no human self guiding or sharing what is told as a detached soul reads out an abstract of the history of the world from above. And the world has not simply fallen into bad times, one kind of "modern" mood of depression frequent enough in seventeenth-century poetry. What is unusual is to find a pessimistic judgment proclaimed with a deliberate and effective impersonality, one assuming that the beholder's eye is indeed an unfeeling instrument for recording only what is there to be seen. Habington's world is presented as bound by the inexorable movements of time as the agent of sin and death. Once it has been set in motion, however, the curse operates as if autonomously, and time the agent acts like universal fate and necessity. As for the otherness of time, it is felt more as a principle than as an enemy and is known only by its effects as these are related in a remote, leisurely statement. If the poem is a *memento mori* it transcends all usual purposes; one would not know to whom it is addressed.

The old-fashioned and the fashionably modern can produce other effects. A poet putting himself at the center of the experience he relates may play his part like an actor whose virtuosity we admire while we observe that his excess of skill contributes to the deliberate unreality of certain aspects of his theme. In his poem "To his Mistress for her true Picture" (pp. 48–53), Edward Herbert treats death as a personified character, the invisible mistress of his life. Death as a body of principles (here not only of time and necessity) creates in the true suitor qualities of detachment that may deserve to court the otherness of death. He sets out to praise a mistress according to the rules governing that subject and a subtheme, that of begging a picture, the true one. She is

> Death, my lifes Mistress, and the soveraign Queen
> Of all that ever breath'd, though yet unseen.

He has viewed only false pictures ("you seem lean"), which do not correspond to the love in his heart or the picture nature drew—figured "by sleep . . . nurse of our life . . . the vision giver," which permits souls to "go play" and recover original innocence. He invokes her to appear as she is, and he strikes a few high notes with witty echoes:

> And if old Vertue's way narrow were,
> 'Tis rugged now, having no passenger. . . .
> Shew me that Goodness which compounds the strife
> 'Twixt a long sickness and weary life.
> Set forth that Justice which keeps all in aw,
> Certain and equal more then any Law.
> Figure that happy and eternal Rest.

> (lines 47–61)

The encomium is carried through with fine verve and comic exploitation. Herbert not only inverts standard attitudes, he cleverly reasons through the potential similarities between what he professes and the orthodox reasonings on love and death. Death imagined as a woman opens unusual opportunities for the courtship of a beloved other, and the self is presented as militantly faithful. Though a mock encomium has its own eccentric freedom, the incongruous humor of this poem may suggest that it draws upon the old sources that treat the universality of death as a liberating theme which moribund readers or listeners are invited to appreciate under the governing law that we all must die. As for the poet himself, he is at the center of the poem as its chief actor, but the self put on display is quite untouched by anything said, and that would seem to be part of the message and the sport. The otherness of death is not engaged, not brought into some bearable relationship with a reasoned process of human feeling and hope. Personified as the invisible beloved, the figure of death becomes the occasion for parading human ideas mischievously out of step, and the appointed function of death remains as vague as the universe she inhabits.

My concluding episode is the "*Sic Vita*" of Henry King, which makes an inventory of familiar images in a borrowed form. The familiar and borrowed may well mislead, and since we conclude here on a remarkable note, I shall undertake approaching the poem by first collecting some background materials. The immediate model was a stanza apparently invented by Francis Quarles:

> Like to the damask rose you see,
> Or like the blossom on the tree,
> Or like the dainty flower of May,
> Or like the morning to the day,
> Or like the sun, or like the shade,
> Or like the gourd which Jonas had:
> Even such is man, whose thread is spun,
> Drawn out and out, and so is done.
>> The rose withers, the blossom blasteth,
>> The flower fades, the morning hasteth,
>> The sun sets, the shadow flies,
>> The gourd consumes, and man he dies.[4]

The durability of the theme is not in question and could not become unfashionable because of dull verse, predictable progression, and stale examples. But Quarles makes too easy a victim looked at so; what surely gave the stanza its particular appeal was the promise of infinite variation, grounded on the placement of "Even such is man" and strengthened by the coda of tighter repetitions ticked off in the same order, concluding with man, who sums up the moral, which interprets itself.

Quarles may have invented the stanza, but he was tapping proved strengths. The conventionality of the images and the basic way they were lined up could be and were used for other purposes. For instance, Giles Fletcher the Elder, in the twenty-sixth sonnet of *Licia* (1593), makes an inventory of a rare, pleasant place, and in the sestet rejects the first three items in order and the rest in a lump: Licia alone makes the only joyous place. Without the turning back on itself, Barnabe Barnes writes (*Divine Century of Spiritual Sonnets,* 1595) an inventory of ephemeral objects that becomes an emblematic definition when man, the last item, finally appears: "Soon born to die, soon flourishing to fade." In the first sonnet of his "A Palinode" (*Englands Helicon,* 1600) Edmund Bolton seems determined to discourage all rivals. The first four lines lay out the system: As withereth/fadeth/vanisheth/melteth, which is followed by a reordering of the verbs while the subjects do not alter:

> So melts, so vanisheth, so fades, so withers
> The Rose, the shine, the bubble and the snow.

These are then translated without ornamentation, which is added only when the items begin to appear again:

> Of praise, pompe, glorie, joy (which short life gathers,)
> Faire praise, vaine pompe, sweet glory, brittle joy,
> The withered Primrose by the mourning river. . . .

The concluding couplet reveals the secret that all items mentioned three times, and interpreted at least twice, really

> Are Emblems that the treasures we up-lay,
> Soon wither, vanish, fade, and melt away.

Alter perspective and the method might serve as well to compose an emblem of Narcissus courting himself. But though an emblematic foreconceit had a recognizable current value, such poems also resemble a familiar kind of riddle organized so that it gradually explains its intended meaning. This is the method of a splendidly intricate sonnet in *The Phoenix Nest* (1593), which may be Raleigh's. "What else is hell, but losse of blisfull heaven?" continues its questioning by the introduction of more paired antitheses: darkness, death, winter (played off against light, life, spring). Then the questions are expanded and the method varied in order to introduce two further terms, *unrest* and *mishap*. In the third quatrain, put in the subjunctive mood, the poet weaves a new, contracted pattern and order out of all his antithetical terms. He ends with a simple answer, how he feels now, by restating his enriched main terms in a final order:

> But loe, I feele, by absence from your sight,
> Mishap, unrest, death, winter, hell, darke night.

Technical grace employed in the service of exploring a labyrinth of pain imposed from without also represents an individual response to the rule of fate (and to the other person who governs like fate). And yet the final turn manages to convey the delicately faint hope of a personal appeal to that mistress of destiny in whose will lies the power of solution and reversibility. "Death" is placed in the metrical center of the last line, and however one interprets the order one must begin by recognizing that "death" cannot be climactic. Nor is "winter" or "hell." The controlling term is the apparently lesser one, "night," reinforced by the only permitted epithet, "darke," which is not redundant and, more to the point, echoes the character of possession in the pronoun of "your sight"—*your* power to restore the light, life, spring, heaven of seeing and being seen.

It is an impressive tour de force of the kind that began to go out with Elizabeth, but the expanding-contracting method of presenting a human problem, one that art can convey as feeling less completely solved than the poetic problems are—that message, and for good reason, has an old and renewable appeal in poetry. But beyond any purpose of negotiating across a gap by means of which the author may figure himself, whatever has been well compressed can be well expanded. The wisdom of sacred writ, wise sayings, proverbs, and images that struck the eye of the mind—these furnished plots for stories, examples, allegories, and arguments. The anonymous wit and wisdom of folk proverbs were remembered and collected. The pithy elegance of classical "sentences" and turns of phrase were treasured and recoined in modern languages. Epigram and paradox, myth, emblem, and hieroglyphic, the deeper tropes of rhetoric, conceit and foreconceit—all served to arouse lethargic thoughts to follow and follow up condensed or hidden meanings.

Fashions and techniques changed, but poets and their readers had been valuing the basic process for a long time, and prized that virtue of intensely focusing upon a part of life which in its vivid clarity could represent a larger part or even the whole. The general method would seem to have some relationship with the favorite trope of holding up a mirror, in which a large subject might be expounded, or a very limited one concentrated, like showing life small as at a view of the end. In the thirteenth-century lyric "Whanne mine eyhnen misten,"[5] twelve symptoms of death are listed, but everything is too late when the bier is ready outside. Then the speaker continues with the future, imminent progress from bed to floor to shroud to grave to the covering of that. It is then more than too late when the house lies upon the nose and the world is not worth a pea to a dead man. The stark arrangement puts the reader/listener in a good position to figure out what the full moral of the scene probably is, but the poet's efforts chiefly go into making the scene powerful enough to evoke a response that will complete and bring home the known meaning.

Many set pieces in the drama, as for example "All the world's a stage," could not satisfy their scenic tasks if they did not hold the audience in alert attention, wondering how the imagistic parallels will be worked out, all the time feeling as an unstated question: What will come next, and how will it fit in? Raleigh's poem "What is our life? a play of passion" signals everything in advance, except its art of choosing particular details and its incremental force. Its power to grip the reader partly depends upon an open, understood secret, as simple and true as the agreement in a child's game that the game will always end with the same surprising climax. For the reader knows that life compared to "a play of passion" will surely move toward the end of the play, and that the poet will try to say something to honor his voluntary obligation and to reward the reader's attention.

Henry King wrote a number of penitential meditations, one of which, "The Dirge," begins each stanza with an image set up to represent man's life. Then the stanza explores and disposes of the image. The underlying linear progress, the minimal expression of moral reasoning, and the open exploitation of well-known materials all resemble tried-and-true practices of the medieval epigram. The surface development, however, is modernized by collecting subsidiary images that make some flourish of minor variation but quickly yield their main effect to a cumulative repetition leading to the same end. In addition to the set problem of beginning each stanza with a dominant image, there is the general purpose of inventorying the sadnesses of life from the perspective of the inevitable ending, and doing so with a quality of mental detachment that is recognizably modern—on speaking terms, let us say, with Raleigh's "What is our life? a play of passion" and with Edward Herbert's "To his Watch." Life is a war, and death signs the peace; a storm leading to the anchor in the grave; a flower that returns where it came from; a dream in which the dreamer vanishes; a sundial that marks the progression of shadows while the dial has light:

> It is a weary enterlude
> Which doth short joyes, long woes include.
> The World the Stage, the Prologue tears,
> The Acts vain hope, and vary'd fears:
> The Scene shuts up with loss of breath,
> And leaves no Epilogue but Death.

As this last stanza illustrates, the images constitute a selected inventory of life from a weary perspective for which there is no dearth of precedents. Religious thought and feeling are simply excluded. The poem is not a testament, and not his only poem, but one that allows itself understood and accepted privileges of working out a particular view in a particular way. Familiar images are turned over with only an occasional touch of freshness: as the spring and fall of life which "faint seasons keep," and the "dream" is fancifully "moraliz'd in age and youth." But the steady effort is not to say, from the perspective of sunset, that there is anything new under the sun. Familiar images and their familiar meanings confirm the feelings. The six stanzas do not progress, do not reach for moments of intensity. Time inside the poem is—the illusion maintains—an accurate version of the time outside the poem. The stanzas keep saying the same thing, as a dirge is expected to do, but say it well, without flagging, or passivity, or mannered leisureliness.

"*Sic Vita*" is not a dirge but an expanding-contracting comparison that moves like a riddle toward its inevitable ending, the particular place of man in a world under the rule of time and inevitability. The set problem is Quarles's stanza and theme, but the handling of these more nearly resembles King's practices in "The Dirge":

> Like to the falling of a Starre;
> Or as the flights of Eagles are;
> Or like the fresh springs gawdy hew;
> Or silver drops of morning dew;
> Or like a wind that chafes the flood;
> Or bubbles which on water stood;
> Even such is man, whose borrow'd light
> Is streight call'd in, and paid to night.
>
> *The Wind blowes out; the Bubble dies;*
> *The Spring entomb'd in Autumn lies;*
> *The Dew dries up; the Starre is shot;*
> *The Flight is past; and Man forgot.*

To begin with, King's exploitation of Quarles's stanza combines a strong epigrammatic concentration with strong but unobtrusive variations. ("What else is hell, but losse of blisfull heaven?" might have served as the inspiration for improving on Quarles.) In the first six lines each couplet presents two related examples, the second of which is lesser in a general order characterized by decreasing magnitude and duration. Power and movement are followed by beauty seen as motionless in its brief moment. The wind both moves and passes; the bubbles disappear in the movement of the line, making their point by no longer being there: "stood." The fourth couplet relates all the comparisons to man and articulates a latent attribute shared by all the *visibilia*, "borrow'd light." Then in the coda everything is abbreviated (except spring); the list suggests that all the actions occur within a single moment of time; there are no epithets or similes, and verbs help make the metaphors. Yet in the tightened form a significant reordering of all the paired items matches man and eagles, the only warm-blooded, soaring representatives of life. When things are spelled out so, they constitute an answer to, what is life like? But in the final repetition the last item, man, feels different and is different.

The answer may seem to be a kind of epitaph, a summation of the old message that all must die. And yet, though everything in the poem is oriented toward death, the analogies that compose the common destiny suggest no sense of a shared destiny. Man is not all men but summary man, as solitary as the falling star that begins the sequence. No lender of the "borrow'd light" may be inferred from the poem, though the phrase troubles; no rationalizable debt of Adam or nature. Instead, a traditional metaphor is applied without the traditional meanings, but with some barriers and gaps. The images of life in the poem are charged with their moment of intensity and reflect something of their nature as they reach toward the cessation of life. The images of death, all but one, are more perfunctory, and what they reflect is limited to something implicit in their kind of movement toward cessation.

Only "Man forgot" makes a new and unexpected turn. The natural things that march more briskly in their final review establish a tempo that leads to the sudden punctuating emphasis of "Man forgot." Man dies like everything else, but being forgotten is not quite like the other examples of evanescence. For though "borrow'd light" may come from an unknown, or unacknowledged, creditor, it is well known whom man is forgotten by—perhaps by God but certainly by fellow human beings. Man cannot be forgotten unless man forgets, and thus involves himself distinctly in the general failure. Man borrowed the light but not the forgetting—unless, by a dubious wrench of sentiment, the human forgetting is borrowed from the seasonal analogy, by which the forgetting of spring may be attributed to autumn, which does not know of its own impending "entombment" by winter.

In any case, the "Man forgot" does evoke a special concentration on man as individualized victim. When his light is peremptorily "call'd in, and paid to night," the human consciousness of time separates man from the other observed victims of time, and he becomes a brief center of pathos to which other human beings may respond and—at the very least—recognize the essential human link, their own ignorance of their individual schedules for dying. *Sic vita.* Man is the climax of all the images of ceasing life; they offer illustrative analogies leading to his "Even such." But the connection is severely limited, and unlike the other examples man is granted no moment of characterizing intensity of his own—except that of the stringent reference to the mental life which separates him from the life and death of nature. His intensity is bare of any evocative sign of grandeur or beauty. It is an intensity of consciousness alone. The poem does not permit death to be felt as an enemy; it is imageless, a kind of nothing, though time and light make known its presence, and the pain of life is knowable to human beings, for they have learned to read the signs around them. Almost everything is summed up by that infallibly ordered drive toward conscious and unconscious extinction.

That observations directed toward the end of life are attracted by the lamentable has not escaped notice. What is new in this expression of dismay is the utter solitude of man surrounded by the busy emblems of dying but with no attachments to other lives or deaths, no enemies or friends, no struggle to resist or accept, no fear, hope, hate, or love. Only the muted anguish toward time and separateness—these and the horror of forgetting make the death human.

Still, one may propose ways by which the poem does maintain contact with traditional contemplations of death. A new reading of the Book of Nature, so many of the lessons of which were known by heart, might simply be read the old way according to the memory of lessons already in place. As for the learned, who have their own ways and may be no more movable than the unlearned: following good principles of moral reasoning, they might have thought, "Though life may be hostile to man's wishes and finally appalling, man forgetting is, however wretched, still a rational and responsible culprit, agent as well as victim, a collaborator of the last enemy, betraying and validating a truth which no one could violate if it did not exist and were not confirmed by the human history of acknowledgment and betrayal." If I may demur, not at the traditional argument but at a difficulty such an interpretation encounters: it seems to require an overgenerous concession to the "borrow'd light" of inherited rationalism and its optimistic adventures in self-containment. For the poem acts as if it were marshaling its familiar images toward a traditional resolution or warning and then seems to forget, as it were, and leaves the organized hopelessness pressing very hard against an open conclusion.

But there is yet another way of looking at the poem that would make a good old sense and most of its new sense. The message King contemplates may have a personal purpose. If we may judge from his own record, man forgetting man would have provided an *exemplum* that made death meaningless except for its shamefulness. He did not himself forget but honored the memory of wife, father, friends, fellow poets, his martyred king, and heroic contemporaries. The life here contemplated may be recognized as an unusual *memento mori* that, however modernized, shocks and warns in the old-fashioned way. Like an epigram or dirge, a *memento mori* does not need to contemplate at large; it may concentrate the negative lessons by which death teaches how to live. Here the lessons review the old message that all must die, but there is a new message that juxtaposes for the summoned man an extreme of isolation, without a friend or an enemy to fix on, and the threat of the indifferent, forgotten death which makes all dying the deaths of anonymous others. The poet sings a traditional elegiac celebration of brevity in the objects of nature, but toward himself and his kind the voice pronounces the summons and the being forgot; the sense of human isolation overrides the bland "Even such is man," and that sense is conveyed without direct statement. The being forgot is bleak and final if human life is ruled by blank, immutable law, and if consciousness can see only extinction everywhere it looks and can glimpse no meaning inside or outside life. But if being forgot is a human fault, or even a half-understood cry of alarm, the fault or the fear might mark a glimmer in the direction of hope.

PART FOUR

Expression

My "unhappiness," so I have always been accustomed to think, was
the result of my father's remoteness and my mother's denial of affection. When my eldest brother died suddenly, and my mother did not
transfer any of her feelings for him to me, and my father did not
become less aloof, I resolved (that resolution made at some time and
for one reason or another by all children) that someday I would
"show" them. But now that someday has come and gone, and no one
remains to whom it would mean anything to be "shown" whatever is
left to show, I myself being the last witness.

Restored to the present . . . I went from Triebschen to the Schwann
Hotel for tea. (In 1890 it was tea and ratafia in, I think, the *En-
glischeviertel*.) Sitting there—where Wagner, not yet amnestied, followed with watch in hand the first performance of *Lohengrin* in
Weimar—it seemed impossible that my own childhood could be so
far away, and impossible that that world of feeling could be extinct,
except in me. Yet not how far away but how close and how real; and

how soon that question in answer to which, like Lohengrin, I must
disappear myself.

STRAVINSKY, 1969

With Homer as their necromancer, the Greeks elaborated a tradition
for heroes in which death was as natural and inevitable as in any quick
conflict between animals, and in which heroism was best expressed,
in a form of art and wit, as an oxymoron. The hero allies a kind of
gallantry of mind to bloodiness of body and purpose. . . . He does
the impossible—combines immortality and mortality, in a fragile
shell steered by some kind of awareness. The hero's life was a hard
one, the only genuine intelligent profession of death, in which attendant glimpses of life were given increased intensity. But mortality
always prevails because it is stronger than immortality, as well as
more common and more natural.

VERMEULE, Aspects of Death in Early Greek Art and Poetry

Many years ago I had a dream, and in the dream I stood by my own
dead body and saw the pennies upon my eyes. I cannot remember at
this distance of time what the rest of the dream was, but it had to do
with the adventures of the soul after death. This dream, while it
convinced me of nothing and gave me no faith in a future life, made a
considerable impression upon me as an artist, and I expanded the idea
and the mood into a novel, which I called *The Glimpse,* the glimpse
being of what lies beyond death. . . . As regards the theory set forth
in my novel, I had naturally made it as plausible as I could to my own
reason. But I never had the slightest belief in it, nor instinctive tendency to believe in it, nor wish to believe in it.

BENNETT, Sketches for Autobiography

CHAPTER FOURTEEN

Preliminary Views

There is a way which seemeth right unto a man, But the end thereof
are the ways of death.

PROVERBS 14:12

In *Western civilization,* since the first golden brevity of the Garden of
Eden, the character of human actions may be presumed to owe something to the imminent presence of personal death and to the quiet fact
that death as universal law exists prior to the existence of intelligence
and will. As an instrument of thought, priority is a hard-working
principle; if excluded, the thinker may have difficulty in controlling the
way its shadow falls. As for the character of human actions, when the
arts of thought turn upon themselves as strictly as they turn upon other
arts, the "something" they may detect is a trace of reaction affecting and
constricting the nature of action as expressed in thought. A mere story-
teller can say as much, demystifying and remystifying, as Kafka's
"Hunger Artist" does when his last words reveal the secret of his pro-
digious accomplishments in the art of fasting: "because I couldn't find
the food I liked."[1]

As preface to what will follow I offer some review, with additions,
of matters previously considered. One learns from responses to the
thought of impending death that variations have been numerous but
major choices few. I mean choices around which thought can organize
and defend its explanations, understanding, and acceptance of the fact of
death. The Socratic model, with its calm and optimistic equilibrium,
displays its easy trust in the life of virtue and the immunity of that life to
external ills. The historical image is that of one freely choosing to accept
the judgment of death, and with modest indifference remaining fully
himself to the last moment—the philosopher who enjoys a gracefully
effortless control of his life and death. Epicurean indifference develops a
more specialized and argumentative version. The Stoic choice builds
upon the wisdom of obeying the laws of nature, and the acceptance of
death becomes a form of control by the rational will, which asserts its

superiority through the arguments it marshals and repeats. The deliberate choice of death may also become the conclusion of a rational process in which the value of indifference is minimal. In these examples from the ancient world a sense of control is important and desired, whatever the differences in the apparatus of acceptance. Among the uneducated and those with small aptitude for thoughtful inquiry, custom and temperament may produce their own modest apparatus, and, to the thoughtful, acceptance, however arrived at, may suggest the presence of a primitive form of reasoning that supports the evident control.

When we turn to the Christian paradigm, it is more difficult to exclude qualifying variations from the essential choice. We begin with a religion based upon revelation, upon the factual events of history, upon the death of Jesus as providential sacrifice, with the rich materials of sacred scriptures offered as the word of God in poetry, story, prophecy, and studied by gifted expositors and ardent schools throughout a long history of exegetical interpretations that contribute to the systematic building of religious philosophy. One important difference is that death is no longer a phenomenon governed by the law of nature but is redefined as the punishment of divine law first declared in the Book of Genesis. Death is made more acceptable by the Christian promise of salvation and resurrection, but also made more terrible by the alternative of damnation and its netherworld of eternity. Everything certain about death continues, but to the uncertainties of the when and the how is added the major uncertainty of the last judgment; and when, as happened, the belief grew that the question of salvation was probably decided at the time of death, balancing the claims of life and death became far more difficult than pagan philosophers had thought.

Yet some of the elements of pagan choices continue under other auspices. Indifference reappears in changed contexts. Voluntary acceptance and the sense of control are still supported by an apparatus based upon reasoning as well as faith. One answer was the severe choice of John 12:25: "He that loveth his life shall lose it; and he that hateth his life in this world, shall keep it unto life eternal." Among other things, the answer reinforces an old suspicion in the world: that life is troubled, its griefs real, its joys deceptive, and death is release (but also, now, a true beginning). If the answer does not supply full directions for living, it is always available as reminder and correction, to mortify exuberant feelings or to authorize melancholy reflections on the state of things. So Donne, perhaps but not necessarily thinking of his dead daughter Lucy:

> If there were any other way to be saved and to get to Heaven, then by being born into this life, I would not wish to have

come into this world. And now that God hath made this life a *Bridge* to Heaven; it is but a giddy, and a vertiginous thing, to stand long gazing upon so narrow a bridge, and over so deep and roaring waters, and desperate whirlpools, as this world abounds with. . . . *As houses* that stand *in two Shires,* trouble the execution of Justice, the house of death that stands in two worlds, may trouble a good mans resolution. As death is a sordid *Postern,* by which I must be thrown out of this world, I would decline it: But as death is the gate, by which I must enter into Heaven, would I never come to it? certainly now, now that *Sinne* hath made life so miserable, if God should deny us death, he multiplied our misery. (*Sermons,* 7:359)

As "the house of death . . . stands in two worlds," it may indeed trouble resolution, and the image of dead bodies as the rubbish of life discharged ignominiously through side or rear gates, and successively thrown out of graves, charnel houses, and common pits, is an image that reflects familiar actuality as well as psychological response. Hamlet, thinking of himself and the dead Polonius linked together by the ways that heaven is pleased to punish, says of the body, "I will bestow him"; but some thirty lines later, "I'll lug the guts into the neighbour room"; and of Yorick's skull, "My gorge rises at it."[2] The house of death in this world "may trouble a good mans resolution," but any man's imagination. In presenting a "sordid" view of death, Donne's language implies or reflects a sordid view of life, as that of one who "hateth his life in this world." But any suggested hatred of life is linked directly to the expressed hatefulness of death in this world. Something other than hatred surely informs the "long," precarious view of life as a narrow bridge over waters and whirlpools. To complete the line of relationship: sin and misery in this world ("now, now") are linked to the house of death but in the merciful jurisdiction of the other world.

Yet elsewhere and often Donne shifts the balance to commend fulfilling the many and good obligations of life. Furthermore, God "loves the Body of Man." "Every man that hath not devested Humanity, hath a desire to have his bones lie at rest," and preferably in consecrated places. Though "Some Nations burnt . . . some drowned their dead . . . some hung them up upon trees . . . Some Nations eat their dead themselves, and some maintained dogs to eat the dead," all these practices may be explained, with minimal figurative effort, as ways of providing "graves." And therefore, to understand the most comprehensive conditions of the Apocalypse, "The state of the dead is their grave, and upon all that are in this state, shall the testimony of Gods love, to the body of man, fall." Donne's most personal voice among these quoted passages is, I believe, one in which the house of death in this world is governed equably by the justice of both worlds: "Still I say, it is a comfort to a dying man, it is an honour to his memory, it is a discharge of a duty in his friends, it is a piece of the Communion of Saints, to have a consecrated grave" (*Sermons*, 6:273–74).

The conduct of burial, then and now, is part of the "justice" of this world, and troubling. Though "God hath made the Body as a House for the soule, till he call her out, and he hath made the Grave as a House for the body, till he call it up" (6:273), and though God loves the body, and the promised triumph in heaven will not be fulfilled until, at last, glorified bodies are there (an unbroken continuity in which Donne passionately believes, as he believes that saints and angels also yearn for the fulfillment)—still, that continuity is subject to the troubling dual jurisdiction of death. For the doctrinal separation of body and soul at death directs climactic attention and religious hope to the "commendation" of the soul. To affirm continuity is to strive, in spite of traditional difficulties, to balance the claims of body and soul. If the soul alone is loved, then the body is corruption and waste and properly hated, not only for itself but as representing the abandoned house of "life in this world." Balancing the claims of body and soul is not the same as, but is an image of, the claims of life and death. As either balance moves, the imagistic relationship also moves, and even small changes may release the surprising appearance of auxiliary images and thoughts. If the desire to have one's bones "lie at rest" is attributed to everyone "that hath not devested Humanity," the dignity of life and the body is affirmed as part of the authentic justice of this world. To dissociate oneself from that affirmation is by inference to reject as worthless the memory of friends, the contiguity of comfort to the dying and duty to the living, and to call into question the reality of the "Communion of Saints." The argument is a very quiet one.[3]

The wish not to have been born if there were any other way to be saved, like the wish to "decline" death considered only as a final, "sordid" state—these are expressive responses that register their forceful sense in the context of the authoritative reasons why they *cannot* represent an actual choice. As I began by saying, it is difficult to exclude qualifying variations from the essential choice of the Christian paradigm. That choice was consciously radical in rejecting traditional ways of thinking about death, but the growth and consolidation of Christian thought also included a careful winnowing and assimilation of what had been thought previously. In addition, there were the inevitable effects of a long history involving the debates of conscientious believers who gained or lost influence, and also the historical effects of social changes that occurred without the benefit of classic arguments to be approved or not. Besides, although citizens of all decades of the Christian centuries did not hold the prevailing tenets concerning death in exactly the same way without diversity of emphasis, there was nevertheless a remarkable stability of belief in basic matters, and unresolved differences were still expected (and the individual was reminded where necessary) not to stray rashly across recognizable boundaries.

Basic matters included thinking of death as divine punishment inherited from Adam and turned into the promise of eternal life through the death of Christ. The right acceptance of death presumed purposive thinking on the subject throughout life, under ecclesiastical direction and periodic reminders, in order to avoid sin, mitigate terror, and prepare for a final acceptance based upon sincere penitence, belief in Christ, and trust in God's mercy. One might then die thinking only of one's love of God and of the life to come. The new premise of human weakness and sin permitted standards of control in acceptance that ancient philosophical practitioners would not have understood, but Christian thought worked out these and other problems with a diligent regard for the value of systematic reasoning. Humility could afford to acknowledge and build upon weakness and fear, and could reason out the good of affliction and the normalcy and uses of fear, and even the benefits of anticipating moments of uncertainty, faltering, and temporary retreats on the course. Christ's death was not only a perfect model, authorizing the normalcy of some impulses of human reluctance ("let this cup pass") and the transitory irruptions of fear at the thought of having been abandoned by God, but finally closing with the deliberate commendation of the soul to God. It was more than a model, and it could inspire some perfect believers who would go on record as moving with no punctuating hesitation or agony of doubt straight to the aim of the appointed design.

I have tried to suggest something of the dynamic complexity and subtlety of the essential choice, supported as it was by the resources of a treasury of ancient wisdom and by the continuing traditions of active thought, which included the results of accurate psychological observations on the motives and responses of human beings under sentence of death. My last word for the moment is to repeat the prominent emphasis on control and reasoned acceptance.

CHAPTER FIFTEEN

Thought and Images

For the force of a similitude not being to prove any thing to a contrary disputer, but onely to explaine to a willing hearer, when that is done, the rest is a moste tedious pratling, rather overswaying the memorie from the purpose whereto they were applied, then anie whit enforming the judgement alreadie either satisfied, or by similitudes not to be satisfied.

SIDNEY, *Defence of Poesie*

To *the thinking soul* images serve as if they were contents of perception (and when it asserts or denies them to be good or bad it avoids or pursues them). That is why the soul never thinks without an image." And further: "When the mind is actively aware of anything it is necessarily aware of it along with an image; for images are like sensuous contents except in that they contain no matter." Thus Aristotle in a statement that exerted great influence (*De Anima* 3.7.8). Augustine, working from other influences and toward other ends, places "corporeal" images at the bottom of his ascending scale, though nothing can be expressed unless it has been preceded by an internal image. "Spiritual vision is superior to corporeal" and does not need the lower faculty, "since the likenesses of absent objects appear in the spirit." At the pinnacle there is "intellectual" vision, which is in effect autonomous, though needed to validate spiritual vision, and never errs, but is also, among other attributes, "ineffable."[1]

In writing on the subject of memory and following Aristotle in the main, Thomas Aquinas adds something else to his description of how the mind acts and reacts:

And those things are *per se* memorable of which there is a phantasy, that is to say, the sensibilia. But the intelligibilia are *per accidens* memorable, for these cannot be apprehended by man without a phantasm. And thus it is that we remember less easily those things which are of subtle and spiritual import; and we remember more easily those things which are gross and sensible. And if we wish to remember intelligible notions more easily, we should link them with some kind of phantasms, as Tullius teaches in his Rhetoric.[2]

Among his precepts for training the memory is the use of "similitudes," preferably unusual ones, "because we wonder more at unfamiliar things and the soul is more strongly and vehemently held by them; whence it is that we remember better things seen in childhood. It is necessary in this way to invent similitudes and images." Further,

> It is necessary that a man should dwell with solicitude on, and cleave with affection to, the things which he wishes to remember; because what is strongly impressed on the soul slips less easily away from it. Whence Tullius says in his Rhetoric that "solicitude conserves complete figures of the simulachra." (p. 75)

As Frances Yates, whom I have been following, points out, Aquinas has misquoted *Ad Herennium* ("sollicitudo" for "solitudo") and added "cleave with affection," thus introducing "a devotional atmosphere which is entirely absent from the classical memory rule" (p. 76). She also observes that the apologetic necessity of providing an image in order to remember the intelligibilia of "subtle and spiritual import" is "a concession to human weakness, to the nature of the soul" (p. 71).[3]

A specialized method of training the memory is not, of course, one of the more prestigious branches of thinking, but inasmuch as the discipline reflects a concept of mind and the relations of the mind to the abstractions it gains and holds, the effectiveness of the discipline was a kind of proof, not negligible, that it was in accord with the true nature of the mind. Besides its practical uses, in thought as well as rhetoric, memory had important functions in the practices of Christian thought and the history of salvation. It was no secret that in one of the more decorous Greek myths Mnemosyne was the mother of the Muses. That memory is immortal was a significant contribution of the Platonic legacy. Augustine's widely influential model of the human soul as based upon the Trinity identified God the Father with memory, Christ with reason, and the Holy Ghost with the affections. Therefore, the inspired messages and images of the affections could be understood as having direct access to memory, and the arts of meditation and devotion were consciously aware of that possibility. Aristotle's quiet corollary, "When the mind is actively aware of anything, it is *necessarily aware of it along with an image*" (emphasis added), presents a dimension of thought in which self-consciousness and a capacity for criticism are endued with

positions for their potential activity. To end this brief sketch: the word
of God in Holy Scripture, accommodating itself to common human
understanding, saw fit to employ images from the whole range of
ordinary human experience. Secular poets were bound by the more
prescriptive laws of decorum developed in their art, but they also
sought images that would stir the mind in the right way.

Particulars, examples, similitudes, which move as well as enlighten
and clarify, were the acknowledged instruments of the reasoning of
poetry and story, but also of that part of religion that concerned individual devotion. Though such uses of the mind were regarded as less
reliable and less well suited to travel over the reaches of intellectual
distance than the disciplines of severe reasoning upon principles, the
less reliable instruments could do some things incomparably well. In
any case, there could be no irreconcilable opposition. Like body and
soul, or the separate faculties of the soul (or in our time the conflicting
claims of basic and applied research), the rule of cohabitation had an
actual force that imposed limitations on the rules of ranking by intellectual eminence. In a religion, one of the foundations of which is love, the
stirring and concentrating of the soul is a proper subject for intellectual
study. So Donne expresses nothing new, but the renewed testimony of
his own conviction, when he says: "For, the object of my understanding
is truth; but the object of my love, my affection, my desire, is goodnesse . . . nothing supplies, nor fills, nor satisfies the desire of man, on
this side of God; Every man hath something to love, and desire, till he
determine it in God" (*Sermons*, 6:232). He can state the thesis in a
redaction of familiar philosophical reasoning:

> *Primus actus voluntatis est Amor;* Philosophers and Divines
> agree in that, That the will of man cannot be idle, and the first
> act that the will of man produces is Love; for till it love some-
> thing, prefer and chuse something, till it would have some-
> thing, it is not a Will; neither can it turn upon any object,
> before God. (*Sermons*, 6:361)

We shall need to return to Donne, but I draw an illustration now
from the leading Platonist of the Renaissance. Ficino, intent on opposing some of the Aristotelians' emphasis on the high value of the visual,
observes that visual images lack motion and therefore move the soul
only a little. (He has a great deal of the best literature of all kinds against
him here.) Similarly, the lower senses of smell, taste, and touch have
their known material effects but cannot penetrate the depths of the soul.
On the other hand, the sense of hearing in the example of musical sound
"excites the aerial spirit which is the bond of body and soul; by emotion

it affects the senses and at the same time the soul; by meaning it works on the mind." It penetrates, flows, floods us with exalted pleasure, and "by its very nature, both spiritual and material, it at once seizes, and claims as its own, man in his entirety." (The lovers of beautifully arranged words might wish to enter similar if more modest claims, mindful that the possibilities of disagreements about the meanings of words and their music make an uncertain basis for anticipating the harmony of other men in their "entirety.")[4]

Paracelsus, reasoning upon a humble phenomenon, is not much less ambitious than Ficino in his explanation. He too is interested in motion and penetration but also in the influential movement of celestial bodies:

> If the pregnant woman begins to imagine, then her bosom is borne round in its motion just as the superior firmament, each movement rising or settling. For as in the case of the greater firmament, the stars of the microcosm also move by imagination, until there comes a sort of bounding, in which the stars of the imagination produce an influence and an impression on the pregnant woman, just as though one should impress a seal or stamp a piece of money. Whence those signs and birthmarks derived from the lower stars are called "impressions."[5]

Part of the interest in these two examples is that each author's mind is conscious of its thought "along with an image," as Aristotle said, and each explanatory method is supplemented by quasi-narrative delineation, which when used formally Ficino calls *apologus*, a fable borrowed or invented for the occasion. A latent figure in Ficino's discussion is the ideal harmony of the Platonic music of the spheres. Part of Paracelsus's case is built upon the ancient similitude that for centuries had compared the human imagination to impressionable wax. Both the accounts depend upon the theory of correspondences and describe the phenomena by drawing upon their believed coincidence with phenomena of the supernal world; both turn the emphasis, however, to the relations of body and soul in this world.

I return to Donne with the limited purpose of drawing upon a few of his many statements on the nature and art of expression. His words on the subject of death are a chief source of this book; he has much to say on my present subject, in statements and asides, chiefly scattered throughout the *Sermons*. We saw him distinguishing between the object of understanding, truth, and the object of love, goodness, but also declaring that the first act of the will is love, and defending that proposition by familiar philosophical arguments directed toward the understanding and its object, truth. Donne keeps insisting on the primacy of understanding; we reach the true assurance of faith and we defend the possession of that happy state by means of the reasoning affirmed by the understanding. And "we know how to worke . . . we know what arguments have prevailed upon us, with what arguments we have prevailed upon others, and those we can use." It is the will which "is so irregular, so unlimited a thing, as that no man hath a bridle upon anothers will . . . no man understands the faculty." What we *feel* in ourselves we *see* in others, that they "persist in errors, after manifest convincing, after all reproofe which can be directed upon the understanding." Therefore, it is an attractive notion, perhaps the best yet produced, but still not true enough, "that the last act of the Understanding is the Will" (*Sermons*, 6:321).

If "no man understands that faculty" of will, in himself and in others, the poet and the preacher are not therefore ignorant; as with arguments, they "know how to worke," and if their instruments do not chart the way to final understanding, there is much they can do, and their effectiveness has been proved by experience and observation, one's own and others'. For the preacher, Donne remarks, "it is a good art, to deliver deepe points in a holy plainnesse, and plaine points in a holy delightfulnesse" (*Sermons*, 9:215). In part the purpose is to prevent the weariness (from not being able to understand) of the unlearned, and the weariness of the learned who understand things before they are said. The practical reason for so doing is explained thus. Quietly implicit is the understanding that only learned members of the congregation will recognize the qualities of the art that can present "deepe points in a holy plainenesse." The immediate reason for the statement, however, concerns the orator's art of presenting himself acceptably while he manages the art of preparation and transition. Donne's next words are, "To day my humble petition must be, That you will be content to heare plaine things plainly delivered." He prevents weariness while explaining how to avoid it, and provides another kind of "delightfulnesse" by concealing the approaches to the plain point of making a necessary transition.

In presenting a more general principle, also in an aside, Donne says:

> The way of Rhetorique in working upon weake men, is first to trouble the understanding, to displace, and to discompose, and disorder the judgement, to smother and bury in it, or to empty it of former apprehensions and opinions, and to shake that beliefe, with which it had possessed it self before, and then when it is thus melted, to powre it into new molds, when

it is thus mollified, to stamp and imprint new formes, new images, new opinions in it. (*Sermons*, 2:282)

Donne is here talking in general about rhetoric and weak men. In a still more general sense what he says applies to all men, and certainly to himself, when the "working" is that of God returning a sinner to the right path. "Melt" is an image that can suggest or describe the controlled, assenting death, or as here also suggest the symbolic "deaths" in life that are part of the recognized process of personal transformation. The emptying of the self is like that *kenosis* by which the "evacuated" man makes room for God to enter. The stamping and imprinting, when it is done by God, is true work and obliterates the distinction between understanding and will.

And so here an instructional aside, formally describing "the way" of rhetoric, steadily moves into broader and deeper ways by which men may be discomposed and recomposed. The methods and consequences of a human art tell one story; the vividness of the images, their cumulative intensity, and the apparently irresistible power of the progression tell another story, based upon two unadmitted similitudes. In Donne's mind the "way" described is also one of the ways God may work in transforming a sinner in order "to stamp and imprint new formes, new images, new opinions." For instance, Saul, a "vehement persecuter," becomes Paul, a "laborious Apostle." "Christ, who is about to infuse new light into *Saul*, withdrawes that light that was in him before; That light, by which *Saul* thought he saw all before, and thought himselfe a competent Judge." "God shut up the naturall way, in *Saul*, Seeing; He struck him blind, But he opened the super-naturall way, he inabled him to heare, and to heare him" (6:211, 214, 217).

As for the way of rhetoric, in its context the development is excessive, as if answering some personal need. For Donne continues at once, "Here in our case, there was none of this fire, none of this practise, none of this battery of eloquence, none of this verball violence, onely a bare *Sequere me, Follow me,* and *they followed.* No eloquence enclined them, no terrors declined them" (2:282–83). But the dismissal of rhetoric is only a convenience of this particular case, and one may suspect a degree of embarrassment on Donne's part as he consciously diminishes the force and import of what he has just said, reducing it to a kind of dubious eloquence, and he provides a minor farewell flourish of his own eloquence.

The ways of rhetoric are often in Donne's thought, and seriously so. "How empty a thing is Rhetorique? (and yet Rhetorique will make absent and remote things present to your understanding)" (4:87). "It is not the depth, nor the wit, nor the eloquence of the Preacher that pierces us, but his nearenesse; that he speaks to my conscience, as though he had been behinde the hangings when I sinned, and as though he had read the book of the day of Judgement already" (3:142). Arguments can be answered, but the forms, images, and opinions of epigrams, satires, libels, and scornful jests "passe more uncontrol'd, and prevaile further, and live longer, then *Arguments* doe" (8:65). The rhetoric that can discompose can also search out what the heart desires, or can offer to the world for admiration those displays that present under disguise the author's own secret life; or, as at the end of the quotation below, the arts of speech can accomplish more general transformations:

> For the most part, the heart affords a returne, and an inclina-
> tion to those things that are willingly received at the ear; The
> Echo returnes the last syllables; The heart concludes with his
> conclusions, whom we have been willing to hearken unto. We
> make *Satyrs;* and we looke that the world should call that *wit;*
> when God knowes, that that is in a great part, self-guiltinesse,
> and we do but reprehend those things, which we our selves
> have done, we cry out upon the illnesse of the times, and we
> make the times ill." (7:408)

The Holy Ghost is the supreme rhetorician and accommodates the language he inspires to the human faculties of understanding and will, but not always to both equally. In moving the affections he is direct, with the "nearenesse" of a felt presence: "The Holy Ghost . . . is a direct worker upon the soule and conscience of man, but a Meta-phoricall, and Figurative expresser of himselfe, to the reason, and un-derstanding of man" (9:328). As Donne notes elsewhere, not wishing to suggest that comments on the ways of the Holy Ghost are to be thought of as rules or as lessons in how to anticipate his expression: "The Holy Ghost pursues his owne way." Yet in the case that prompts this remark he goes on to say that the Holy Ghost does here "as hee does often in other places, he speakes in such formes, and such phrases, as may most worke upon them to whom he speaks" (2:304). The direct way that touches the soul is easily recognizable and requires little or no in-terpretation. But the figurative expressions tax the minds of the best exegetes. The accepted standard of Donne and his co-religionists was to establish "the literall, that is, the principall intention of the Holy Ghost," but that standard could not always be met or the results attain the agreement of others. There were ways to manage the problem, such as by the discreet charity and toleration toward other opinions Donne himself liked to practice when he could.

Another way, which has its counterpart in more personal unargued practice not obliged to attempt the persuasion of others, as we shall see in a moment, is this:

> In the figurative exposition of those places of Scripture, which require that way oft to be figuratively expounded, that Expositor is not to be blamed, who not destroying the literall sense, proposes such a figurative sense, as may exalt our devotion, and advance our edification. (6:63)

Donne then proceeds, as one may among friendly listeners, to induce a figurative exchange, mild and smooth by social usage. He will decide, as if by an analogy discovered and affirmed by reason, to accept the invitation "of the day, which we celebrate now," by proposing to add something of his own to the "three expositions authorized by persons of good note in the Church." It is, he says with winning modesty and candor, "a fourth sense, or rather, use of the words; not indeed as an exposition of the words, but as a convenient exaltation of our devotion." In another sermon preached four years earlier, he had prepared the way for "a convenient exaltation" by referring to the fact that there are plenty of "direct proofes" in Scripture and "undeniable arguments" in the possession of the church. Following Luther, Donne acknowledges, "We must not proceed alike with friends and with enemies." The issue is a possible reference to, or adumbration of, the Trinity, which Donne thinks "is a lovely and a religious thing, to finde out" and meditate on. There is no good proof, however, and the literal sense plainly means something else, as Luther avers. But there are other considerations too. Though Augustine is right to say that "a figure, an Allegory proves nothing; yet sayes he, *addit lucem, & ornat*, It makes that which is true in it selfe, more evident and more acceptable." Besides, as Luther said, there are passages in Scripture where no proof is needed for us to exercise meditation and devotion, as we may use a wooden sword for purposes of exercise. Therefore, "to exercise our owne devotions, we are content with similitudinary, and comparative reasons" (3:143–44).

This brief selection from Donne's thought and practice in the pulpit is made for "similitudinary and comparative" purposes, not as an argument but to illustrate and explain some of the conditions and circumstances that influenced thinking and speaking with images and "along with" images. We have also had occasion to observe in passing some of the potentialities when separation and divergence develop between the thought and the image. When noted by a strict Renaissance critic, such self-indulgent straying from "the purpose whereto they were applied" was to be condemned. Another attitude was required while facing up to the problems experienced in trying to interpret the figurative expressions of the Holy Ghost.

I point to some problems in human expression easier to solve once than to make the solution thereof continuous: where and how by its laws thought should conduct itself and the attending image; where the image may tend, by its nature and its attachments scrutinizable like a text, but also partly hidden, perhaps wayward, perhaps inspired and discovering or illuminating the true, making it beautiful, releasing its power to convince. I have touched on other problems that share some resemblances. In Aquinas the grosser images of sense are easily remembered, but to be remembered the subtle and complex matters of higher thought need an image, preferably one felt with affection. The nature of the relationship between body and soul could be fixed in a definitive judgment, but the claims of each in any particular case could make the scales of justice quiver; so too the claims of life and death and their relations to this world and the next. The Holy Ghost, with or without an image, acts directly on the affections and will, but by figurative expressions indirectly on the reason. Because of the nature of the Good it is possible to chart by the principles of reason the desire of the will which leads to its source in the first cause. But Calvin "discomposed" and convinced many that the mind is more easily endowed with thought than the heart furnished with that assurance which is a major effect of faith. Devotional thought had its own reasons, and some would think these both nearer and more effective than the outmoded reasoning of the Scholastics and pagan philosophers. "*Houses* that stand *in two Shires,* trouble the execution of Justice."

CHAPTER SIXTEEN

Images of Reflection

Consider the lilies of the field.
MATTHEW 6:28

As *Donne said,* following scriptural example and the traditional understanding of that example, "No metaphor, no comparison is too high, none too low, too triviall, to imprint in you a sense of Gods everlasting goodnesse towards you" (*Sermons*, 7:369). His basic standard is that of conveying the "imprint" of God's intention. The preacher using his own metaphors and comparisons derives support from another comparison: the analogy of how the Holy Ghost works, directly on the affections or indirectly on the mind, or both at once. It is "the principall intention of the Holy Ghost" in that place which authorizes and governs the meaning of the expression. So the story Donne has been telling, of a mother, a wolf, and a child, and then defending in the first quotation above, is called not a fable but a parable. The story is charming but is defined by the moral intention. Elsewhere Donne notes with admiration the appropriate and delightful use of words in the Scriptures,[1] and we know from reading him the many strong or delicate ways by which Donne knows how to register meaning, or how shades of meaning may be lightly intimated or deliberately placed. We have already noticed how Donne's account of "the way of Rhetorique" tells a story based upon unadmitted similitudes, and I remind the reader of the related examples from Ficino and Paracelsus that tell a story like a reasoned argument. But let us leave for a while the practices of religious expression and turn to some other sources.

"Cowards die many times before their deaths." The confident pronouncement by Shakespeare's Julius Caesar (2.2.32) is a familiar kind of limited figurative truth which easily overextends its credit. In dramatic expression the limited truth has many valuable functions, not least of which is its pointing toward alternative potentialities in every pronouncement. "Be absolute for death," says Duke Vincentio in a grand set speech of *Measure for Measure* (3.1.5–41). Shakespeare's Cleopatra, among her other accomplishments in variety, combines pagan *eros* with both pagan and Christian *thanatos*. "She hath pursu'd conclusions infinite / Of easy ways to die" (5.2.358–59). She can say, almost in the same breath, that "The stroke of death is as a lover's pinch, / Which hurts, and is desir'd," and that the despised world "is not worth leave-taking" (5.2.298–301). And she can reject the world of change and illusion in terms that, out of context and as far as they go, the most severe theologian might commend:

> Which shackles accidents and bolts up change;
> Which sleeps, and never palates more the dung,
> The beggar's nurse and Caesar's.
>
> (5.2.6–8)

For the moment I mention the dramatic example only as a reminder that recognizable potentialities of great scope did exist. The lyric obviously must deal with its limited truths and latent alternatives differently and within a narrower compass. Yet almost all of the familiar ways of thinking about death, including the profession of limited truths and the contemplation of standard subjects, could be turned to yield a lyric discourse answering particular circumstances and expressing the individual character of the poet.

First, by way of illustrative example it will be useful to recall the topic of time again. In the lyrics confronting personal death, time emerged as a central subject only for Tichborne and for the Raleigh of "Even such is time." But time is not in the same way central in Raleigh's "The Passionate Man's Pilgrimage," Donne's "Hymne to God my God in my sicknesse," and Herbert's "Death." In these poems the imaginative encounters with time are indirect, instrumental to talking about something else, but nevertheless most powerful and widely ranging. In many lyrics, however, ones that take time or an aspect of time as a direct subject, both the scale and the immediacy of the imaginative experience are less; so are the conceptual grasp and the quality of the ordering.

For instance, that valuable injunction of the love poets, *carpe diem,* lent itself to the purposes of lyric argument because the promised rewards were backed by the alternative threats of punishment. Poets had little difficulty in making the rejection of present pleasure appear to be the deliberate choice of consequent pains, and these could be drawn variously and suggestively from aspects of the character of time. The most threatening images evoked thoughts of death or euphemistic substitutes appropriately veiled. "For having lost but once your prime, / You may for ever tarry" is a mortal thought (spinsterhood as an image of dying) gently presented "To the Virgins" by Herrick

(H-208). "Corinna's Going A-Maying" saves for the last stanza a summary statement of the alternative to making the most of our brief time
and then partly softens, with no retraction, the penultimate word of
"Then while time serves, and we are but decaying" (H-178). Daniel
exploits the conventional reluctance of women to think of age and
threatens "Delia" with a darkness her vanity will be forced to prefer, as
a cosmetic concealment:

> And *Delia,* thinke thy morning must have night.
> And that thy brightnes sets at length to west:
> When thou wilt close up that which now thou showest:
> And thinke the same becomes thy fading best,
> Which then shall hide it most, and cover lowest.[2]

These were ways of construing the lessons of time to love's advantage. There were, of course, other ways. The absence of time from
Marlowe's "The Passionate Shepherd to his Love" is not overlooked in
"The Nymph's Reply," which deserves its attribution to Raleigh.
Though questions of sincerity are raised, the chief points of wit depend
upon the "reckoning" time exacts in a world where joys are not without
"date" nor age without "need." "Time drives the flocks from field to
fold," and the "pretty pleasures"

> Soone breake, soone wither, soone forgotten:
> In follie ripe, in reason rotten.[3]

Edward Herbert, while making the conventional argument to "the
April of your youth," draws up his either/or in ways calculated to
express more than the art of persuasion:

> Then think each minute that you lose, a day,
>   The longest Youth is short,
> The shortest Age is long; time flies away,
>   And makes us but his sport;
> And that which is not Youth's is Age's prey.[4]

And one further example. The conclusion of Donne's "A Lecture upon
the Shadow" is entirely different. It does not aim at a carefully limited
point but at something central in the conflict between love and time.
The effect is that of an apparently categorical answer that has the power
to delay for a moment and then release threatening questions that turn
back on themselves:

> Love is a growing, or full constant light;
> And his first minute, after noone, is night.

Love is and is not time's fool. The images prove adaptable, and this is the main point I wish to emphasize and shall return to. For the chosen aspects of the poetic subject, or the controlled limitations imposed upon certain familiar truths—these may be made to serve personal circumstances or purposes while other considerations linger about the edges of the subject in varying states of potentiality and may or may not be engaged. The images prove adaptable, and they are mostly simple ones, inexhaustibly used: day, night, the seasons, objects produced by the seasons and enduring objects held up for confirmation or contrast. Governing them all, in frivolous or serious ways, is what the poet wishes to think, or needs to think, or wants his reader to think, as he interprets the reflections made available by his images. The seasons provide a large encyclopedic entry with a major section on flowers. The rose is best for love; the lily is a special flower for other uses:

> "Behold, O man, that toilesome paines doest take. . . .
> The lilly, lady of the flowring field. . .
> Yet nether spinnes nor cards, ne cares nor fretts,
> But to her mother Nature all her care she letts.
>
> Why then doest thou, O man, that of them all
> Art lord, and eke of Nature soveraine,
> Wilfully make thy selfe a wretched thrall."
>
> *(Faerie Queene* 2.6.15–17)

In the "love lay," the excerpted lines of which suggest the familiar plot, the lily is standing in for the rose in Spenser's calculated temptation. Yet the lily also represents a deceptive image of human life escaping from "toilesome paines," for man may consider the lilies of the field while secretly longing to kiss the image of his death. "Gather the rose of love whilest yet is time" is the burden of the "lovely lay," which Spenser enters on another page:

> So passeth, in the passing of a day
> Of mortall life the leafe, the bud, the flowre,
> Ne more doth florish after first decay,
> That earst was sought to deck both bed and bowre
> Of many a lady, and many a paramowre;
> Gather therefore the rose, whilest yet is prime,
> For soone comes age, that will her pride deflowre:
> Gather the rose of love, whilest yet is time,
> Whilest loving thou mayst loved be with equall crime.
>
> (2.12.75)

But accompanying the song, and heard most clearly in the opening lines, is an underside of the message—the sung brevity of life, which blossoms into bright reasons for gathering "the rose of love" but has no word for the dark desire to forget about time "whilest yet is time."

Spenser is not speaking for himself overtly, but we may think that the unacknowledged feelings are valid and that the orchestration allows them to be heard under the formal dominance of the main theme. What is heard is a reflection of mortality, though mortality here is not the formal subject of the reflection.

In the usage I am sketching and introducing, reflections of mortality are not for the most part directed toward the subject of death in general but toward dying—and, again, not toward the act itself but aspects of the act, the figurative meanings that may be won from considering the reflected instances of dying outside and inside the self. In moral theology this dying constitutes the discipline of "mortification," preparing soul and body for actual death by rehearsing the mind, emotions, and will. One may practice "dying to the world" on a regular schedule or from time to time, dying to particular sins on the official lists, or one may follow a more personal order of priority; or one may single out for special attention aspects of that which is deemed illusory or excessively attractive or distracting. The spiritual discipline, like its informing similitude of "dying to," proved applicable and useful in expressing human responses to analogous circumstances—those, for instance, produced by the stimulus and perplexity of love, ambition, and the like, and the unlike.[5] So reflected instances of dying might be evoked with no apparent purpose that answered to the direct aims of spiritual mortification.

I come to my main set of examples, a brief review of George Herbert's procedures which will both illustrate the problems of my subject and, I trust, make some gains in clarity.

"The Church" contains many poems that are formal mortifications. Most of the thoughts, themes, and images are part of a long European tradition and could be catalogued as such. By their proved history, Herbert's poems are public and didactic. They instruct others, but their success depends, like that of much good teaching, on a valuable effect that convinces because it does not aim only to do so. The poems are personal, they speak for and teach the poet himself, they are no less overheard than heard. Given the nature of the subject and its long history, no new basic ideas had been overlooked by predecessors, but Herbert's temperament and lyric genius, his resources for speaking the personally imagined truth for himself, could express the intimations of mortality in fresh and moving ways.

Death holds no dominion over his thoughts and feelings. In this respect two poems I have considered, "The Forerunners" and "Death," are reliably characteristic. Those poems of Herbert's which take up the subject of exemplary "dying" do so with many of the kinds of distinction expressed in his other poems. They too are singularly free of morbidity and the alluring excesses of self-regard.

Herbert's personal standards appear to be laid down most directly in "The Church-porch," where he counsels against "trifling in thy wo." And he often treats aspects of dying as no more than the summing up at night which balances the books in preparation for the morning's activities. Judgment is coming, "make thy accounts agree," neither neglecting nor striving to oppose the familiar ways by which time rules over human affairs and life itself: "Dresse and undresse thy soul: mark the decay / And growth of it." The last stanza counsels the kind of balance he recommends to others and tries to practice himself—if one accepts the lyric poet's privilege to express occasional feelings with an intensity that matches their rule over him, and if one observes how moments and poems conflict with, dare, and encourage one another as they compose a full and true record of the inner life. Here he is quietly summing up in a discursive way, but it is noteworthy that two images of dying—the transiency of pleasure and the brevity of life—are subordinated to the privileges and dues of living:

> In brief, acquit thee bravely; play the man,
> Look not on pleasures as they come, but go.
> Deferre not the least vertue: lifes poore span
> Make not an ell, by trifling in thy wo.
> > If thou do ill; the joy fades, not the pains:
> > If well; the pain doth fade, the joy remains.
>
> (lines 457–62)

I shall first briefly survey five poems of mortification. Throughout I shall be mindful that I have already discussed many poems at length in *George Herbert's Lyrics* and considered one whole group as mortifications. The frame and emphasis of the present discourse are necessarily different.

The poem entitled "Mortification" accords a single stanza to each of five stages of human life marked by ceremonies that reveal the anticipation of death. The message is a clear one:

> Yet Lord, instruct us so to die,
> That all these dyings may be life in death.

From infancy to old age, aware or unaware, we practice dyings. Herbert's wit imposes itself masterfully from without and discovers to our greater surprise, from within as it were, correlations between the stages of life and their individual acknowledgments of death. Each scene is complete and perfectly separate, at once a framed episode and a linked sequence indispensable to the whole. The point of view is directed as lesson toward man in general. The achievement, considered only as mastery of style, engages powers of character and art in flowing grace and minute precision, as if the poetic art itself were wholly natural and any man might think and speak and act so. The last stanza opens the point of view and brings in the inclusive "us" for whom the poet has been acting as personal spokesman.

My second example, "Church-monuments," tightens the address and alters the quality of detachment. The physical scene is located in and held to one place and time. These are not, however, particularized, and the poem admits brief mental excursions that involve episodes touching on three kinds of indefinite future: when the body will grow "wanton in thy cravings," when death which "Drives all at last" will bring about "thy fall," and when the monuments themselves will "fall down flat" and be indistinguishable from the remains "which now they have in trust." The soul is praying in church among monuments but pauses to instruct the body, which is "entombed" by the act of prayer. The detachment of the soul is more impersonal and rigorous than the poet's detachment in any stanza of "Mortification," where the scenes imagined are allowed some free and sympathetic expansion in their own existence and in their claims on our interest. Here the speaking soul treats the body as an alien "other," which must be schooled hard, as if incapable of learning through gentler methods.

The rigor of attitude matches the strict attention to the objects that reflect, not the admonitions of dying which may serve as guidance to living, but the single compendious lesson of death. The objects are the dust of those already dead, their crumbling monuments, and the living body that will join that company. Although there are small touches of wit, they do not deflect or lighten the rigor. At most their minor extravagances add some play of light and shadow to the substantial invulnerability of the lesson. Throughout, the rhythm is restless and driving; pauses come irregularly, not when they are anticipated and never at the end of any stanza but the last. The rhymes, being widely separated (abcabc), accommodate themselves to Herbert's rhythmic design, and the design carries its own contributing message—of life driven by time, careering toward its end always in the control of an outside force:

That flesh is but the glasse, which holds the dust
That measures all our time; which also shall
Be crumbled into dust.

The lesson is a limited one, strictly limited, with no departure permitted from the course of time leading to death. What lies beyond is here only dust returning to dust.

Since the schooling is deliberately elementary, a spelling lesson for the body learning its elements, all of the distracting complexities of more advanced instruction are excluded. Among these are that side of the process which otherwise might include the first divine animation of the original dust, the episodic recurrences of "life," and the hopes and promises thereunto subscribed. The body listening is one episode in a closed system, an orderly procedure in a single direction, and the rhythmic signature is that of death's "incessant motion." It is a microcosm in which "the good fellowship of dust" seems like a brief, punctuating eccentricity; the governing truth is best discerned in the certainties that "dissolution" plainly demonstrates. It is a microcosm in which sin seems to be the sole executive of time, and death the prime mover. The images are memorable in their power, and they gain from what they are free to exclude by their concentration. And yet at least one touch of unacknowledged wit does allow an entrance (if not an exit) for Herbertian mirth. The soul's remarkable virtuosity in lecturing is only an aside, simple instruction to the rigid body kneeling obediently, an aside while the soul is chiefly engaged (or will be, we cannot tell) in her devotion—"Deare flesh, while I do pray, learn here."

In "Vertue" the soul is distinguished, not from the body, but from everything else in the created world. The evidence of death is, however, now more varied; an important exclusion is part of the record, and the speaker includes himself and also the natural attachments of human feelings. The representative examples illustrating the principle that "all must die" are, with one major exception, drawn from the common world of nature: the day, the rose, and springtime. The manmade art of music is the exception and concludes the series: "My musick shows ye have your closes." Each object is accorded a tender, elegiac celebration, appropriately individual, as it is filed in testimony. The day is a "brid-all," and dew "shall weep thy fall to night"; the rose "Bids the rash gazer wipe his eye." Only the virtuous, constant soul will be more alive at the last day. No mortification could be more gentle in accepting death and its rules while expressing human affections for the mortal.

My fourth example is "Dotage," a poem that never mentions death but teaches the strict lessons by another method. The objects considered are drawn from a summary human experience of pleasure and pain, and these are locked in a juxtaposition for which, it becomes clear, some easing remedy must be sought. As an argument based on the deceiving illusions of life, nothing could be more familiar and—from our impatient perspective in time—equally disposed to convince or to bore. But Herbert is the kind of scrupulous artist who almost never becomes passive and insensitive when deploying familiar materials. The poem acquires an unusual power from staccato phrases of compressed brilliance and passion which are also phrases of definition and do the work of the precisely drawn scenes in "Death" and "Mortification." False pleasures are, among other things:

> Shadows well mounted, dreams in a career,
> Embroider'd lyes, nothing between two dishes.

Sorrows are:

> True earnest sorrows, rooted miseries,
> Anguish in grain, vexations ripe and blown,
> Sure-footed griefs, solid calamities.

The necessary answer is that men pursue and prefer "griefs in earnest, joyes in jest" because they center themselves "here." But perhaps the greatest severity of the poem is an underlying one that is, we know, contradicted elsewhere in Herbert. The pleasures are unqualifiedly false but the sorrows are, however multiplied and intensified by folly, nevertheless true—less true than the delights of heaven, yet joined to these along an axis from which pleasures are excluded.

Finally we come to the priest's own mortification, "Aaron." Only in its limited scope does it bear resemblance to "Church-monuments"; everything else is different, and "Aaron" has nothing to do with the natural facts of death. Nor does the poem so much as recognize as an issue the turning away from the pleasures and pains of life. But if one is willing to overlook its kind of concentration and its purpose, "Aaron" does resemble "Mortification" and "Vertue"—at least insofar as it proposes a disciplined process by which thoughts related to death may be made to influence the course of living. The subject is not death, but as most often in Herbert the subject is purposive "dying," the discipline and directions to be acquired from thoughts of death and applied to the thoughts and acts of living. In "Aaron" the intensity and concentration are unrelieved; the same materials and rhyme words ring out their repetitions in the same place in each stanza, while absolute contrasts are made by substituting a few key words, many of them the smaller parts of speech: pronouns, prepositions, and adverbs. Dressing and undressing are not, as in "The Church-porch," imagistic advice to the soul, but an image for the infallible measuring of the true, and all departures and returns as well. Music, which in "Vertue" reflected only its message of finality, varies and transforms the issues of life and death.

> Holinesse on the head,
>   Light and perfections on the breast,
> Harmonious bells below, raising the dead
>   To leade them unto life and rest:
>   Thus are true Aarons drest.
>
> Profanenesse in my head,
>   Defects and darknesse in my breast,
> A noise of passions ringing me for dead
>   Unto a place where is no rest:
>   Poore priest thus am I drest.
>
> Onely another head
> I have, another heart and breast,
> Another musick, making live not dead,
>   Without whom I could have no rest:
>   In him I am well drest.
>
> Christ is my onely head,
>   My alone onely heart and breast,
> My onely musick, striking me ev'n dead;
>   That to the old man I may rest,
>   And be in him new drest.
>
> So holy in my head,
>   Perfect and light in my deare breast,
> My doctrine tun'd by Christ, (who is not dead,
>   But lives in me while I do rest)
>   Come people; Aaron's drest.

If we let these five poems represent the general range of Herbert's treatment of the subject, we may find in many other poems echoes and variations that extend the range and strengthen the texture of his thought on the purposes of imaginative dying. For instance, Herbert's delight in the art of narrative makes of "The Pilgrimage" a story of outward and inward movement and response which is a complete parable of seeking death along a path marked only by emblematic objects. The rightness of the conclusion has been well demonstrated: "After so foul a journey death is fair, / And but a chair." Two departures from the standard emphasis of Christian thought seem to suggest more than a momentary or wandering interest on Herbert's part, but we may only note these in passing. "Content" deals with the restlessness of life and the war of "mutt'ring thoughts" by counseling a "gentle measure"— one by means of which life and death are contemplated with philosophic calm. The seeking and the finding are both directed inward to the self. "Decay" looks not at individual but at historical life, celebrates the "sweet days" of the good Old Testament, and concludes that "the world grows old" and toward its end of time.

"The Flower" is one of several poems that compose a full personal conflict within a single lyric. The continuous point of reference is that standard object for symbolic reflection, the flower: in its winter death ("dead" only to the world, but keeping "house unknown" at the root), in its springtime of true pleasure, in its summer pride, painful oppressions, and mysterious budding again amidst the joys of dew and rain. The flower is more than contemplated; the lessons of its history reflect the poet's, and advise. The most important lesson is that of mastering, as "but flowers that glide," the wonders of love and life while obeying the wonders of power and death. "Life," another sustained contemplation of flowers, limits itself to flowers that wither in the hand and to a simpler human analogy ("deaths sad taste," "my fatall day"). The personal reference is made authentic with brief imaginative power, and the concluding identification, while balancing matters of smaller scope than "The Flower," achieves a kind of purity and state of graceful indifference which may bear comparison with the ending of "Death":

> I follow straight, without complaints or grief,
> Since if my sent be good, I care not, if
> It be as short as yours.

Altogether different is the sustained analytical contemplation of "The Rose," which produces witty and original variations for a standard rejecting of "this world of sugred lies."

Images, I say again, prove adaptable, and the imaginative encounters with aspects of time which mirror death at some distance are characterized by their flexibility. Their disposition and use can be varied for any occasion. Thus images may simply be stationed for mute notice where they are to be passed on the way to or from another subject. So in "The Collar" the invoked flowers, fruit, and other seasonal signs are less distant than they may appear to be from the death's-head and fears that are desperately rejected. To illustrate another inventive variation: in "The Answer" images related to death enclose a mental landscape that dissipates energies similar to those grimly concentrated in "Church-monuments."

Herbert's inventiveness is hardly in dispute, but it is worth dwelling, at least a little longer, on examples of imagistic adaptability. In "Church-rents and schismes" the image of a rose represents the church in its miserable state: "Brave rose, (alas!)." Dust in "Longing" and "Frailtie" has meanings and functions but distantly related to the dust of "Church-monuments." In the latter poem the image of monuments that "fall down flat" in dissolution anticipates a surprising image of destruction in "The Jews," when "the Church falling upon her face" performs a vitalizing, restorative office. Time itself in "The Discharge" is relieved of the larger part of its customary burden and does not "encroach upon deaths side." The central optimistic doctrine is that "Man and the present fit"; all the calm wisdom is directed against anxiety over the future. But wholly absent from consideration are perplexities drawn from the past, which do not go unremarked elsewhere.

In addition to the vocabulary of images that Herbert shares with other poets, his religious intentions make available the particular symbols of ecclesiastical tradition and of the church calendar and practice. Another large source, partly shared by secular poets but with obvious differences in application, is certain states of mind which by familiar usage acquire emblematic currency. Thus the desire to escape from oppressive longings can reflect the experience of the love poet or the religious man's conflicts, in which both the longing and the desire to escape are figures related, however differently, to actual and analogical instances of dying. That simple formula can contain many variables and their combinations. So too the states of languishing, or dullness, or glib hopefulness. So too the storms of nature from without, and the storms within, and those produced by the beloved. Thoughts of God's justice can evoke extended images of terror or hope ("Justice II"), or directly demonstrate the record of inner dissipation in outward efforts ("Justice I"). "Miserie" can undertake a full inventory of its nature, causes, and lamentable effects—all described with righteous passion but from a detached and privileged point of view. The last line reconstrues the whole discourse: "My God, I mean my self."

Because of his religious and poetic gifts and discipline and the sensitive responsiveness of his common humanity, Herbert is admittedly a special case. Still, what he shows is not different in kind from what other poets do. He can be "absolute for death," as in the rigorous concentration of "Church-monuments." At the other extreme he can apply some of the lessons of death with more than a token sympathy toward the limited but just claims of life in this world. They too, as the simple joys and the griefs and the sympathies of living, are sanctioned by God. One stanza of "The Flower" tells that story best:

> And now in age I bud again,
> After so many deaths I live and write;
> I once more smell the dew and rain,
> And relish versing: O my onely light,
>   It cannot be
>   That I am he
> On whom thy tempests fell all night.

Like other writers, he can explore the many and differing reflections of an image, or base his lyric discourse on the implications of an unstated similitude such as "mortification," the practice of purposive "dying," a free imitation expressing what passes between considerations of death in life and life in death.

His uniqueness does not lessen the value of his example. No one in English has so combined these three great powers: that of the inspired prophet or psalmist; that of being able to speak to God with perfect courtesy in a range that extends from the common to the exalted; that of commanding a sensitive personal art of veracity.

Expressed so, my admiration for Herbert declares a large optimism that may seem to reduce real difficulties—in the general subject of this book as well as in the use of images. We must not let Herbert's achievement overencourage our optimism, but also remember the exacting standards that govern his poetic methods and his personal art of veracity. As poet he draws on the more general sources of lyric: longing, apprehension, the desire for release. As a religious lyricist of the highest order he shows himself to be at once magnanimous and scrupulous in recognizing and honoring the dignity inherent in the particular truth of the individual occasion. This I believe to be close to the very center of his effective power over lyric feeling. To which I would add: the known answers, which are to be obeyed, do not stifle the truth of feelings which are to be composed.

In other writers, and not only in their didactic and hortatory works, the adaptability of images may become an invitation to abuse privilege. The literature of death is rife with images as with arguments that dominate expression by the unmitigated power to select, and to omit or divert some reflections in order to concentrate only those reflections that serve the chosen purpose.[6]

CHAPTER SEVENTEEN

Reasoning by Resemblances

Bentham judged a proposition true or false as it accorded or not with the result of his own inquiries; and did not search very curiously into what might be meant by the proposition, when it obviously did not mean what he thought true. With Coleridge, on the contrary, the very fact that any doctrine had been believed by thoughtful men, and received by whole nations or generations of mankind, was part of the problem to be solved, was one of the phenomena to be accounted for.

JOHN STUART MILL, *"Coleridge"*

So in divine learning we see how frequent Parables and Tropes are: for it is a rule, *That whatsoever science is not consonant to presuppositions, must pray in aid of similitudes.*

BACON, *The Advancement of Learning*

The preaching of the word hath been made a servant of ambitions, and a shop of many mens new-fangled wares. Almost every meanes between God and man, suffers some adulteratings and disguises: But prayer least.

DONNE, *Sermons*

In the study of sacred Scripture there were recognizable differences between the latitude of interpretation acceptable for purposes of individual devotion and the stricter methods expected from reputable theologians, old or new, presenting, to others, pious, learned, and reasoned arguments. To a hostile or impatient view the differences may seem negligible. To a sympathetic view, tempered by the knowledge that the differences were real to intelligent citizens of another age, but also tempered by the knowledge provided by historical perspective, further discriminations are available. One can observe singular opinions, however produced, becoming general and acquiring a history of their own. Moreover, in reading history and its interpretations one can observe major and minor shifts in the methods and some of the aims of scriptural interpretation. The Reformation broke with the old four-level method and its permissible elaborations of allegory. Instead, the Reformation stressed the importance of the literal, historical level and therefore needed to develop, not without some strain, a new interpretation of what "literal" really meant. Furthermore, the needs and dangers of the times, whenever these were recognized, were likely to influence casual interpretations of the moment but also the serious handling of texts by authoritative champions. In addition, there was always the transitory work done in sermons to a special audience for a special occasion. Nevertheless, in spite of the qualifying remarks I have been making, serious religious thinkers believed that the truth was there in the text and, in spite of human fallibility, a system of reasoning was available which had developed its own principles and applications and ways of discriminating among the degrees of probability. The learned might argue about the relative worth of resemblances and the stricter methods of logic, or about the weight as evidence of any pattern of resemblances or any disposition of analogies; still, in religious reasoning a linking of resemblances accepted as authoritative could not be denied as having the force of reasoned analogy. What moves a private insight or a public argument to the stage of a dominant historical career is a humbling question in all branches of human endeavor.

Members of the militant church, the community of the living who aspired to join saints, martyrs, and the blessed dead who would rise to membership in the triumphant church in heaven, could not be indifferent to the obvious fact that all competing arguments concerning doctrine and interpretation could not be equally valid. The reformed churches encouraged individual study of Scripture, not without guidance and the kinds of control exerted by authoritative agreement on crucial points, but not able or willing to furnish institutional validity to established rules and sanctifications assuring salvation. As fact, the death of every person is an individual event. The fact lends itself to psychological bewilderment, traumas of incredulity, and transferences but can also be muted or molded by patience, knowledge, and skill. The general loosening of institutional supports, along with the increasingly widespread sense that the moment of death was, in relation to the last day of judgment, a preliminary hearing, or trial, or more, unquestionably released old feelings latent in the knowledge that all die, but each dies once, old feelings in new surges that had to be mastered. To emphasize the connections between death and salvation by scrutinizing and explicating them with prolonged attention could and did heighten and extend the individuality of personal death. I am reviewing matters that have been touched on before, but now for another purpose: to bring together the acknowledged feelings related to all stages of striving for salvation and the value of reasoned acceptance traditional in the ideals of Christian death. For the individual feelings must do their part and carry their share of a good argument not to be read in the study by the learned but acted upon.

However great his desire for exact knowledge in formal discourse, a good poet cannot be indifferent to both the indispensability of, and the rightness of choice involved in, the uses of resemblances in poetic discourse. I draw another example from George Herbert. In "The H. Scriptures II" he begins by affirming his knowledge that all the separate "lights" of Scripture "combine"; they are "configurations" and "constellations of the storie." But how the unity of the whole was made is a subject that exceeds human understanding while it inspires human longing to know:

> This verse marks that, and both do make a motion
> Unto a third, that ten leaves off doth lie:
> . . . .
>
> Such are thy secrets, which my life makes good,
> And comments on thee: for in ev'ry thing
> Thy words do finde me out, and parallels bring,
> And in another make me understood.

While believing in the inexhaustible profundities of scriptural meanings, and well aware of conditional uncertainties in interpretation ("both do make a motion / Unto") and of the need to temper inspiration by sound discipline, he nevertheless makes a characteristic personal statement in the poem. He chooses not to exclude the personal evidence concerning the efficacy of the "word" from the intellectual analysis of meaning. To the speaker of the poem, who certainly did not regard himself as unlike the probable reader of his poem, the most important acts of commenting on Scripture are the demonstrations of understanding communicated by the life he lives. These will make him *understood in another,* the comments expressed by one life entering the very structure of another life. The human "secret" is to study both the word and "Gods Worke in his heart through the Word."[1]

There is an implicit correspondence between the absoluteness of divine initiative and the human initiative of marking resemblances, motions, and parallels. God's words in Scripture "do finde me out, and parallels bring." So divine communication is felt as immediate. The right human response is partly that of discursive reasoning and analysis, to understand, and partly that of assimilating the recognized parallels into the structure of personal life, to confirm and demonstrate the conclusions. Though the unity of God's "configurations" is not be understood at the level of "how," it is nevertheless to be answered at the level of "why," as an intuitive understanding of God's purpose. (That understanding is not itself the subject of analysis.) The human answer that is presented imitates the divine unity in the smaller world of personal life, by an architectonic unity of living thought. And so the mystery of God's "secrets" is repeated on a modest human scale. For the immediacy of communication made by direct contact, or the sense of contact, with one of blessed life speaks in ways not open to the eloquence of words or the convincing power of thought. With the assistance of some brief explication, Socrates would have understood the argument and might have thought another understood him.

What we see in Herbert's sonnet is a bona fide argument in which personal feelings are presented as the contributing materials of inference. The argument is figurative and subtle, making and requiring interpretations, but also precisely reasoned within acceptable rules of both theology and poetry. The discourse does not depend on fiction or pretense or other privileges of poetic speech, though it surely owes much to the kinds of exacting discipline good poets impose on themselves. Once again Herbert's example provides a special case. His figurative argument is a tour de force of convincing personal integrity, at once complete and brief, brilliant and humble in its combining intuition and plain good sense familiar to all. But when we step back from this height of dazzling realization, we should not be blinded to the existence of other possibilities of making poetic arguments out of similitudes, human feelings, and reason.

Certain images by long usage acquired something of the capacity of scriptural verses to "make a motion" toward another image, to "combine," and to generate "parallels." When Donne wishes to persuade his mistress to make their lovers' parting peaceful and optimistic, he produces as the right model a scene of the good and happy death of the virtuous:

> As virtuous men passe mildly away,
>   And whisper to their soules, to goe,
> Whilst some of their sad friends doe say,
>   The breath goes now, and some say, no:
>
> So let us melt, and make no noise.
>   ("A Valediction: forbidding mourning")

The large similitude between death and parting makes available a wealth of arguments concerning the desirability of a good death. A small similitude, released by the choice of a single word, may go unnoticed. The melting is not, as John Carey proposes, one more example of Donne's obsession with thoughts of dissolution, but is instead a translated echo signifying the peaceful death of the man of reason and self-control.[2]

The vocabulary of death is well furnished with standard indirections and is hospitable to new figures of speech. When Milton's Eve eats the apple and delights in the taste and in the high expectation of knowledge, Milton combines death and eager ignorance and invents the idiom and syntax that tell a strange story under the auspices of indistinct "constellations," as if one were speaking around the impediment of food: "Greedily she engorged without restraint / And knew not eating death" (PL 9.791–92). An old image often coming to mind was the brief narrative contained in the thought of life as a loan called in by death. That it was a pagan invention, like death as law, did not disturb the proper Christian definition of death as divine punishment. The image was useful and well worn and offered a kind of expressive neutrality which suited some circumstances of feeling. So Donne can write, opening a sonnet on his dead wife, "Since she whome I lovd hath payd her last debt / To Nature." And Jonson can write, not without bitterness, on the death of his first son:

> Seven years thou wert lent to me, and I thee pay,
> Exacted by thy fate, on the just day.

I conclude this stage of the discussion of similitude and reason by illustrating the use of three basic images for reflecting death: sleep, time, and love. They have the virtue of not seeming tired when repeated in the same ways, and they also possess a considerable range of unusual suggestiveness. First, sleep, the irrepressible similitude spreading easily through the obvious likenesses of appearance and illusion and the unlikenesses of common reality. If the life of the body is thought of as unreal, the further comparison of life as the dream of existence suggests itself. If only the life of the soul is thought of as real, the actual or metaphorical sleep of the body can be thought of as the waking time of the soul.[3] Sleep is an entrance to thoughts of periodicity, such as night, winter, time, and eternity: "One short sleepe past, wee wake eternally." It is a time of restoration, safety, and comfort, or of premonitions and terrors. Dreams may comment on past or future life or act as the authorized messengers of death, or one may imagine their bringing unknown contents to the sleep of death.

These patterns are familiar in literary and other usage, but particular examples often have both expected "motions" between sleep and

death and some unexpected turns. When Shakespeare's Octavius Caesar
looks at the dead Cleopatra, he becomes, against his bent of nature and
destiny, a poet:

> If they had swallow'd poison, 'twould appear
> By external swelling; but she looks like sleep,
> As she would catch another Antony
> In her strong toil of grace.
>
> (5.2.345–48)

After his coroner's eye rejects the cause of death as poison, he takes
another look and sees a figure in repose, inviting erotic thoughts, which
are prudently transferred to "another Antony." Implicit in the beauty of
sleep there would seem to be a strange heightening of the kind experienced in some works of art and here also influenced by the knowledge
that the imagined sleep *is* death. The last act of nature seems to be
surpassing or here reversing the standard Renaissance aesthetic doctrine
and to be completing art. But if I have gone a little too far now, let me
add that Caesar is no spokesman for the later Romantic obsession with
the beauty of death.

Among the slowly changing styles of tomb sculpture, in the kneeling or recumbent figures the sense of sacred, waiting repose expresses
an image of religious sleep as tranquil hope. My next example is concerned with such and is also from drama, so I hasten to admit that the
poetry of drama is often a special case. For the poetry is part of a larger
argument in which movements and actions corroborate, contradict, or
increase the density of meaning in spoken words. When a principal
actor speaks, it is from an evolving function and individuality of character; where, when, and to whom he speaks are factors of what is then
said. In a separate lyric poem the speaker does not have these advantages
and their space, but can manage his limitations well enough and even
provide some valuable lessons for the dramatic poet.

I come to the example, Shakespeare's Lady Macbeth on the subject
of sleep. There are two preliminary remarks, one a natural observation:

> When Duncan is asleep
> (Whereto the rather shall his day's hard journey
> Soundly invite him).
>
> (1.7.61–63)

The second is a contemptuous comparison of sleep and death. She will
ply Duncan's chamberlains with "wine and wassail" and so alter the
nature of memory and reason that Duncan will be left "unguarded":

When in swinish sleep
Their drenched natures lies as in a death.
(1.7.67–68)

Then, alarmed that Macbeth has failed, even though she has done her part and has also carefully laid out the grooms' daggers ("He could not miss 'em"), she mentions a moment of her own encounter with the sleeping Duncan:

Had he not resembled
My father as he slept, I had done't.
(2.2.12–13)

Whether she is remembering her father laid out in death or simply asleep, her memory ("the warder of the brain") responds to something essential in the physical likeness—for her, perhaps irrepressible feelings of filial reverence or a disturbing thought of the common exchangeability, now a planned exchange, between sleep and death, but also surely a sense of sleep lying "as in a death" of sacred repose. Then, after Macbeth has spoken his anguished poetry of sleep and has refused in fear to return to the place of murder, she declares:

Infirm of purpose!
Give me the daggers. The sleeping and the dead
Are but as pictures; 'tis the eye of childhood
That fears a painted devil. If he do bleed,
I'll gild the faces of the grooms withal,
For it must seem their guilt.

(2.2.49–54)

Resemblances are renounced with contempt, along with what "the eye of childhood" may see or remember, and whatever fear she felt in her experience with the sleeping Duncan is now transformed and dismissed in the image of "a painted devil." She confirms her resolution by the verbal play on "gild" and "guilt," and by her own determination of what "must seem."

My last two examples are less intricate and more playful. In them sleep "bears a taste of death," as Denham wrote, but then clarified excessively, as others would not: "And both are the same thing at last."[4]

Unlike time, sleep does not lend itself well to arguments based upon the condition of antagonism. Its threat of unattainability may approach alienation and otherness but chiefly as an estrangement, like a dear love that has turned away or a familiar part of one's life that can be "murdered" in ignorance as by Macbeth. Or sleep may abscond from its due resemblance of death, as Henry King discovered while inventorying the ills of life from the perspective of the sickbed, where "all forms of death" surround him, and "He copies death in any form but sleep."[5] Another poem ends, "I long to kiss the image of my death." It sounds like a modern poem, but it is the conclusion of a sonnet by an insomniac William Drummond who seeks ease, even "feigned solace" for "a true-felt woe." If the usual terms of praise, such as rest, peace, comfort, forgetfulness, will not move the "deaf god" to wonted grace,

> Come as thou wilt, and what thou wilt bequeath;
> I long to kiss the image of my death.[6]

In the great lyrics discussed in Part 2 of this book, in which the poet drew upon thoughts of his own death, the imagining of time evolved as if by a spontaneous creation, an apparently collateral action that when it is finally in place is revealed as a master configuration. In "The Passionate Man's Pilgrimage," "Hymne to God my God in my sicknesse," and "Death," each evolving movement is unique, responding, one may think, to an intuitive necessity not acknowledged or explained in the body of the discourse. Time was not a theme, or a concept for purposes of reference or examination, but a force clear in its effect though indeterminable as cause or motive. What we may recognize, at the very least, is that the effect is a certain sign of the poet's depth of engagement and control of his subject.

Poems on the death of another, discussed in Part 3, did not need to master a personal struggle with past, present, and future. In the public elegies fixed obligations were prominent—the necessity of giving place to the traditional parts of praise, grief, and consolation. When solemn, enclosed time was completed, the shared time of the living could be acknowledged as beginning again. These are poems directed toward reconciliation. To those alive, much of human experience can be measured by, referred to, commented on, by time or by the many images that serve as passages toward remembering and anticipating the properties of time. For the dead, the engagement with personal time has ended; mourners may prefer to talk of other things.

In the more private poems on the death of another, the weight of time was felt and responded to; still, the more urgent thoughts of present loss left no opening for the shaping imagination of time.

Time and its agents, mutability and death, haunted the Renaissance mind and aroused thoughts of human aspiration and constraint, of man's proud, reaching spirit and the extremes of grandeur and reduction. Images of time can reflect the intimacies of breath or pulse, or furnish the materials for arguing against a fixed antagonist, and time can figure the absolute otherness of death. Speeches on the seven ages of man do not need to mention death, but in Herbert's "Mortification" every stage of life offers a pregnant image of dying, like the stanza on middle age:

> When man grows staid and wise,
> Getting a house and home, where he may move
> Within the circle of his breath,
> Schooling his eyes;
> That dumbe inclosure maketh love
> Unto the coffin, that attends his death.

The verses Raleigh left at the Gatehouse the day of his execution begin, "Even such is time," which "takes in trust" and "pays us" and "Shuts up the story of our days." To the man about to die time is the agent of death. To the author writing the last paragraphs of his *History of the World,* death has a force that, however derived from time, seems to act as if autonomously and, like an oracle immediately believed, sums up the wisdom of the world (and especially to the "great lords of the world" who have complained against infidelity, time, destiny, and fortune):

> They neglect the advice of God, while they enjoy life, or hope
> it; but they follow the counsell of Death, upon his first ap-
> proach. It is he that puts into man all the wisdome of the
> world, without speaking a word. . . . It is therfore Death
> alone that can suddenly make man to know himselfe. . . . O
> eloquent, just, and mightie Death! whom none could advise,
> thou hast perswaded; what none hath dared, thou hast done;
> and whom all the world hath flattered, thou only hast cast out
> of the world and despised. Thou hast drawn together all the
> farre stretched greatnesse, all the pride, crueltie, and ambition
> of man, and covered it all over with these two narrow words,
> *Hic jacet.*[7]

In discussing "Images of Reflection," I touched on *carpe diem* poems and their ways of interpreting the lessons of time to love's advantage. Images that could be made to reflect aspects of time and mortality were not in short supply, and the book of nature was always open for ready reference. Henry Vaughan demonstrates a standard method of moralizing "natural histories":

> This *bird* may very well signifie our *life,* and by the *river*
> we may understand *time,* upon whose brink we are always
> pearching. *Time* runs faster then any *streame,* and our *life* is

swifter than any *bird,* and oft-times all the pomp of it comes to an end in one *day,* yea sometimes in an *houre.* There is no *object* we can look upon, but will do us the kindnesse to put us in minde of our mortality, if we would be so wise as to make use of it. The *day* dyes into *night,* the *spring* into *winter, flowers* have their *rootes* ever in their *graves, leaves* loose their *greenenesse,* and drop under our feete where they *flye* about and *whisper* unto us. . . . And if from these *frailer objects* we turne our Eyes to things that are more *permanent,* we may by the doctrine of *contrarieties* make them as useful as any of the former.[8]

I think I may spare further examples. Others less naked have appeared in previous pages, and Spenser's use of lily and rose and the contextual complexity of "So passeth, in the passing of a day" illustrated the finer possibilities of what may be done. I shall end with a couple of examples of another kind.

The factual measurements of time, when taken as a figurative reference to one's own day of death, may exert some direct torsion on the unguarded feelings. In *Measure for Measure,* Isabella tries to shame her brother with numbers chosen as if at random:

> O, I do fear thee, Claudio, and I quake,
> Lest thou a feverous life shouldst entertain,
> And six or seven winters more respect
> Than a perpetual honor.
>
> (3.1.73-76)

Robert Parsons does not use such numbers with uncalculated spontaneity. He offers his religious patient a generous prediction of future life, doubles that, and then divides by ten and what remains by twelve—all preparatory to a deathbed scene in which time is measured by the expectation of moments:

> Imagine then (my frende) thow I saye which art so freshe and froelicke at this daie, that the ten, twentie, or two yeres, or perhaps two monethes, which thow hast yet to lyve, were now ended and that thow were even at this present, stretched out uppon a bed, wearied and worne with dolour and paine, thy carnall frindes aboute the weepinge and howlinge, the phisitions departed with theire fees, as havinge geeven the over, and thow lyinge alone mute and dumme in most pitifull agonie, expectinge from moment to moment, the last stroake of death to be geeven the.[9]

George Herbert could deploy the numbers casually, in a detached manner, measuring not the time until death, and its latent anxieties, but the probable span within which, depending on the soil and contributing factors, a buried body might be expected to decompose sufficiently to make room for a new corpse, or for whatever reason become a visible object. This follows the opening stanza of "Death" and extends the erroneous former concept of death as something represented by the "hideous" remains of skull and bones. Though the subject is not inviting, and though there is a brief, erroneous opportunity for the reader to mistake the time as referring to his own approaching death, there is no personal threat intended, but only a dry comment in the process, not yet finished, of correcting an error of the past:

> For we consider'd thee as at some six
> Or ten yeares hence,
> After the losse of life and sense,
> Flesh being turn'd to dust, and bones to sticks.

Finally, I want to mention one image of an entirely different kind in Marvell's "To his Coy Mistress." It is not the extravagant unrolling of time in the first stanza, or the distinction, for purposes of assessing time, between dust and ashes, or the devouring of time at once rather than languishing, or the "Desarts of vast Eternity"; it is:

> But at my back I alwaies hear
> Times winged Charriot hurrying near.

Images of time prefer to speak to the mind and emotions through the eye. Here we have an exception, an allegorical vehicle that is named but exists chiefly because it is heard, behind one, always; its "hurrying" motion addresses the individual ear, which is the chosen access for measuring the degree of closing distance.

We reason by means of similarities and differences. *Eros* and *thanatos* have a long history of opposition; they are not unacquainted with each other's secret thoughts. Human love and love of the divine use each other's images and vocabularies but try not to forget the differences. Love of the divine, among other benefits, grants reasoning about death certain prerogatives. For those writing about love or death all differences had their convenient and necessary uses, and so did all discoverable affinities.

Though the speech has personal resonances in the mouth of Cleopatra, she is not saying what no one else might have thought when, about to die herself, she witnesses the sudden, quiet death of Iras:

> If thou and nature can so gently part,
> The stroke of death is as a lover's pinch,
> Which hurts, and is desir'd.
>> (*Antony and Cleopatra*, 5.2.294–96)

The chaste heroine of a serious comedy finds herself saying more than she might intend about the hidden connections between death and sensuality. Thus the Isabella of *Measure for Measure* can proclaim to Angelo:

> That is, were I under the terms of death,
> Th' impression of keen whips I'ld wear as rubies,
> And strip myself to death, as to a bed
> That longing have been sick for, ere I'ld yield
> My body up to shame.
>> (2.4.100–104)

A masculine voice as from her "father's grave" speaks less colorfully, and the brother's desire seems much indebted to resolution:

> If I must die,
> I will encounter darkness as a bride,
> And hug it in my arms.
>> (3.1.82–84)

Other images are almost as familiar. Among the many "feigned deaths" of poetry, lovers' partings begin with a known basis in "sweet sorrow" and are free to draw on analogies, of which the separation of soul and body is not to be forgotten. Nor are the metaphoric exchanges among spiritual ecstasy, sexual climax, and death. In meditative compliments, the lover can renounce all the world for the beloved and imagine "one little room" into "an everywhere"; or, alternately, summon the "soul" of the world as an appropriate essence that love possesses.[10] Between the lover and his dead beloved the earth "such a strange eclipse doth make / As ne're was read in Almanake," but may be read in the witty schedules of love:

> And the conjunction of our lips
> Not kisses make but an Eclipse.[11]

Or the lover, neglecting the whole world of appearances and others, and transcribing a conclusion of his own feelings, can say, as in Shakespeare's sonnet 112,

> You are so strongly in my purpose bred,
> That all the world besides methinks are dead.[12]

Or the lover can slowly turn over an image of winter (with lingering retrospection of "yellow leaves, or none, or few," and bare, cold, shaking boughs "where late the sweet birds sang") and can draw out twilight after sunset fading in the west, all of which night will take away, "Death's second self, that seals up all in rest"; and can dwell on the past and future history of the last glowing embers of a fire: so Shakespeare in sonnet 73 reviews what the person addressed will surely know but will be reminded of by another argument of love:

> This thou perceiv'st, which makes thy love more strong,
> To love that well which thou must leave ere long.

Time being what it is, the warning images are free to adjust their evolvement in whatever sequence the mind chooses. So the lessons of *memento mori* do not quite exclude the younger lover.

In reasoning about the griefs of love, poets feel entitled to draw upon all the records of human misery and feel no more obliged to observe strict decorum, or the rules of logic, or a balanced view, than do those who meditate on death by arraigning all the illusory evidence of life. When love is denied, both the absence and the presence of the beloved "kill." In *The Phoenix Nest,* 1593, a poem that may be Raleigh's ends its mixed survey of grim cheer with the retrospective summation, "Death was the end of every such desire."[13] But the denial of death may also be part of the torment of living and loving and may exact ingenious pain. For the lover who sees and hears laughter and scorn from without may turn the view inward as he sees his life wearing away and finds himself despising himself:

> And most of all wherewith I strive
> Is that I see myself alive.[14]

Or the poet in pain may recognize a surprisingly simple analogy: that his personal necessity is quite like the higher law that declares that willingness to accept the gift and good of life requires an equal assent to the ill. Since love "is a care that doth to life belong," therefore, in spite of the "torments,"

> Yet had I rather thus for to remain
> Than laugh and live, not feeling lover's pain.[15]

In the seventeenth century the standards and taste for poetic reasoning responded to the currents of a new age. Marvell, who took full advantage of coming late, reworked old and new with a perfection that signaled the end of one age as the beginning, and the necessity, of another. To be brief: he can write triumphant exercises on the issues of love and death. The violent history of "The Unfortunate Lover" ends with a posthumous chapter:

> Yet dying leaves a Perfume here,
> And Musick within every Ear:
> And he in Story only rules,
> In a Field *Sable* a Lover *Gules*.

In "On a Drop of Dew" and "A Dialogue between the Soul and Body" the love of the soul is entirely directed toward dying "here" in order to regain life at the source—old themes, and answers, elegantly revived and refined.

In other poems he can cultivate naivety, for instance in "A Dialogue between Thyrsis and Dorinda," where a small dramatic narrative discovers and pursues the simple conclusion to all the passionate praises of the life of immortality. Thyrsis instructs the innocent Dorinda as if he were a "shepherd" Adam acting in a small, rhymed version of *Paradise Lost* intended for a children's performance. She brings up the subject of death, very prettily, and he moves by adjusted steps to a description of the life of eternity "accommodated" to the experience and dreams of shepherds. She is troubled and demands proof that the story is true, requiring in her own story-language that he convince her "By bidding, with mee, all adieu." Thyrsis answers in the oldest language of love:

> I cannot live without thee, I
> Will for thee, much more with thee dye.

Upon which they speak in chorus, Dorinda's voice perhaps a little more emphatic as they propose to arrange for the "charge o' the sheep" and to make a potion of poppies. They will drink until they "weep" (unexplained): "So shall we smoothly pass away in sleep." The poem is an extraordinary feat, and we know little of its provenance except the state of confused transmission. The inner logic of its irony matches the more relentless single-mindedness of some Tudor love poetry, but the splendid simplicity is another matter. It reads like a serio-comic miniaturization, translated for another genre, of the human drama in *Paradise Lost*. And if the pastoral dialogue did (one wonders) precede all acquaintance with the epic and its plans, we may still think with conjectural delight of the connoisseur's pleasure Marvell's great friend might have had in listening to this entertainment.

Except for some of Marvell, however, and some of the darker poems of Donne, poets in writing of love and death are usually writing about love while drawing upon the expressive resources of death. The one major exception is Crashaw, who is more than half in love with strenuous death. Magdalene, "The Weeper," is a walking example of love as death-in-life. The world itself is "lovesick," but that is almost incidental: "Love thou art absolute sole Lord / Of life and death." Love is also the self-consuming "sacrifice," the divine "annihilation(s)." St. Theresa, being denied simple martyrdom, must be Love's victim until her "numerous" religious deaths "shall all at last dye into one."[16] And most to my point, the powerful prayer of invocation that ends "The Flaming Heart" of 1652:

> O thou undanted daughter of desires!
> By all thy dowr of *Lights* and *Fires;*
> By all the eagle in thee, all the dove;
> By all thy lives and deaths of love;
> By thy larg draughts of intellectuall day,
> And by thy thirsts of love more large then they;
> By all thy brim-fill'd Bowles of feirce desire
> By thy last Morning's draught of liquid fire;
> By the full kingdome of that finall kisse
> That seiz'd thy parting Soul, and seal'd thee his;
> By all the heav'ns thou hast in him
> (Fair sister of the *Seraphim!*)
> By all of *Him* we have in *Thee;*
> Leave nothing of my *Self* in me.
> Let me so read thy life, that I
> Unto all life of mine may dy.
>
> (p. 65)

This has been an intentionally brief survey of some of the images, their use, and their adaptability. Whenever love radically disturbs the orientation toward living in the world, the lover's fancy turns to thoughts of death or to images at one remove or more. When it creates the acute sense of loss of self, love suggests obvious analogies with death; so may the disastrous losing or the ecstatic winning of the other. On union with the other in death, poetry says little worth saying that is not quoted from religion, though Donne and Milton show how much can be said by not quoting too much. But I do not want to leave the subject without a word in behalf of the independent inventiveness of love. Even the myth of Narcissus and its link with death, actual and metaphoric, can be rescued from that association as well as from the familiar scandal of self-love. So Raleigh, prevented by the reasoning of love from gouging out his eye or stabbing his heart, thinks further:

I found my selfe was cause of all my smart,
And tolde my selfe, my selfe now slay I will:
But when I found my selfe to you was true,
I lov'd my selfe, bicause my selfe lov'd you.[17]

CHAPTER EIGHTEEN

Intricacies

Nor I, nor any man that but man is,
With nothing shall be pleas'd, till he be eas'd
With being nothing.
                    SHAKESPEARE, *Richard II*

And if you, at the youthful age of fifty-four, can't help thinking so
often of death, are you surprised that at 80 1/2 I keep brooding on
whether I shall reach the age of my father and brother, or even that of
my mother, tortured as I am by the conflict between the desire for
rest, the dread of renewed suffering (which a prolonged life would
mean), and by the anticipation of sorrow at being separated from
everything to which I am still attached?
                    FREUD, *Letters*

Dear Madam (or Miss?)
Your mysterious and beautiful book has pleased me to an extent that
makes me unsure of my judgment. . . . And with it such a diffident
letter! Can it be that your modesty causes you to underrate your own
value? Who are you? Where did you acquire all the knowledge expressed in your book? Judging by the priority you grant to death, one
is led to conclude that you are very young.
Won't you give me the pleasure of paying me a visit one day? I have
time in the mornings.
                    FREUD, *Letters*[1]

D_{ead} is certain, but almost everything related to its advent, especially
the when and the how, is uncertain. These are truths everyone can
understand, but it is the kind of knowledge that bristles and swarms
with human efforts to gain and to hold a reasonable control over
the certainty and the uncertainties. That too is a common truth, of im-
mense bulk in its known history of manifestation, to which we can add
the private histories we know; there are also innumerable lost and un-
disclosed private histories. The record of human response, whatever
else one may say of it, and its venturing to explain other matters important to human life and death would appear to be the kind of truth that

depends upon an earlier discovery and derives from the original certainty and (at least in more advanced societies) the secondary uncertainties.

The purpose of beginning so platitudinously is to center attention
on the uncertainties, for these are shared by life, which provides indispensable materials by which and against which most of the uncertainties (and the unknowns) of death are to be explained. Why we die and
the significance of our deaths are subjects religion has both embraced
and inherited—so too, therefore, the responsibility of preparing individuals for death and setting the forms and limits of grief and consolation. Grief has its practical necessities rooted in human nature, learned
by experience and observation, and respected by those who have the
cure of souls. The needs of consolation are partly similar but are more
capable of listening to intellectual and spiritual persuasion. The records
of consolation are more ancient than writing and speak to archeologists.
Though the nature of consolation may have changed very little, the
terms, like the objects and subjects, have changed many times.

I mention these matters with some abruptness, for though they are
an inextricable part of my general subject, grief and consolation are
central only to the experience of survivors and mourners. To grief
uncertainty can have little real interest until grief has lapsed into sadness
or melancholy. Consolation has already turned to thoughts of deaths
still to come before it can make out, with any usefulness, murmuring
about the uncertainty of life; all such thoughts must be kept safely
distinct from thoughts of the certain rest, peace, and salvation of the
dead. In the following discourse I look at topics and examples that
illustrate the presence and something of the character of uncertainties as
they are expressed in the language of those who write about dying and
death to those who will have in mind their own death.

I return to a passage that furnished an example for another context,[2] Donne's powerful description of how rhetoric works upon the
weak:

> The way of Rhetorique in working upon weake men, is first
> to trouble the understanding, to displace, and to discompose,
> and disorder the judgement, to smother and bury in it, or to
> empty it of former apprehensions and opinions, and to shake
> that beliefe, with which it had possessed it self before, and
> then when it is thus melted, to powre it into new molds, when
> it is thus mollified, to stamp and imprint new formes, new
> images, new opinions in it. (*Sermons*, 2:282)

The account is remarkably full in its compressed, imagistic brevity
when it tells how men are taken apart; how they are put together again is

more general: when they are ready they are stamped with "new formes, new images, new opinions." Let me add two other remarks by Donne also quoted in the previous context: "The Echo returns the last syllables; The heart concludes with his conclusions, whom we have been willing to hearken unto" (7:408); and "It is not the depth, nor the wit, nor the eloquence of the Preacher that pierces us, but his nearenesse, that he speaks to my conscience . . . as though he had read the book of the day of Judgement already" (3:142). The preacher who "pierces" by his "nearenesse" resembles the Holy Ghost who works directly "upon the soule and conscience" but is "a Metaphoricall, and Figurative expresser of himselfe, to the reason, and understanding of man" (9:328). (The preacher who makes one think "he had read the book of the day of Judgement already" is also figurative to the mind.)

The description of rhetoric need not be limited to its effects on "weake men," for it applies well enough to all sinners and in particular to those whom God or His servants convert from old ways to new. As for those "whom we have been willing to hearken unto," though Donne does not mention it, they may echo the heart's desire for good as well as ill; for they may also speak to the conscience by means of a more intimate "nearenesse" that may not pierce but still may, as consciousness discovers the truth of its real desire, draw the heart's "conclusions." The passage describing the way of rhetoric does not include an image of piercing; its way is one that first disorders and then undoes thoroughly in order to recreate as it wills material as pliable as the clay out of which God made Adam. The last step is brief and general. The power as described lies in the destructive process, which is both systematic and cumulative. Both are necessary, but it is the cumulative that takes control of the power. Piercing *nearness* can act at once, and the willing heart, which has listened for an indeterminate length of time, can *conclude* with no more delay than the return of an echo. But in the paradigm of rhetoric, acts of psychical force repeated like blows gradually reduce the listener to the condition of complete receptivity. If the subject is death, strong men may turn weak under the weight.

If the work is to strengthen readers against the anxieties and disasters of life and death, or to reconcile them to a great personal loss, the way of rhetoric (and philosophy) will also be systematic and cumulative in assembling the arguments that heal and renew the order of life. After the death of Beatrice, Dante turned to Cicero's *De Amicitia* and Boethius's *The Consolation of Philosophy.* In Canto X of *Paradiso,* Boethius is "l'anima santa" of the eighth light: "through seeing every good, the sainted soul rejoices who makes the fallacious world manifest to any who listen well to him."[3] If the reader of Boethius is to see every good, he must listen well to arguments that repeatedly dismantle false thoughts in a dialogue that leads error into chosen positions and then silences it by the privileged intensity of rebuttal. Even in the best of consolations the fixed purpose cannot permit much lingering on alternative views, and the purpose cannot be achieved without accumulating a considerable pressure of evidence leading in a single direction.

For more than five centuries the *contemptus mundi* was a favorite topic for earnestly piling up all the evidence against the worth of life in this world. Being more than loosely systematic was less important than being thorough in collecting quotations, commonplaces, vivid examples, clichés—whatever had been thought and written. A new example, or turn of argument, or phrase, was likely to be incorporated in subsequent collections, but novelty was no more than a minor, random grace in a subject that maintained its steady appeal long after it had been effectively ransacked. The most successful work, judged by its popularity, was *De Miseria Humane Conditionis,* written in 1195 by Cardinal Lotario dei Segni who would become the respected Pope Innocent III. It was, though relatively short, an encyclopedia that included the best and much of the rest that had been said: (1) on the more repulsive miseries of life from conception to old age; (2) on the vanity of human desires for riches, pleasures, and honors; (3) on the decay of the body, the pains of hell, and the coming of the Day of Judgment.

That so much could be said on the subject, and that it could be repeated with satisfaction, certainly contributed to its settled authority. But one cannot ignore the enduring appeal of the thesis itself. It provided a single answer to everything that seemed wrong and could go wrong in the experiences of life and fitted smoothly into other systematic arguments that explained the prominent problems of life and death. In the early seventeenth century, writing on the death of his first son, Ben Jonson reached out to touch the theme. Fifty years later, contemplating the "leaden slumber" of Cromwell's dead body, in a moment unlike anything else in his long "Poem upon the Death of O. C.," Marvell burst out:

> Oh! humane glory, vaine, oh! death, oh! wings,
> Oh! worthlesse world! oh transitory things!
>
> (lines 255–56)

In his *Flores Solitudinis* of 1654 Henry Vaughan, writing in "sicknesse and retirement," published his translations of two treatises on the subject; for "we live in an age, which hath made this very Proposition (though suspected of Melancholie,) mighty pleasing, and even meane witts begin to like it; the wiser sort alwaies did." In his "Advertisement" to the translation of Eucherius, whose arguments rendered riches and honors "not only contemptible, but odious," he concludes by defending the relative brevity: "Much more might have been spoken against them, but (seeing the Age we live in hath made all his Arguments, Demonstrations) he hath in my judgement spoken enough."[4]

In *Measure for Measure* the Duke delivers a thirty-five-line lecture to Claudio on the theme, "Be absolute for death." It is a compendium of the main traditional argument, long enough to make Claudio reply, "I humbly thank you. . . . Let it come on"; and long enough to fill and prepare the stage time before Isabella's entrance. But this is drama, and the privileged argument is opposed by other forces. When Claudio catches a glimpse of hope in Isabella's clumsy exposition of what Angelo has offered, the repressed fear of death pours out with the eloquence and convincing originality of a true nightmare. He ends:

> The weariest and most loathed worldly life
> That age, ache, penury, and imprisonment
> Can lay on nature is a paradise
> To what we fear of death.
>
> (3.1.128–31)

The potential for complexity when there is conflict shows a different side when Uncle Claudius, in the second scene of *Hamlet,* goes to work upon the unreasonably extended "mourning duties," as Claudius calls them, of Hamlet for his father. It is not a long speech but it seems very long, for Claudius lays on Hamlet an unbroken succession of the appropriate reasons and well-established wise thoughts for setting a "term" to "sorrow." He calls in other arguments to prove the grief "unmanly" and "unschool'd," perilously tending toward impiety. The cumulative effect produces growing discomfort as the rhetoric of the speech turns us into strong and unwilling listeners. The use of personal prerogative, the exhibition before a public audience, and the motives—all are lightly concealed under the thin veil of power administering benevolent correction. The tone is self-congratulatory, the adornments are crude; though almost everything is repeated wisdom intended to be systematic and cumulative, the man in the speech keeps edging toward personal emergence. He comes closest when the rhetoric of his "common theme," the "death of fathers," leads him to cite the doctrine of necessity as the operative law of reason "From the first corse till he that dies today." He is covered by a slight error: Abel was not a father.

In his *Anniversaries* Donne tries hard to be systematic and to cover all the old topics but not in the old ways, and he certainly aims at a cumulative effect. But I want to turn to a related effect that depends on one's awareness of the familiar arguments concerning the miseries of life that lead to death. This awareness gives unexpected body to the opportune image entering into a traditional way of thinking and its familiar images, a way that has gained a special authority augmented by an unchallenged continuity of repetition. Life is a journey, we know, and the end is rest and salvation for the faithful:

> This unspeakable, this unimaginable happiness is this Salvation, and therefore let us be glad when this is brought neer us. And this is brought neerer and neerer unto us, as we come neerer and neerer to our end. As he that travails weary, and late towards a great City, is glad when he comes to a place of execution, because he knows that is neer the town; so when thou comest to the gate of death, be glad of that, for it is but one step from that to thy *Jerusalem*. (*Sermons*, 2:266)

It may be hard "to repress a shudder," as a recent critic has written,[5] but that personal experience cannot be trusted as if it were sufficient evidence for pronouncing a literary (or psychological) judgment. The peculiar discovery of "a place of execution" (recognized by a gibbet, perhaps, and other signs that do not require much light to be known?) and what it signifies would make a welcome example and a convenient argument for a *contemptus mundi*. The old context brings to the new context an image of the uncertainty of living, and by a single turn recalls to memory the old inevitable grinding forward of the argument that life in this world is full of deception, change, pain, and painful surprises. All of these contribute to the new context as the certainty of death and the desire of the weary traveler for rest find in the "place of execution" a fixed sign of death; yet the traveler's own spontaneous feeling of gladness (and relief and hope) translates a symbol of death in life into the nearness and accessibility of life in death. In the strange paths along such borders, certainties and uncertainties may interchange, and the traveler, "weary, and late," may hardly notice the difference. The same cannot be said for the listener/reader, who is not this traveler, and though he may not be able to make a good account of what has happened to him as he heard or read, he should feel no mental weariness.

Not the place but the act of execution furnishes Donne with an image that brings the certainties and uncertainties of death directly together. The context concerns the Resurrection, in which the damned will also be immortal (Lucifer no less than Michael, Judas than St. Peter) but in a state of "continuall dying." Therefore, "it is impossible to separate the consideration of the Resurrection, from the consideration of the Judgement; and the terrors of that may abate the joy of the other. . . . If I can put off all feare of that Judgement, I have put off all imagination, that any such Judgement shall be." The image I have in mind concerns the wicked and their immortality:

> But the wicked begin this feare, when the Trumpet sounds to the Resurrection, and then shall never end it; but, as a man condemned to be halfe hang'd, and then quartered, hath a fearfull addition in his quartering after, and yet had no ease in his hanging before. . . . That which we call immortality in the damned, is but a continuall dying; howsoever it must be called life, it hath all the qualities of death, saving the ease, and the end, which death hath, and damnation hath not. They must come forth; they that have done evill, must do so too: Neither can stay in their house, their grave; for, their house (though that house should be the sea) shall be burnt downe; all the world dissolv'd with fire. But then, They who have done evill, shall passe from that fire, into a farther heat, without light, They who have done good, into a farther light, without heat. . . . Remember with thankfulnesse the severall resurrections that he hath given you; from superstition and ignorance, in which, you, in your Fathers lay dead; from sin, and a love of sin, in which, you, in the dayes of your youth, lay dead; from sadnesse, and dejection of spirit, in which, you, in your worldly crosses, or spirituall tentations, lay dead; And assure your self, that that God that loves to perfect his own works, when you shall lye dead in your graves, will give you that Resurrection to life, which he hath promised to all them that do good, and will extend to all them, who having done evill, do yet truly repent the evill they have done. (*Sermons*, 6:277–79)

The wicked who are "halfe hang'd" represent the certainty but also the uncertainty of death itself. Their brief reprieve represents the final judgment to come. But the process of being quartered, which might or might not be efficient in protracting life while still being unspeakably inefficient, does not quite correspond to the certainty of judgment or the uncertainties of how infinity will be spent. Death is like going to the house of the grave or being "halfe hang'd," except for "the ease, and the end." "They must come forth": which brings into death some of the "qualities" of life, as the apprehension of uncertainties.

I have quoted more of the passage that follows the image than was needed to make my modest point. I did so because it is a convenient place to illustrate that inherited love for the piling up, the rhetorical way of reducing resistance by the cumulative effect of a series of blows that makes the willing listener fully receptive to the alternative, which then can be "imprinted" with a gentler application of force. But this too need not come all at once, for hope also needs the process of repetition, to be tempered and strengthened, and to be remembered by the application of "sensible" images of the kind that, as Aquinas wrote, the soul may be "held by" and may "cleave with affection to." Donne inherited that love for the cumulative effect and a taste for the vivid example, but he was not one to imitate the more naive aspects of the earlier art, though he knew their uses in the pulpit. The "severall resurrections" available to individual memory are a bridge to the final Resurrection, and God "will *give you*" what he has promised "to all them that do good, and will *extend to all them,* who having done evill, do yet truly repent the evill they have done." This is handsomely precise in its discriminating emphasis. But what he does with the "halfe hang'd" and the weary traveler is to coordinate closely the certainties and uncertainties of death and life and the intricacies that bind and separate them.

I*n seventeenth-century* England one could separate reason and revelation in the traditional manner of a philosophical Christian trying his hand, with proper acknowledgment and deference, at a limited experiment of explaining by analytical reason alone how to organize the practical knowledge of nature. Bacon's *The Advancement of Learning* is a diplomatic, statesmanlike book that promotes an intellectual revolution already in the making. One could separate the business of life from revelation so, but not the business of death. Few would have listened; most of those who heard of the proposition by report would have been incredulous at the novelty and would have suspected atheism. Besides, analytical reason, directed toward the materials of recently acquired knowledge and ways of regarding that knowledge, had little new to offer on the subject of death, and what was on record in earlier thought was either opposed to revelation or had been absorbed into Christian thinking. Accepting death as a part of life may have been the resigned attitude of whole societies in the Middle Ages and may have continued to persist, as in Montaigne's country folk and Tolstoi's peasants, but it was an acceptance gained like a habit without much formal thinking. It could not have defended itself against the standing array of powerful arguments. Even the church, whatever its contribution to that simple acceptance, was committed to treating death as related to life chiefly in special ways; death was made to seem both separate and more important.

To think of death in ways that further increased its separateness from life required thinking of life in ways that increased its separateness from death. The early Montaigne avers: "Our religion has no surer human foundation than contempt for life" (1.20.64). The late Montaigne advances his personal opinion that the measure of human felicity is "living happily," not "dying happily" (3.2.619). And further: that there is "no knowledge so hard to acquire as the knowledge of how to live this life well and naturally; and the most barbarous of our maladies is to despise our being" (3.13.852). It would have been still harder to acquire the knowledge of how to defend the knowledge of living well against the tested arguments on the side of death. As the value of living well began to gain some purchase in the world, the new absolute primacy of faith to salvation found it necessary to separate itself emphatically from the traditional importance of "good works," while of course making formal acknowledgments that good works were still good in their place. Late in *Paradise Lost* Milton's careful phrase is "faith, not void of works" (12.427), which resembles his "love with fear the only God" (12.562).

There were acknowledged and unacknowledged unknowns in death, some of them locked up in mysteries attributed to God's will. Yet the literature on death offered reasoned answers in an unhesitating flow and with the air of comprehensiveness, by means of arguments privileged to explain all apparent contradictions, to ignore all omissions, and to treat like laws the established habits of selecting only certain kinds of evidence and proof. Anomalies could be attributed to official mysteries or to the faulty performance of the living person who was dying.[6] To be "Absolute for death" one needed only to "Reason thus with life," and so forth. If the will, that acknowledged theater of moral action, faltered, it was immediately subject to demotion or exclusion as a recreant or enemy of the rational soul. In *Measure for Measure* Claudio's fearful imagining of the condition of being dead would make a clear case. Yet Shakespeare's Juliet hesitating over the Friar's sleeping potion and swept into waves of fear, hysteria, and hallucination still does what she decided to do, with no visible help from reason but only from a love remembered at the lucky worst moment, a love stronger than the fear of death or madness. She presents a difficult case, but thinkers from Plotinus into the seventeenth century do not hesitate to deprive the recreant will of its freedom, or its name and place in the psyche, if it departs from the regulated precincts of the rational.[7]

I cannot solve these problems, but I can review them and go on. A serious work of the imagination can juxtapose arguments without using one side as a foil to set off the convincing reasons of the other. In

Milton's *Samson Agonistes* Samson refuses his father's proposal of seeking by ransom to gain his release from prison and hard labor. Samson prefers his deserved punishment, and to "expiate, if possible, my crime." He implores God's pardon, "but as for life, / To what end should I seek it?" He can see no hope of recovering the lost purpose of his life:

> Here rather let me drudge and earn my bread,
> Till vermin or the draff of servile food
> Consume me, and oft-invocated death
> Hasten the welcome end of all my pains.
>
> (lines 573–76)

Manoa's answers to that dangerous admission of desiring death are of a practical sort and superficial; he seems to have intuited that desire already when he presented his strongest argument:

> Be penitent and for thy fault contrite,
> But act not in thy own affliction, son;
> Repent the sin, but if the punishment
> Thou canst avoid, self-preservation bids;
> Or th' execution leave to high disposal,
> And let another hand, not thine, exact
> Thy penal forfeit from thyself; perhaps
> God will relent, and quit thee all his debt;
> Who ever more approves and more accepts
> (Best pleased with humble and filial submission)
> Him who imploring mercy sues for life,
> Than who self-rigorous chooses death as due;
> Which argues over-just, and self-displeased
> For self-offense, more than for God offended.
>
> (lines 502–15)

The heart of Manoa's argument poses pride against piety, death against life, self-judgment against trust in God's mercy. Samson does not answer these arguments directly; either he cannot or chooses not to, a classic ambiguity that defies resolution. We recognize that Manoa's arguments offer a plausible but not an authoritative explanation of Samson's behavior, and that in general they have the authority they bring from the history of human experience in its relations with the divine. That authority, however, is subject to doubts when it is represented by a spokesman whose own thoughts and feelings we do not trust to be represented fully by what he chooses to say. But a good argument may have its own integrity, weakened in a particular context but not dissolved by our perception of the questionable motives of the speaker. As for Samson: the prospects of release cannot answer the depths of his feelings; these we cannot know, and Samson cannot know where outraged pride passes into an authentic conviction that his penitence for the betrayal of God still is incomplete. The verbal arguments are inadequate on both sides; what they say is what may be said, but they are no direct guide to the truth, which will come in a form beyond the reach of their arguments. There can be no meeting of minds between a tragic sinner refusing to act before his will recognizes the right signs, by which it will be proved rational and a father who is being true to his obligations as he understands them. Milton gives us in a story what arguments cannot: a view, from the human and the divine perspectives, into a corner of the untabulated mysteries of death. Again we may acknowledge the advantages of dramatic writing, which has its own special relations with the inevitable and no need to present a mimesis of the comprehensive, and which enjoys a different range of freedom in choosing and ordering questions.

In the didacticism of sermon or argument the need to explain will often suppress any sense of alternative or the possibility of a more complex or a deeper view. For example, Donne illustrates the reckless indifference to life in a "picture" of one who dies "upon the wrack of a distracted conscience":

> When the devil imprints in a man . . . I care not though I were dead, it were but a candle blown out, and there were an end of all: where the Devil imprints that imagination, God will imprint an *Emori nolo,* a loathness to die, and fearful apprehension at his transmigration. (*Sermons,* 8:188)

A long passage of description follows, more than proving what his listeners well knew, that even if death ended there, to escape "that manner of death were worthy a Religious life." One would not guess from this account that the writer could support a different view of "a loathness to die," or that such reluctance could be anything but a sign of the wicked. But there was, always to be remembered but not always adduced, the example of Christ's death, his "*colluctations* with *death,* and a *sadness even in his soule to death,* and an *agony* even to a *bloody sweate* in his *body,* and *expostulations* with *God,* and *exclamations* upon the crosse." The day Hilarion died he said: "*Hast thou served a good master threescore and ten yeares, and now art thou loath to goe into his presence?* Yet *Hilarion* was loath. He was a devout man." Donne's message is: "Make no *ill conclusions* upon any mans *loathness* to dye." This is true of malefactors too, for Christ was *reputed* and *executed* as such, "and no doubt many of them who concurred to his death, did beleeve him to bee so." And "make no *ill conclusion* upon *sudden death* nor upon distempers neyther, though perchance accompanied with some *words of diffidence* and distrust in the *mercies of God*."[8]

This is didacticism of a larger spirit not absorbed by the rhetorical needs of a single view. If we read the sermons of one who is also a great writer, we may still expect that his chosen text and his intentions to edify will keep him from straying into expressions that trouble the clarity and effectiveness of his purpose. There may be moments, images, and digressions that suddenly, as from a personal imaginative impulse, enlarge or complicate matters that a stricter didacticism would have suppressed. But in general he will avoid a change of opinion or emphasis that might weaken or distract from the main line of his purpose. In the second part of the sermon quoted above, Donne's last, he is intent on undermining human presumption in trying to understand death and to turn *examples* into *rules* for private purposes. Donne's message is that to God alone "belong the issues of death." Conformity to and dependence on Christ is the one answer. Still, a significant part of undermining presumption concerns the ambiguity of reluctance to die, elsewhere castigated; and Donne with unexpected and touching generosity enters a defense of human passion and "distempers" even when they speak, against the sacred reason of faith, in the language of diffidence and distrust. Usually we must encounter the other side of an opinion or emphasis in another, more hospitable place—as in the righteousness, but "agony," "vehemence," and "bitterness" of the passion of the Widow of Zareptha who importunes the prophet to restore her dead son: "A storme of affections in nature, and yet a setled calme, and a fast anchorage in grace, a suspition, and a jealousie, and yet an assurance, and a confidence in God, may well consist together" (*Sermons*, 7:383). But even here the context clearly safeguards the essential piety, though it significantly enlarges the decorum usually expected of piety and does something to temper the habits of rational suspicion and to make the easy impulses of illiberality a little harder to indulge.

In imaginative literature the uncertainties of death not tied to the when and the how, and not tied to any of the usual relationships between questions and answers, can say unprecedented things. The odd imaginations that sport or stray across the mind under stress may startle and give strange pleasure. Their intimations of source and motivation may forestall their being censored as fantastic nonsense. They may, rather, be accepted as legitimate surprise, demonstrating a recognizable aptness in the circumstances, which nevertheless remain open-ended and cut off from any established pattern to which they might be referred. We are finally unable to settle these odd imaginations into a reassuring position, or blunt their point, or forget their "wayward" interest, or develop their implications into a compelling argument. The best, though still inadequate, description I know is what Enobarbus in an aside to Cleopatra says in answering her question, "What means this?" The occasion is Antony's preparing for "one other gaudy night" but falling into the language and behavior of a last farewell. Enobarbus answers, " 'Tis one of those odd tricks which sorrow shoots / Out of the mind" (4.2.14–15). The fourth act of Shakespeare's play has many such, as part of a discontinuous process of the soul and body, which "rive" in parting before death but secretly anticipate death. Other statements are single, isolated—such as, in the sleepwalking scene, Lady Macbeth's "Hell is murky." When Lear's death arrives, his last words are terribly related and unrelated to everything else in the play. Edmund, half-forgiven by his half-brother ("The dark and vicious place where thee he got / Cost him his eyes"), produces a mysterious toy to clutch and wonder at: "Yet Edmund was belov'd!" (5.3.240).

Nor are poems, in spite of their smaller range of multiple actions, without similar moments. I think of Tichborne's dark speaking, "My tale was heard, and yet it was not told," and of Donne's precognition of death caught sight of in an image of light:

> Thinke then, my soule, that death is but a Groome,
> Which brings a Taper to the outward roome,
> Whence thou spiest first a little glimmering light,
> And after brings it nearer to thy sight.
> (*The Second Anniversarie*, lines 85–88)

This is indeed strange, like directions to a baroque painter; or Donne may have derived the image from a painting he saw. In any case, the imaginative impulse stands by itself; however it came, this image has nothing further to do or say. A less portentous (and final) example is Jonson's eleventh "Epigram," "On Some-thing, that Walkes Some-where." This is a brief, sketchy narrative on an "it" encountered at court. The clothes, looks, and adjustment of countenance are all pretentious; the speech goes further:

> It made me a great face, I asked the name.
> A lord, it cryed, buried in flesh, and blood,
> And such from whom let no man hope least good,
> For I will doe none: and as little ill,
> For I will dare none. Good Lord, walke dead still.

Jonson's wit has managed to extract from the mixture of spiritual affec-
tation and true confession a new, dehumanized meaning to go with the
usually painful idea of death in life. But his is different from the preceding examples. Its surprising uniqueness is based on known distinctions;
once these are put together by Jonson's summary definition, any loiter-
ing interest we might have in the eccentricity of person and motives is
turned to the definition, which is not open-ended.

In the Expostulation of Devotion 17, the echo of the bell tolling for
an unknown dying man continues in Donne's thought. If God wills,
any sounds may convey His music, and Donne declares, "Thy *voice*, thy
hand is in this *sound*, and in this *one sound*, I heare this *whole Consort*." He
hears Jacob prophesying to his sons when it was time for him to die. He
hears Moses blessing his people before his death; this too is part of
God's music, "within the *compasse* of this *sound*." And Isaiah to Hezekia:
"Set thine house in order; for thou shalt die, and not live." ("Hee makes
us of his familie.") He hears the apostle Peter stirring up remembrance
when he knows that he must soon "put off this my tabernacle." And he
hears God's Son saying, "*Let not your hearts be troubled*." Then Donne
expostulates with God:

> The *legacies* in thy first *will*, in thy *old Testament* were *plentie*
> and *victorie; Wine* and *Oile*, *Milke* and *Honie*, *alliances of friends*,
> *ruine of enemies*, *peacefull hearts*, & *cheerefull countenances*, and by
> these *galleries* thou broughtest them into thy *bed-chamber*, by
> these *glories* and *joies*, to the *joies* and *glories* of heaven. Why
> hast thou changed thine old way, and carried us, by the *waies*
> of *discipline* and *mortification*, by the *waies* of *mourning* and
> *lamentation*, by the waies of *miserable ends*, and *miserable antici-
> pations* of those miseries, in appropriating the *exemplar* mis-
> eries of others to our selves, and *usurping* upon their *miseries*, as
> our owne, to our owne *prejudice?*

He then asks why the absolute joy and glory of heaven have no counterpart here but only contrast, and answers that there the joy and glory are
real and owe nothing to comparison and contrast. The only true comparison is with the being of God: "*Essentiall joy, and glory Essentiall*."
Then he concludes:

> But why then, my *God*, wilt thou not *beginne* them *here?*
> pardon, O *God* this *unthankfull rashnesse;* I that aske why thou
> *doest not*, finde even now in *my selfe*, that thou *doest;* such *joy*,
> such *glory*, as that I conclude upon *my selfe*, upon *all*, They that

finde not *joy* in their *sorrowes, glory* in their *dejections* in this
world, are in a fearefull *danger* of missing both in the *next.*

That Donne elsewhere calls death in the Old Testament a threat but
a promise in the New Testament is not to my purpose here; nor that he
obtrudes upon all these Old Testament deaths the later pedagogy of
reminding witnesses to think upon their own deaths. (He attributes to
Jacob a "prophetic" version of the popular gnome, more suitable to
decaying or skeletal remains: What you are I was, what I am you will
be.) And we may also disregard the fact that Jacob's prophecy was not all
milk and honey, or that Hezekia heard some bad news along with the
good. Up to a point Donne's main intention is to identify the tolling
bell with God's music; all the deaths referred to are "within the *compasse*
of this *sound*"; both testaments contribute to a single harmony. But this
intention is broken off, and two testaments are aligned in contrast,
though moments later even the conceivability of comparison and contrast will need to be rejected when he moves to his own personally
anguished questions of why earthly and heavenly joy and glory have no
relationship. One may sense but cannot be sure that a reflexive action
has occurred and that an invalid effort to apply the reasoning of comparison (earthly and heavenly rewards) to one manifestation of God's
will has weakened or disabled the personal expression of eloquent certainty in comparing the old and new ways of death. No connection is
acknowledged, but human certainty arguing with God acts against the
background of authoritative precedents on record, and these do not
need to be cited for their influence to be felt. The new development
begins with a contrast between Christ's saying, *"I goe to prepare a place
for you,"* and the voice in the tolling bell, "this man in this *sound* saies, *I
send to prepare you for a place, for a grave."* In his own voice Donne then
speaks the warm praise of the old way of death with something of the
special tone of celebrating pastoral innocence in a remote Golden Age,
in contrast to the new ways, not all of them God's doing, for there is the
human contribution of borrowing miseries from others. The main link
is shifted from the binding metaphor of music to the passage from life
to death to heaven, from the rewards of the "first *"will,"* which led and
induced us to heaven by *"glorious* and *joyfull* things,"* to the new ways of
the Christian life. Like the Widow of Zareptha and others, Donne
speaks with "vehemence" and "bitterness": "A storme of affections in
nature . . . and a confidence in God, may well consist together."

But the outburst of natural passion, however justified, cannot restore the formal unity of the discourse. Nor would it help if we borrowed from our next example, the preceding, sixteenth Expostulation.

There Donne thanks God for permitting Christians to remember that they were "*naturall men* before" and for permitting the church "to have taken in from *Jew* or *Gentile*." But in the present Expostulation he has done something else. He is not demonstrating an assimilative unity attributed to God, nor demonstrating that any "harshness" or "hoarseness" (like that of his protesting voice) may become musical if God "set" His voice to the sound. This last is, I think, too fine a thread and too remote from the entrance of joy at the end; one may, however, hesitate to exclude that tenuous connection absolutely. Still, the character of the change is sudden, and so much something in itself, that it demands to be recognized as an event that is not merely serving or concluding a process. We have to take his word for the joy; he does not discuss the details of its arrival or analyze its contents. That such an occurrence is most rare in his book does not lessen our willingness to believe him now. We may want the personal satisfaction of explaining his joy as part of the impulse that will cause him in the next part of this Devotion to pray for the soul of the man for whom the bell has been tolling. If the Holy Ghost is the enabling agent, it would be hard to decide which causes which, in the matter of the joy and the subsequent prayer. Donne says nothing to the point. We may well be reluctant, however, to accept as given the moral lesson of his last sentence, that those who do not find joy and glory in the antithetical experiences of this world are in danger of missing joy and glory in the next world. The application seems easy and opportune, like an afterthought presented by a self-conscious teacher as if it were the conclusion toward which everything else had been pointing.

But the joy remains a thing apart, and precious. The interrupted continuity of intention and the loosening of the unity, common faults in writing, here seem to do homage to the joy. In sum, the expostulation with God is transposed by God and heard by God as a prayer; the feeling of joy is the answer that identifies the prayer.[9]

My second example from the *Devotions* I have already introduced, and it will require no fine labor to present. Though it strays a modest distance from my subject and does not touch death directly, the sixteenth Expostulation is instructive in its presenting a moment of certainty while Donne makes his way through materials that have been and are controversial and uncertain. His interpretive exposition is carefully pitched and paced. It begins with announcing that his argument is with men who "dare expostulate" with God over the ceremonial use of bells at funerals. He continues reviewing and defending Christian practices that have a pre-Christian history and then returns to his own case, cut off as he is from the full church service he hears only in brief and fragmented form. In his own voice, and in the special circumstances of dangerous illness, he cries out, "We cannot, we cannot, O my *God,* take in too many *helps* for religious *duties.*" Then he confesses to God and thanks God for a personal practice of his own, followed by a general and diplomatic comment on God's purposes as he understands them:

> I know I cannot have any better *Image* of *thee,* than thy *Sonne,* nor any better *Image* of *him,* than his *Gospell:* yet must not I, with thanks, confesse to thee, that some *historicall pictures* of his, have sometimes put mee upon better *Meditations* than otherwise I should have fallen upon? I know thy *Church* needed not to have taken in from *Jew* or *Gentile,* any supplies for the exaltation of thy *glory,* or our *devotion;* of *absolute necessitie* I know shee needed not; But yet wee owe thee our thanks, that thou hast given her leave to doe so, and that as in making us *Christians,* thou diddest not destroy that which wee were before, *naturall men,* so in the exalting of our religious devotions now we are *Christians,* thou has beene pleased to continue to us those *assistances* which did worke upon the affections of naturall men before: for thou lovest a *good man,* as thou lovest a *good Christian:* and though *Grace* bee meerely from thee, yet thou doest not plant Grace but in *good natures.*

His reasoning attributes God's permission to things the church has admitted and seals that matter by acknowledging to fellow churchmen that nothing really needed to be "taken in," and seals the matter again by thanking God again for the gifts received. At the end, good men, good Christians, and good natures are linked together as objects of God's love. His personal confession of having been moved by *"historicall pictures"* of Jesus receives its justification indirectly. It comes under the general permission but is acknowledged by a separate thanks to God for the good he has received. The effect of improved devotion is as real to him as the sudden exaltation of joy in the Expostulation that follows. I think we may conclude that his general argument would not be affected by the omission of his personal evidence, but that he has felt a personal desire to include this, perhaps intending to produce a favorable context for its expression. He is quite silent about Puritan and other hatred of any form of devotion associated with Roman Catholic practices, as in the use of images to promote devotion. Donne does, however, carefully use a technical term of art, "historical pictures," widely current since the eighteenth century but not so in the 1620s: the first use recorded by the *OED* is 1658.

By most standards, the rhetorical diplomacy is superior to the reasoning, but this is religious reasoning into which Providence must be coordinated. Still, the personal experience, in spite of the graceful writing, stands apart in a special position, like the joy of my previous example. On the other hand, this personal experience is not advanced as the climax of the discourse but is placed in a guarded position. Donne knew that some readers would respond with aroused suspicion.[10] In other respects the private experience resembles the announcement of joy, a personal certainty arising from conditions subject to further arguments and uncertainties but stated briefly. It is a truth that does not require an explanation that will satisfy all: it is what it is.

I end this part of the discussion by returning briefly to the more familiar way that the preacher changes the thought of an image, not suddenly or by unexpected juxtapositions more at home in imaginative literature, but by changing what he actually says in different places.

Donne's "house of death that stands in two worlds, may trouble a good mans resolution," not only the mental firmness of the dying person, but his physical termination, in the medical sense of "resolution," and his spiritual passing from dissonant to consonant, in the musical sense. Those who attend the death may also be troubled. They may see a spectacle ranging from visible struggle and compulsive pain to lethargy or coma; the arrival of death may appear as a steady, swift, or abuptly neutral closing down, or a calm, masked neutrality, or a scene of ecstasy, or quiet, peaceful arrest, or gradual dimming. What the witnesses see and what they remember will be affected by what they think of that life and its loss, and by how they are affected by the particular accouterments and ceremonies, domestic and public, that attend the disposal of the body. What they see will also be troubled by their thoughts of human and divine justice, human and divine mercy.

Donne frequently uses imagistic properties of "house"; it is a convenient figure for purposes of organization, and at the same time will help the attention and memory of listeners. He can divide the country into the houses of state government, the church, the place of the family, and the individual, for whom the body is the house of the soul and the grave house of the body. The image has other uses, too, for houses have grounds, foundations, rooms, roofs, furniture, inhabitants; and the person as house has "bodily" and other "endowments." The sermon speaking of the house in two worlds was probably delivered in 1626/7. What it says and releases for imaginative response has an indisputable force, but it is a force involved in questioning. It cannot be regarded as an indisputable answer; and it will not be adequate to many occasions of grief or faith. If the sermon was delivered a month after the sudden death of his eighteen-year-old daughter Lucy, my commentary migh find itself composing a story that could not ignore that dangerous "long gazing upon so narrow a bridge [to heaven], and over so deep and roaring waters, and desperate whirlpools, as this world abounds with" (7:359). But since the date is only "probable" and I have another story to tell, I note indispensable items of the plot and pass on.

In a sermon of 1622, a confirmed date, Donne had already written, "For we know, that they which are gone, are gone but into another room of the same house, (this world, and the next, do but make up God a house) they are gone but into another Pue of the same Church (the Militant and the Triumphant do but make up God a Church)" (4:63). In an undated sermon assigned by the editors to the most probable date of 1626/7, Donne writes a firm revision of his house of death in two worlds (and of the seventeenth Expostulation):

> The pure in heart are blessed already, not onely comparatively, that they are in a better way of Blessednesse, then others are, but actually in a present possession of it: for this world and the next world, are not, to the pure in heart, two houses, but two roomes, a Gallery to passe thorough, and a Lodging to rest in, in the same House, which are both under one roofe, Christ Jesus . . . so the Joy, and the sense of Salvation, which the pure in heart have here, is not a joy severed from the Joy of Heaven, but a Joy that begins in us here, and continues, and accompanies us thither, and there flowes on, and dilates it selfe to an infinite expansion. (7:340)

In his Easter day sermon of 1627, a confirmed date, Donne makes another revision of the image of the house of death in two worlds:

> That if the dead, and we, be not upon one floore, nor under one story, yet we are under one roofe. We think not a friend lost, because he is gone into another roome, nor because he is gone into another Land; And into another world, no man is gone; for that Heaven, which God created, and this world, is all one world. . . . This is the faith that sustaines me, when I lose by the death of others, or when I suffer by living in misery my selfe, That the dead, and we, are now all in one Church, and at the resurrection, shall be all in one Quire. (7:384)

I think we may decide that this change is not a binding article of doctrine or faith, arrived at and to be defended by an open consideration of evidence and analysis. I mention this inapplicable extreme in order to say that the statement here is closer to and resembles more the expostulation with God that discovers itself to have been a prayer that has been answered. The image is a vehicle that is capable of representing intellectual conception and intuition, but is also an expressive instrument of immediate desire and has no means of examining the durable truth of that desire and its image. The arbitrariness is not like that used in arguments designed to sway others—as, say, when Lotario dei Segni in *De Miseria* cites John 11:35, "Jesus wept," and acknowledges the obvious pity for the suffering of those who grieved for Lazarus but prefers to single out the odd but serviceable interpretation: "troubled himself, and wept, but more for the reason that he called a dead man back to the miseries of life."[11] Insofar as Donne is "arguing," it is with himself, and whether he has changed his opinion or admitted a flaw of inconsistency into his thought would be a trifle. He confesses to his hearers: "This is the faith that sustaines me." The "death of others" and "living in misery my selfe" are not two distinct categories, though Donne makes a gesture in that direction and writes "or"—"or when I suffer by living in misery my selfe." By the death of others one loses and suffers to be "living," and "my selfe" is more than a grammatical reflexive; it intensifies the solitude of suffering and loss. Donne shared the admiration and reverence of his age for the Psalms, and there he would have found the authority and example for the expression of immediate feelings true to their circumstances, a divine poetry not composed to satisfy the clenched fist of logic as taught in the schools.

The death of others, not only considered but deeply felt, may make the image of the house of death in two worlds appear to be a kind of intellectual luxury, better suited for considering the uncertainties of death, and one's own death, than for responding to the death of another, a beloved other. If indeed there is only one house of the world, one is relieved of troubled "resolution" and double justice, and of the problems of despising the world and human life in accord with one set of reasons and of defending them by a carefully selected different set of reasons. A few casualties may have to be put out of mind, such as the discomfort of "a good mans resolution," who is only a good man and does not, as do "the pure in heart," travel the felicitous path from beginning to end. Faith in the Resurrection is a single answer to the misery of loss, and it does enable grief to accept limits and turn its passion into something else.

Mourning for the dead is also inherited from the affections of "natural man." Beyond its due season of time, inconsolable grief for the dead is mingled with the misery of one's own life and involved in the certain uncertainties of one's own death; and would have no answer to the accusation that faith in the resurrection of the dead beloved has been proved to be deficient. An even bleaker thought, one that is more possible to keep out of sight, for it does not challenge faith and is already shrouded in the mysteries of God's will, is that one can hope but not know that the salvation of another is assured. (Resurrection without salvation is not to be thought of in the house of the family; it is for designated times of warning the wicked.) Faith can believe it is difficult but possible to receive assurances of one's own salvation. One may continue to hope to know oneself and to discipline the raw desire for assurance, but the secret inclinations of others will be less well known, and how God may act on His knowledge it would be arrant presumption to entertain. Hope is more proper than faith, prayer than any reasoned weighing of evidence.

The natural franchise of consolation liberates the mind from the disturbance of unwanted thoughts, and so the unity of the world of one house opens love's doors on death but silently closes other doors; the architect's plans do not mention windows. God's love for the world is magnified, and life in the world will be relieved of conflicting purposes. The human expressions of love for the divine will be concentrated in the "faith that sustaines," directed toward the Resurrection. Many of the uncertainties of life may thus be set aside or suspended. But once we step back from the special dues of consolation, the intricate relationships of self and other will again have to find their own ways of trying to think-and-not-think of the unknowns and mysteries of life that touch on death but do not belong to death alone.

In *other parts* of this book I have gone over some of these grounds with various other tasks in mind. Now it is time to look again.

If the sensitive balance that exists when the house of death stands in two worlds can be put out of mind when there is only one world, the fixed orientation toward death can also be reversed, and the witty pursuit of pleasure, the love of life and love in the world, can turn old objects of anxiety and complex reference upside down, if only in the freedom of play. So Suckling manipulates his wonder at the death of love as he examines a former source of disturbance:

> She every day her Man doth kill,
>   and I as often die;
> Neither her power then, nor my will
>   can question'd be,
>   what is the mystery?
> Sure Beauties Empires, like to greater States
> Have certain periods set, and hidden fates.[12]

Whether the death of love is referred to the lightly contradicting evidence of daily episodes of sexual consummation or to the awesome episodes involved in the fate and fall of empires, the comparisons are trivializing and intended to demystify both love and the death of love. Thomas Carew varies the method and the subject when in "A Rapture"[13] he prepares a new paradise for a new innocence. There famous victims of "cancell'd lawes" are making up "for their time mispent." History rewritten also demystifies, perhaps with more surprise or shock when the private lives of individuals are revealed in their new freedom. Tarquin's Lucretia studies Aretino's "lectures," and in knowledge and performance she is the equal of Laïs, who needs no second chance. Penelope has given up weaving and unraveling, "And th'amorous sport of gamesome nights prefer, / Before dull dreames of the lost Traveller" (lines 129–30).

To make a parallel step before circling back: Carew, refusing the invitation of Aurelian Townshend to write an elegy on the death of Gustavus Adolphus, deftly puts his refusal through some elegant paces. He writes an elegy while protesting his unfitness for so high a subject and then turns to praise his friend and encourage him to undertake "subjects proper" to the England of "Our *Halcyon* dayes":

> Of peace and plenty, which the blessed hand
> Of our good King gives this obdurate Land.
> Let us of Revels sing.
>
> (p. 75, lines 47–49)

The sweet of life is not Henry King's only true subject. When he first hears the bad news, his thoughts hang on him "Like a cold fatal sweat which ushers death." When he praises the dead hero of Protestant Europe, he matches him not only against Caesar but against his own urgent yearning for a hero he can honor properly. These are not good times, and that news is not altogether recent. His elegy for Sir Walter Raleigh spares lament and makes the praise effectively brief. It is the scandalous behavior of Raleigh's political enemies that provides the foil and "made thy ag'd fame / Appear more white and fair, then foul their shame." When he comes to write on the death of Charles I, he casts aside all restraints, and Charles is memorialized against a "foil" several hundred lines in length. King's excess tells the other side of Carew's story.

Carew is not without the suggestions of a darker side, and he can praise Sandys's translation of the Psalms with some sense of being touched by personal perplexity; skill comes to his aid, however, and he defends his inclinations by translating the language of religious aspiration into his own amorous idiom. It is a witty exhibition of winning words, a moderated penitential psalm directed toward a possible future, "Who knowes . . . may . . . may . . . may" (p. 94).

Cowley is a professed adherent to the new age of reason: "Bacon, like Moses, led us forth at last," and Hobbes is praised as "Thou great Columbus of the golden lands of new philosophies." But there is also a side of skeptical diffidence: "neither ought any man to envy *Poets* this posthumous and imaginary happiness, since they finde commonly so little in present. . . . a warlike, various, and a tragical age is best to *write of,* but worst to *write in.*"[14] And there is a part of him that longs for his friend Crashaw's faith, though he holds his opposing position very well in their joint poem, "On Hope." His elegy "On the Death of Mr. Crashaw" calls him "Poet and saint. . . . The two most sacred names of earth and heaven." Crashaw's Muse, "like Mary, did contain / The boundless Godhead," and he died at Loreto, "In thy great Mistress' arms." Elsewhere in "Christian land" idols persist, and we "the monster woman deify"; our Muses are variously corrupted: "Wanton as girls, as old wives fabulous." As the religious praise crosses doctrinal boundaries, he asks pardon of his own Church, but continues:

> Ah, mighty God, with shame I speak't, and grief,
> Ah, that our greatest faults were in belief!
> And our weak reason were ev'n weaker yet,
> Rather than thus our wills too strong for it.
> His faith perhaps in some nice tenets might
> Be wrong; his life, I'm sure, was in the right.
> And I myself a Catholic will be,
> So far at least, great saint, to pray to thee.

Though the tendency may have its fashionable aspects, Cowley is for personal reasons attracted by the Horatian ideal of the simple life; he also professes the desire for a less fashionable retreat:

> to retire my self to some of our *American Plantations,* not to seek for *Gold* or inrich my self with the traffique of those parts. . . But to forsake this world for ever, with all the *vanities* and *Vexations* of it, and to bury my self in some obscure retreat there (but not without the consolation of *Letters* and *Philosophy*). . . . As this therefore is in a true sense a kind of *Death* to the *Muses,* and a real *literal quitting* of this *World:* So, methinks, I may make a just claim to the undoubted privilege of *Deceased Poets,* which is to be read with more favor then the *Living.* (2:82)

Under the pose and the witty turn at the end (he *is* writing a preface to the 1656 volume), there is a strain of mid-seventeenth-century Christian melancholy in the half-serious cultivation of death.

I pause to borrow for comparison a casual sketch by a nineteenth-century writer of a fifteenth-century king trying to avoid death in earnest. Measured by time, Cowley is almost midway between them, and all the outward actions are different when Stendahl describes Louis XI in his fortified castle of Plessis-lez-Tours:

> Hidden in the palace, this melancholy Louis XI had all those he was afraid of hung from the nearby trees. There he died in 1483, sighing and trembling at the idea of death like the last man in the world, making his doctor rich and summoning a saint from the depths of Calabria. To me, this king was Tiberius with the fear of hell added.[15]

But even the differences make the comparison worth a moment's consideration. Louis is a terrified monster, Cowley a civilized poet entertaining the thought of an *image* of death, with all the advantages of peace and uninterrupted contemplation, to which may be added the companionship of books. There is no acknowledged fear of death or fear of isolation; one may, though, surmise that his chosen image of death reflects, if not fear, at least some disaffection with life and some proclivity toward isolation, or at least an intermittent inner sense of being a stranger to the world and cut off from the reinforcing relationship with others. There is no hint that he will contemplate death and the other world in the old-fashioned way; his way is new and cast in an aesthetic attitude. Though he will die to the world, as the phrase went, it is the world and life out there that will die to him. Interest in the quality of life leads him to imitate the selected parts of death in life that offer attractive present advantages.

The performance and its staging are mannered and play with the recognizable exploitations of a commonplace of thought. That he can do so is more significant than what he says, for his process of selectivity, whatever the mixture of his motives, is in the mainstream of writing about death. In the worst moments, which are many, one encounters in that specialized literature a rigorously disciplined orgy of remembering everything that can add to the argument of one side, and a different kind of orgy of forgetting anything that might be thought on the other side.

The fear of hell had been in steady decline for some time.[16] The *logos* of Christianity was still in place and would remain so, but the capacious entirety of the *mythos* (many houses, many rooms and passageways) had begun to waver under a change of times and the irreconcilable hostilities of sectarian forces. As for death, it ceased to be thought of regularly as the last enemy to be destroyed; the drama of the deathbed was gradually changing some of its character and getting ready to accommodate new sensibilities. The fear of death was what it had long been, but some of the *dicta* and some of the folklore commanded less belief, and the expression of the fear made adjustments to the altering ways in which death could be regarded. One symptom was the tendency, discussed earlier, to think of death as an "idea," or a kind of image that represented all that was other to the sentient self and its desires. But these changes do not proceed systematically in a fixed order; old ideas, attitudes, and images keep reappearing in new contexts.

For example, I single out Waller's "Of the Last Verses in the Book" to illustrate the minute changes that compose the large difference between, say, Tichborne, Raleigh, Donne, Herbert, Nashe's "Adieu! Farewell Earth's Bliss," Shakespeare's "Fear no more the heat o' the sun," Milton's "Lycidas," and the Waller of 1686. Granted, as always, there are differences in imaginative endowment, art, and the hold of the subject on heart and mind; still, a new form of sentimentality has now appeared on the scene. Without either conflict or celebration, the house of pessimism is reduced to a nominal existence like a forgiven because mostly forgotten error of youth; the house of optimism leaves the other house in shadow while not gathering much light itself:

> Leaving the old, both worlds at once they view,
> That stand upon the threshold of the new.

But the reader must unaided imagine both, for in the world of the poem old age serves as an image of death, but not in a traditional way. It is a cheerful old age well furnished with remembered aphorisms from good books. Purged of passion, it sees "that emptiness" concealed from younger eyes, and the decayed house of the soul "Lets in new light through chinks that time has made"—presumably the better to review the emptiness of the old world and to preview the glory of the new. The faith that is required to see this must be content with the intimacy of a sentimental image in an appropriate rhythm. As a figure of death old age talks like an imaginary companion who is both faintly self and faintly other, a wise, kindly, fading friend. If there are touches of senility, one cannot be sure whether they are indebted to art, nature, or the times.

In the optimistic tradition of Neoplatonism the rational soul was capable of judging the part of reason against other claimants from within or without. Those more impressed by human fallibility and weakness, at least during times of stress and doubt, advised seeking the counsel and trusted judgment of another. Yet as the new age evolved, for which Bacon was a significant spokesman, the traditions of Neoplatonism declined in effective influence. To turn the attention more toward living well in the world (though not therefore to be indifferent to the aim of dying well) was to admit the value of intuitions and other knowledge derived from life in the world as capable of contributing to human wisdom and one's own wisdom. Direct observation of experience, and knowledge gained from the writings of other keen observers not repeating each other and not engaged in composing a *summa*, vastly increased the available knowledge of the diversity of human life. If knowledge of diversity added some finer precision to the knowledge of uncertainty, that was part of another question, whether new knowledge was indeed better knowledge. The old answer of the old knowledge was not forgotten. How could it be? But the recovery of neglected knowledge and the pursuit of new learning did not have as their purpose the composing of an improved argument to demonstrate the essential fallacy of studying the world and human life, and to do so in order to conclude with a new unanswerableness that such knowledge was the insidious merchandise of death in the world and that it was leading away from the one true human knowledge. "Worldly" wisdom and "carnal" thought continued as terms of opprobrium, but they were on the way to having their confident and coercive usage become limited to a specialized vocabulary.

I *have been* offering some comments and illustrations of certainty, uncertainty, and their ways when brought up against the subject of death. For the next few pages I turn to some of the relations between self and others when death is involved. (I shall not enter into modern explorations of the subject, which would require setting up an apparatus and a vocabulary and would require a high level of initial and continuous belief if one is to profit from their subtleties.)

"Others" may represent the community: the house of the family and its extensions and of the state and the church. Of this last there is the visible militant church and the invisible triumphant church in heaven. The loss of a living member of a church necessitates stirring the memory of mourners and their hope in the communion that will at last reunify all the dead and all the living. During his lifetime the individual has various obligations to his communities, and these are thought of as reciprocal. Afterwards, it is the religious community that will pray for him and identify his hope for salvation with theirs. Some individuals, perhaps many, must have been aware that personal death contained the possible consequence of personal annihilation. But such a thought seems to have been well repressed. Still, the forbidden thought of annihilation makes an occasional appearance in literature: it is implicit in some of Hamlet's grotesque jokes in the graveyard, in Claudio's ecstasy of fear, and in "man forgot" as the last words of King's "*Sic Vita*"; it is explicit in the oration of Milton's Belial (*PL* 2.145–51), a vivid hypothesis intended to frighten listeners who might be resisting his eloquence. From one point of view, the community was there to witness against the image of annihilation implicit in being forgotten and to affirm the impossibility that God would forget. The religious community must have nevertheless felt, without needing to form the thought or voice it, the threat of its own annihilation among rivals and enemies.[17]

Witnesses also represent the community; the dying person, by his life, by the circumstances of his death, may act as witness to the values of the large or small community that claims him. He may also bring scandal, to increase the number of the diffident and to encourage the boldness of the wicked. In the traditions of law and oratory, witnesses and their varying rights to authority were well established; the religious witness testifies by deed and word, by the life and by the death. Those intimates who gathered around the deathbed were to some degree witnesses. They were also mourners feeling what they imagined the dying person to be feeling; without needing instruction, they would imagine their own death and improve their sense of certainty or discover new materials for uncertainty. Those attending public executions or, as in eighteenth-century France, crowding into an "open house" where someone was known to be dying, were also to some degree witnesses.[18] For the intimate group at the deathbed, their obligations and benefits were obvious, though their individual experience might vary widely. The obligations and benefits of the dying person were too variable to be obvious and did not lend themselves to effective analysis and codification.

As for the self, the individual, the death that is only and all one's own, we have the oral and written reports, and we may have had personal messages ourselves to help collate what we have heard and read, the better to interpret these or our own messages. Whether any individual experience of death can free itself from acquired knowledge, no one can say; or whether finally knowledge, as we understand it, is an applicable concept. In any event, it seems probable that almost no one dying, and certainly no one reporting, could entirely escape the influence of acquired knowledge, a large part of which consists in what one ought to think and feel.

Death is always the same: "eadem sunt omnia semper." But to whom? The religious moment of the departing soul resembles, at least in its tangle of potential questions, those raised concerning when the soul is first infused along with its normal blemish of original sin, and how, and whether it is a newly created soul for each individual or some other kind. But the moment of the departing soul awaiting judgment had a practical urgency for definite answers, and these were forthcoming. Doctrinal differences were not unimportant, but they were perhaps less moved to be speculative than in other matters.

Death, or what we can see of it, was not always the same, and it is useful to be reminded of a few singularities. In his funeral sermon Jeremy Taylor reported of Lady Carbery, "She feared not death, but she feared the sharp pains of death."[19] Montaigne observes that some people at their execution are obviously in a hurry, "hastening and urging the carrying out of the sentence." This resembles but is not an act of resolution: "They want to deprive themselves of the time to consider it. Being dead does not trouble them, but dying does indeed" (2.13.460). In his last sermon Donne rigorously excludes friends and witnesses from the most important communications between the dying person and God. He offers almost no comfort to mitigate the recognition of that silent, closed place into which witnesses cannot enter. Facing the mystery of a sacred place, they may feel themselves to be outsiders, forbidden and profane intruders even by the desire of their love, but these feelings are their own personal problems. Donne allows only an austere article of faith, that God's mercies are invisible but are known to the dying person. The unspoken advice of the exclusion is that one must practice waiting. For his own death we have to depend on Walton's story, but Donne took the trouble of making a public preface and postscript. He delivered his last sermon while already in the visible grip of his final sickness; it was "stiled the Authors owne funeral Sermon." And it was published after his death with an epigraph and frontispiece, an engraving based upon the drawing Donne himself had arranged, the shroud opened to frame his face, eyes closed—a drawing, not a death mask, and the expression of voluntary repose was assured by the intention of the subject and the skill of the artist. I agree with Helen Gardner's "suggestion"

> that Donne's last sermon, with its splended title: *Deaths Duell, or a Consolation to the Soule, against the dying Life, and living death of the Body,* and with this striking frontispiece prefixed, was published in accordance with instructions which he himself gave; and that we should add to his activities in his last illness, the arrangements for the publication of his last sermon and the composition of this epigraph. He wished that, being dead, he might yet speak.[20]

Raleigh, in the verses on time left at the Gatehouse the day of his execution, would have had the same wish, however different the circumstances and the divergent strands of motive.

Related to the desire to speak after death, there would seem to be as well a particular desire to create the sense that this expression is a last statement, and as such it creates an image of the death, both picture and frame. To speak of Raleigh and Donne: each participated in the shaping of his death and the image it would leave, and in doing so they presented themselves as voluntary participants in what was happening to them. So far as the parallel goes, we may think that both were also shaping themselves, which can seldom be done without at least mental rehearsal if one is to act in a single command performance. But their expression was directed toward others, perhaps as witnesses, perhaps as audiences. None of the central expression was directed toward God, for obvious reasons, and yet one characteristic of the expression, at least in the case of Donne, would have been a prominent part of his preparations for death—that is, the desire to exercise his own will as a participant in the waiting and the dying.

Willing one's own death was perilous, and Donne had a professional interest in the problems of suicide.[21] The resolution of acceptance was the trusted right way; when that was achieved and death was coming unwilled, then the acceptance might express joy in which the individual will was allowed its place. (Saints and martyrs might die by their own rules.) Sir Thomas More had a lawyer's competence in these delicate matters:

> It was also said unto me that if I had as lief be out of the world as in it, as I had there said, why did I not speak even out plain against the statute. It appeared well I was not content to die though I said so. Whereto I answered as the truth is, that I have not been a man of such holy living as I might be bold to offer myself to death, lest God for my presumption might suffer me to fall, and therefore I put not myself forward, but draw back. Howbeit if God draw me to it himself, then trust I in his great mercy, that he shall not fail to give me grace and strength.[22]

If Walton's story is true, or true enough, that Donne closed his own eyes at the moment of death, that is an astonishing act of will, a virtuoso performance that could not possibly impress God but could prove something to oneself. The acceptance of the dying man was then translated into a self-initiating act assenting to death. He was the actor-witness, himself and another and at one edge of the moment a dead man.

Montaigne preferred it to happen without much ado, while setting out cabbages, or on horseback, or among strangers, without a framed moment of time. "Dying is not a role for society; it is an act for one single character. Let us live and laugh among our friends, let us go die and look sour among strangers" (3.9.748). He mocks the vanity of preferences in part by exhibiting his own; he always knows which, if not why, one of two choices seems less bad to him. "It is only an instant; but it is of such gravity that I would willingly give several days of my life to go through it in my own way" (3.9.752).

The sameness and the singularities of death are the purview of others, witnesses and observers, many of whom tell different stories in the same way and the same story differently. As for the death that belongs to the individual person, too many of the certainties and uncertainties become unclear and wander. The uncertainties have their own ways of appearing and shifting. We may be tempted to substitute our own rigid explanation for their stubborn states and predicaments of recurrence. We are at the mercy of the truth in reports, autobiographical accounts and essays, stories, poems; or, of late, the conclusions of medical and psychological research, or the shape certain facts assume when gathered from the observations of clinical practice. I find myself believing most in the messages of poetry, but that belief is not identical with one's belief in facts or in a master truth that the workaday world honors and dishonors as best it can with intermittent attention. My belief in poetry does not depend upon and is not identical with the truth of my own interpretation.

Some of the vagueness that creeps into a discussion of the death that belongs to the self is relieved if we add someone else, another. In Part 3 of this book the poets writing on the death of someone else illustrated many different kinds of relationship between the self of the poet and the dead other. I do not propose a review, but within the general terms and focus of a chapter entitled "Intricacies" I have a few last points to bring forward. They are not intended to simplify the intricacies.

Freud's insight is very hard to resist, that no one can imagine his own death, "and whenever we attempt to do so we can perceive that we are in fact still present as spectators."[23] His insight comes in support of a larger statement, that the unconscious is convinced of its immortality, but it is the spectator as other that interests me now. Freud seems to have in mind a fantasy scene, a visualized inner narrative, but the poets who furnished my main examples of writing on one's own death did not center their material on the physical event. Whatever the motivating force of responding to the certainty of their death, the most deeply imagined moments were centered in a past or future, or in a present this side of the threshold. (As partial exceptions I note the extraordinary moment of his own beheading in Raleigh's "The Passionate Man's

Pilgrimage" and the exuberant fantasy of the celebration in which Herrick himself participates at the close of the last act in "*Plaudite*.") Poets are trained and gifted spectators who are used to moving from one presence to another when composing a poem. They may have more than one kind or degree of presence or detachment even in a single word or pause. There was, however, the example of Donne's fantastic staging of his own death early in *The Second Anniversarie*. There the soul was an active and hostile spectator of the dying and then of the dead body, with some overt coaching by the poet and other use of a heavy hand. The weeping friends were also spectators, but organized like a claque, and the poet was busily present conspicuously interpreting the death and the scene. I do not take the scene seriously for what it pretends to be but regard it rather as an example of manhandling death as if it were an object existing in, and subject to, the familiarities of the mind.

The poets show how the simple or extraordinary other can move into or out of the self. (At the simplest they, like us, can always produce a speaker or listener if necessary, as the "you" commonly invoked and answered in the course of an internal monologue.) Ben Jonson the grieving father speaks to his dead son so that he can listen to himself expressing the double vision of early death and protracted life, the pains of loss, the pains and perils of living and loving. Donne writing on his wife's death presents his one true, soaring answer, the remarriage in heaven, and then begins a "dialogue of one" on the elementary problems of spiritual infidelity. At the end of "Lycidas" a new speaker seems to emerge from the monody; until he says it we do not realize, among other things, how justified he is in speaking that boldest of words, "Tomorrow."

The poets of the best poems were often actors and spectators. There are many other kinds of spectators, such as those identifying their own divided responses and desires with the spectacle they witness:

> The people, which what most they fear esteem,
> Death, when more horrid so more noble deem;
> And blame the last *Act,* like *Spectators* vain,
> Unless the *Prince* whom they applaud be slain.[24]

Ben Jonson, who distrusted audiences, longed for "judging spectators," whom he distinguished from both actors and ordinary audiences. Like other masters of illusion, he has moments when the basis of his art seems to pose an uncontrollable threat: "*I have* considered, our whole life is like a *Play:* wherein every man, forgetfull of himselfe, is in travaile with expression of another." It is our nature to imitate, and so we may lose our ability to "returne to our selves." On the other hand there are the master spirits of their times who "look'd downe on the Stage of the world, and contemned the Play of *Fortune*. For though the most be Players, some must be *Spectators*."[25] Ambivalences aside, the idea he has in mind is that traditional figure of unmoved contemplative wisdom who understands the causes of things. Here for the moment he parts company with his hero Bacon and his fixed principle: "But men must know, that in this theatre of man's life it is reserved only for God and Angels to be lookers on" (*Selected Writings*, p. 321). Nor would Jonson have been comfortable with Dr. Johnson's application of the aloof concept to the metaphysical poets, who "wrote rather as beholders than partakers of human nature; as Beings looking upon good and evil, impassive and at leisure."[26] In his elegy on Shakespeare, Jonson wrote what he himself practiced: "To write a living line" the poet must hammer it out "Upon the *Muses* anvile: turne the same / (And himselfe with it)."

All good writers moving others are *in* the words they write and have written, but some part of them will always have separate work to do in examining, encouraging, and controlling the sources of the words, and the flow and shape of the words, and the rejections and selections made before and after the words were first written. We are not privileged to observe much of this creative spectatorship, and poets do not always remember well their own side-glances and half-perceptions of rapid activity, shifting its centers of location, concentrated within, but also receiving messages that may deliver themselves from somewhere else. The house of art, if it is one house, stands in several figurative worlds endowed with marvelous systems of communication; those parts that have been brought to their highest phase of perfection find themselves in a state of comparative disuse, while the most ambitious development is directed toward those parts that appear to have been neglected.

This last is familiar, perhaps a hard fact, perhaps wholly understandable. But a touch of wholesome absurdity may help remind us of what we all know. The good writer who is *in* the words moving others has not pledged all the rest of his life to maintaining the sincerity and truth of a convincing scene or moment he composed. According to report, Robert Parsons, the great Jesuit master of the didactic exhortative death scene, died quietly, "in the midst of work,"[27] as if he were the unexpected beneficiary of one of Montaigne's expressed options.

When Montaigne wrote about friendship he drew from the life, or the former life, of his one great friend, La Boétie. The efforts at description are consciously extreme and inadequate, for good reason: "Our friendship has no other model than itself, and can be compared only with itself" (1.28.139). But he can compare the rest of his life with that four years of friendship ending in death: "There is no action or thought in which I do not miss him, as indeed he would have missed me" (1.28.143). In old age he returns to the subject and reveals by implication something latent in the passage of time:

> In true friendship, in which I am expert, I give myself to my friend more than I draw him to me. . . . And if absence is pleasant or useful to him, it is much sweeter to me than his presence; and it is not really absence when we have means of communication. In other days I made use and advantage of our separation. We filled and extended our possession of life better by separating: he lived, he enjoyed, he saw for me, and I for him, as fully as if he had been there. One part of us remained idle when we were together; we were fused into one. Separation in space made the conjunction of our wills richer. This insatiable hunger for bodily presence betrays a certain weakness in the enjoyment of souls. (3.9.746–47)

The paragraph is a stray reflection in an essay on many things, "Of Vanity," and the paragraph is notable for its retrospective omissions. It is filled with the certainties of friendship in life and is silent on the personal uncertainties discovered in the friendship after death. The brief "In other days" keeps the focus on past "separation," in the days of reciprocal life, which he has chosen to write on. A few pages later he breaks out, "And if I had not supported with all my strength a friend that I lost, they would have torn him into a thousand contrasting appearances" (p. 752). Another detached thought is limited to the subject of traveling alone, with chance companions, or with someone you like and who likes you: "I have missed such a man extremely on all my travels. . . . No pleasure has any savor for me without communication" (p. 754). We knew this last of the author of the *Essays* but are reminded of La Boétie again, to whose absence not a few of the personal bypaths discovered and followed in the act of writing may perhaps be attributed. He hopes that "some worthy man" pleased by his writings will try to meet him before he dies. Such a person could gain in three days of reading the equivalent of "long acquaintance and familiarity." And if the signs were right, "I would go very far to find him. . . . Oh, a friend!" In between the being sought and the seeking he inserted a later thought: "Amusing notion: many things that I would not want to tell anyone, I tell the public; and for my most secret knowledge and thoughts I send my most faithful friends to a bookseller's shop" (pp. 749–50).

For Montaigne or anyone in his position, there was no replacing of what the other "saw for me, and I for him." Without the reciprocity, the self had only its own resources; Montaigne would never know the "extended . . . possession of life" he had been deprived of by the loss of the other self. La Boétie, however immediate his presence, would remain the young friend of a man steadily growing older. If one cannot imagine one's own death, as Freud declared, without imagining someone else as acting the part, is it more probable that one could seriously construct the changes and developments in one's own future and then trust the authenticity of one's particular responses to imagined circumstances? Could one do this for another? But even if one could see with the eyes of the other and overcome for both all the obstacles created by the passage of time, how could one imagine *his* seeing "*for me*"? Where and how does one accommodate in the psyche the inescapable burden of conscious failure to see and to communicate the experience of two separated by the death of one? An oblique remark in another place admits the plain answer:

> For time . . . furnishing our imagination with other and ever other business, it dissolves and breaks up that first sensation, however strong it may be.
>
> A wise man sees his dying friend hardly less vividly after twenty-five years than in the first year; and according to Epicurus, no less vividly; for he attributed no alleviation of afflictions either to their anticipation or to their old age. But so many other thoughts traverse this one that in the end it languishes and tires. (3.4.635)

The kind of certainty and uncertainty isolated here may be glimpsed by grief and its anticipations but realized only through experience examined and reflected upon.[28] The example here is one more special case both like and unlike other intricacies considered in these pages. I am not bold enough to say with Montaigne, "It is the inattentive reader who loses my subject, not I," but I should like to think so. If we assume a more modern stance, the example of Montaigne and La Boétie may make it easier to measure the relative superficiality (however intimidating) of unmentioned instances that need only to be mentioned. I have in mind the otherness that is a contrived inversion of self, a holiday spree to experiment or purge; or the intermittent impersonation of an imaginary other (as in lending or borrowing voice); or the assuming of various disguises to mislead death, or to warm the hands at the sacrificial deaths that may add a moment of reassurance to the private person's, the tyrant's, or the crowd's immortality.

Expression has been the general subject, and I conclude: To express a reasonable acceptance of one's own death and life, one will need to consider the ways in which the experience and imagination of life affect our thoughts of death, and the ways in which the knowledge and imagination of death affect our thoughts of life. One will need to draw on the available thoughts and their language. One probably must, aware or not, include some discreet choices between thinking and not thinking, as in the instances of Montaigne and La Boétie or of Donne on the house of death in two worlds or one world. And one must reckon with the fortune or fate of the times one lives in and through, and what the house of art then makes available, or possible, or necessary.

CHAPTER NINETEEN

The End

As a stream falls from a single crack in a glacier
and its taste has two faces, one forward
one backward, and one is sweet and one hard,

so I die for the last time through each moment of these days,
and one way the old sighing frees me no longer,
and the other way the goal can no longer be seen.

OSIP MANDELSTAM, *"Moscow: December 1933"*

Who knows his own name at the last?
How shall he speak to a soul that has none?
"Tell me that name," I cried, "that I may speak
In a dire hour." The dire hour
Is the time when you must speak
To your naked self   never
Before seen, nor known.

ROBERT PENN WARREN, *"Sunset," Altitudes and Extensions*

The imagistic exchanges between the experiences of life and the observations and imaginations of death are, one concludes, necessary and instructive. They tell us things we might not otherwise know, even if the
knowledge becomes inert or restive. As we have had some occasions to
witness, images are true, or true in their place, or no truer than they
should be. They are also marvelously adaptable for all kinds of purposes, better and worse. They faithfully serve, and they may equally
divert, insinuate, dominate, rampage. As Bacon declared, from the
vantage ground of his time and wisdom, the imagination is not "simply
and only a messenger." Nor is it only a Janus:

> This Janus of Imagination hath differing faces; for the face
> towards Reason hath the print of Truth, but the face towards
> Action hath the print of Good; which nevertheless are faces.[1]

We may read in David E. Stannard's excellent book, *The Puritan
Way of Death,* how New England Puritans of the earlier period were
unable to reconcile the differences between their apprehensions of

dying and their concept of death. By the nineteenth century "the print of Good" on the Janus face turned toward "Action" was the one face in public view:

> In large measure, if not entirely in response to the growing individual anonymity brought on by changes in their social world, Americans sought a return to their lost sense of community in the graveyard and the heavenly world of the dead; in the process, paradoxically, they effectively banished the reality of death from their lives by a spiritualistic and sentimentalized embracing of it. (p. 185)

Here the imagistic exchanges familiar in literature may be discovered by the historian in ways of life that characterize a whole society. The differences in our concentration make what I have learned from Stannard's book most helpful in a few places where our interests converge. On the other hand, I have been deeply impressed by another work of history, the study of death in Western civilization by Philippe Ariès. Though I have made my basic acknowledgments earlier, I should like at this point to offer a brief critique of his book and to select from his magisterial work those thematic motives that illustrate and may help to focus the similar and different aims and interests of a book on literature.[2]

Two clearly articulated presuppositions direct the course of the study. The first is an anthropological insight: that the "tame death" is best, by which the social instincts and experience of human beings, "by prohibitions and concessions," protected themselves "from the violent and unpredictable forces of nature" (p. 604). The controls of "ritualization" and "ceremony" prevented "natural extravagance" and "solitary adventure" while developing into a necessary "public phenomenon involving the whole community" (p. 604). The second presupposition is that the truest guide to the history of death is the collective unconscious—though the discoveries of individuals may intuit or recognize that force and its current tendencies. One infers that such individuals may also produce the models of expression that represent the consciousness of the times.

The basic model is that of the "tame death," and a sturdy thread of his continuity is the demonstration of examples that express a characterizing abstract of their times and that exhibit suggestive currents and undercurrents of relationship to past and future examples and to the basic model. Each main phase of the history, besides its exemplary patterns, is augmented by a deliberate wealth of illustrative historical materials from a great variety of sources.

To continue: In its second major phase death moves toward becoming individual, something apart from the continuity of life, and develops into a dramatic concentration on the death of the self.[3] In its third phase death is thought of more as happening to someone else, part of "the idea of mortality in general" (p. 314), and characterized in the nineteenth century as the "beautiful" death of the loved one, and in the twentieth century by various forms of "invisibility."

The modern era is characterized by a collective "denial" of death, by unacknowledged evasion, silence, and suppression. Death becomes invisible and private, "medicalized" in hospitals, for which the most vivid example is the solitary death protracted by the determination and skills of technology. The extremes of history repeat themselves:

> The death of the patient in the hospital, covered with tubes, is becoming a popular image, more terrifying than the *transi* or skeleton of macabre rhetoric. (p. 614)

That is the kind of irony which talented moralists have always been alert to discover. More to the point, however, the history of the collective unconscious records many examples of the return of the repressed, often in the shape of exchanges under disguise. For instance, in the twentieth century the liberation of sex coincides with the growth of taboos surrounding death. So children are shielded from direct knowledge of death, but sex education begins early. A trained observer may speak of the "pornography" of death.[4] The "remoteness" of death "has aroused . . . strange curiosity . . . fantasies . . . perverse deviations and eroticism" (p. 608). Though for centuries the messages kept coming—as the personal warning by which one recognized, by some trusted signal, that death was at hand—these messages have now generally lapsed. The modern midlife crisis may, however, still be on the rise. Excessive attention to the soul of the dying person has been replaced by excessive attention to the body.

I now begin to work back toward the Renaissance again but pause on the "beautiful" death of the Romantic era. In the analysis by Ariès, fear, supplemented by the emotions of a new sensibility, was transferred from the self to the other and centered in the feelings of loss; these were transformed by a new pathos and by easy, domesticated thoughts of reunion in the next world.

> The compromise of beauty was the last obstacle invented to channel an immoderate emotion that had swept away the old barriers. It was an obstacle that was also a concession, for it restored to this phenomenon that people had tried to diminish an extraordinary glamour. (p. 610)

Death was "exalted as a moment to be desired." This last was of course not altogether new, but now the motives and the attendant feelings of the exaltation and desire were different, and in some ways new.

The death of the self of the earlier phase, in spite of the intensity of its highest development, is in Ariès's historical perspective characterized by hidden motives and disguised exchanges. For instance:

> In the spiritual treatises of the sixteenth and seventeenth centuries the main purpose is no longer to prepare the dying for death but to teach the living to meditate on death. . . . in this new economy, death has become the pretext for a metaphysical meditation on the fragility of life that is intended to keep us from giving in to life's illusions. Death is no more than a means of living well. It could be the invitation to pleasure of the Epicureans; actually, it is the rejection of this pleasure; yet the skeleton on the goblets of the pleasure-seeking Epicureans of Pompeii is the same as the one in the engravings of the *Spiritual Exercises*. (p. 301)

On the other hand, there is "a model of the good death" in the sixteenth and seventeenth centuries, "beautiful and edifying," with no identified repressions or evasive exchanges, and up to a point resembling the old model of the "tame death." Ariès describes and admires it but is unusually sparing of examples. He explains its existence from the rise of the value of moderation at a time when man accepted the responsibilities of living in the world, without either excessive attachment to the things of the world or total renunciation. Death can no longer "call everything into question when its shadow falls upon a life," but is also "subject to the law of moderation":

> This is the death of the righteous man who thinks little about his own physical death when it comes, but has thought about it all his life. This death has neither the excitement nor the intensity of the death of the *artes moriendi* of the late Middle Ages. It is not exactly the death of Roland, La Fontaine's laborer, or Tolstoi's peasants, but it is not so unlike it either. It has their serenity and their public quality, whereas the death of the *artes moriendi* was dramatic and internalized. Everything happened out of sight of the circle of friends. (p. 310)

The emphasis on the "public quality" would seem to owe more to the original model in the author's mind than to the volume of historical evidence. Yet this good death could at times be witnessed, and certainly heard of and read about. (Though not what Ariès intends to include, there are some affinities between his model and the public deaths of More and Raleigh, and those of the Jesuit martyrs Campion and Southwell.) The kind of death Ariès seems to have in mind is examinable and so is "public" in the attributes demonstrated, but it is nevertheless an individual achievement, a death intended to reflect the control of reason and will. It is related to the death Milton's Michael teaches Adam to accept as a basic guide to living outside the Garden of Eden. Sir Henry Wotton's death as Walton describes it resembles the model. The calm summation of Herbert's poem, "Therefore we can go die as sleep," represents a workaday ideal available to the individual reader. With minor adjustments the model is applicable to Donne's "Hymne to God my God, in my sicknesse" and "A Hymne to God the Father," and even to Raleigh's "The Passionate Man's Pilgrimage."

One may note that the death of the righteous man expresses, in the efforts mastered and transformed into graceful serenity, a singular possession of personal freedom before death. The terms would seem to limit the number of successful candidates, with even more restricted availability to those in the midst of life—though a modern political hero who has learned not to desire what his masters have to offer may be fortified by the modest joy of that freedom.[5] Some tragic heroes make the lights and shadows of the territory more knowable. The equipoise achieved by conscious refusals cannot be common to all, and the model is not one likely to be transmitted by social forces and their driving needs. Still, I want to enter the demurral: an achieved balance belongs to the history of death and continues, as consciousness does, though communal and other supports have dwindled.

In the model that Ariès admires, he nevertheless identifies a cause of its historical ineffectiveness and its contribution to a deteriorating change. Because the man "who thinks little about his own physical death when it comes, but who has thought about it all his life," by exhibiting a personal success helps increase that relative neglect of "the historical reality of the moment itself." As a result, the moment became "diluted and distributed over the whole of life and in this way lost all its intensity." The substituted "idea" was that of "mortality in general." He concludes: "This life in which death was removed to a prudent distance seems less loving of things and people than the life in which death was the center" (p. 315).

One of his approaches to his Renaissance model of the good death is by way of an example from Erasmus's *Colloquies*. In "The Shipwreck," an apparently simple person displays an exemplary calm in the face of imminent death. Amidst the competing voices raised to heaven in prayers and vows offering gifts and services, and these to be delivered at specific holy places on earth, " a certain woman who was suckling a baby. . . . was the only one who didn't scream, weep, or make promises; she simply prayed in silence, clasping her little boy."[6] Later, when she was lashed to a plank in a special way and given a small board and pushed out clear of the ship, "Holding her baby with her left hand, she paddled with the right" (p. 144). She made it safely to shore, the first one to do so. Her practical action of resisting death (both arms doing their proper work) is a piece of silent eloquence, a memorable image of balance. The balance owes much to the skill and economy of Erasmus's narrative art, which creates, mostly out of what is not said amidst the noise a certain sense of her mental preparation to accept the death she effectively resists. For direct comments we may look to, and borrow from, another colloquy, "The Godly Feast." There one speaker asks:

> What else does Christ proclaim to us than that we should live
> and watch as though we were shortly to die, to exert ourselves
> in good deeds as though we were to live forever? (p. 67)

Another speaker recites a list, too long, of Christian ceremonies (these are approved of in spite of the way they are presented, but the spirit in which they are performed is not approved of). He then concludes with a grim travesty of the ceremonies that accompany, and often hasten, the approach of death. Still, no criticism is intended of ceremonies "sanctioned by ecclesiastical usage . . . yet there are also other, more interior means of helping us to depart from this life with cheerfulness and Christian trust" (p. 69).

Expecting death before long, but doing good as if we were to go on forever and, whenever death comes, seeking to leave cheerfully, with Christian trust: that is an interpretation of life, one man's wisdom lifted out of a couple of instructional exercises that have the character and charm of good fiction. What Erasmus shows is not an interpretation of history. But Ariès insists on translating these views of Erasmus into historical evidence, part of the case for showing that interest in death chiefly served interest in life. And that program for wisdom seems to lead toward a long, downward path, after "the historical reality of the moment itself" (i.e., death) lost its place at the center of life, and a process of deterioration became inevitable, and life became or "seems less loving of things and people." Though the statement comes as a large interpretation of history, one recognizes that this too is an interpretation of life, one man's wisdom.

On the other hand, I find myself with little resistance to Ariès's proposition that the idea of death was "replaced by the idea of mortality in general." Indeed, I have tried to follow some of the evidence in poetry. But poetry has its own ways and rhythms of "replacing" the old with the new, and so does the history of one life, if it is thoughtful and imaginative. Approaching old age, Montaigne wrote (I quote again):

> I saw death nonchalantly when I saw it universally, as the end
> of life. I dominate it in the mass; in detail it harasses me.
> (3.4.636)[7]

The details are never "replaced," but whether or when or how they are thought of can influence both "the idea of death" and "the idea of mortality in general."

For example, Jeremy Taylor was a master of the "new" Protestant art of casuistry and of the Protestant art of dying. As part of his general approach to the problems of dying, he shifts the emphasis from the crisis of the last moment and treats many of the standard preparations with a sympathetic practicality. For instance, the likelihood of a last sickness and its unavoidable weakness: weakness opens the understanding to doubt, and then faith has to stand while lacking the old supports of health; therefore, "let the sick man fear a proposition, which his sickness hath put into him."[8] It is good advice, though some Puritans would have regarded it as an impotent palliative. It is advice that owes something to rational analysis, but is also motivated by a practical kindness not unlike that which one admires in Tolstoi's peasants. The example of Taylor would seem to have more roots in the history of critical rationalism than in the collective unconscious. When he reminds the healthy community of witnesses that what is happening is between the dying man and God, not "between him and the friends that stand by the bed-side"[9] (3.2.81), he does not himself seem "less loving . . . of people."

To return to the matter of sickness: the casuist does not neglect the rational difficulties in a theoretical choice that may instruct one facing a decision that has been made elsewehere, and he offers alternatives that test and refine the answer, whichever it is. On the one hand, men dread a sudden death; on the other hand, "though a sicknesse tries our vertues, yet a sudden death is free from temptation: a sicknesse may be more glorious, and a sudden death more safe" (4.5.188). Then he turns to a troubling subject, the mockery of God in deathbed repentances. Though "sorrow for sins upon any motive may lead us to God by many intermediall passages," repentance is to be completed, not begun, on our death-bed (4.6.199). And yet, as in the relative safety of sudden death and the possible glory of a long sickness, he would weigh the alternatives in a rational balance. For there is also a "heroic action of vertue" to be recognized as possible in a late repentance; indeed, it is a "huge compendium of religion." If sudden and true ("which is seldom seene"), it may jump the ordinary steps of virtue from inclination to act, to habit, to abode, to reigning, to perfect possession, to "extraordinary emanations." For "it is certain, that *to some purposes* God will account for our religion on our death-bed, not by the measures of our time, but the eminency of affection" (4.6.205).

Besides the kindness and the application of rational analysis intended not to increase the intensity of the last moment but to increase the possibility of a calm acceptance of death, he does not forget his regular spiritual obligations and purposes. These do not prevent him from giving dignified comfort and instruction. So on the major subject of fear he sorts out the kinds that are unreasonable if one believes in a merciful God. Fear and trembling are normal and to be expected, "parts of our duty," and not be diagnosed as symptoms of "our calamity."

> The fearing man is the safest, and if he fears on his death-bed, it is but what happens to most considering men, and what was to be looked for all his life-time, he talked of the terrours of death, and death is the king of terrours: and therefore it is no strange thing if then he be hugely afraid: if he be not, it is either a great felicity, or a great presumption. (5.5.285–86)

My questioning of Ariès derives in part from the study of a different kind of literature which is less obedient to the methods of his own discipline. I am sympathetic with his enterprise and applaud the achievement, and being a fellow citizen of the present I have a share in some of his ways of seeing problems, the shadows they cast and the shapes they contain. On the other hand, I think it reasonable to note that Ariès does not grant religious traditions enough credit for their contribution to the history of disciplining resistance and fear. In any case, the smaller body of distinguished materials I have studied in my own way, asking other questions, yields some partly different answers and some irreducible half-answers.

I think of Montaigne, who is perhaps too sprawling and elusive to find any place in Ariès's book but keeps slipping into mine, though he is not an Englishman or only a Frenchman and does not quite represent his times by his peculiar combinations of material from ancient books, modern observations, and self-consultations. We find him returning persistently to Socrates as a true model in the significant agreement of his life and his thought. On the other hand, there are Montaigne's unembarrassed sidelong acknowledgments of his own disinclination or inability to measure up to that example of human perfection. He will die, we learn elsewhere, peacefully in bed listening to Mass—not at all

ERRATUM

Arnold Stein, <u>The House of Death</u>

The first five lines of page 267 should read as follows:

in accord with his announced whimsical truths of the moment, such as preferring to die while planting his cabbages or while going off to look sour among strangers. In the disciplined indulgence of his essays he stubbornly refuses to look "elsewhere" to understand death. Yet, like others, he would himself shut his eyes when leaping into the sea.

"hospice" and a practical means of recovering for some the benefits of the "tame death." Social history in the making now has an increasing number of those striving to educate the collective unconscious, about which new knowledge has discovered an appropriate instrument of leverage and hope:

> It belongs to the one and only Socrates to become acquainted with death with an ordinary countenance, to become familiar with it and play with it. He seeks no consolation outside the thing itself; dying seems to him a natural and indifferent incident. He fixes his gaze precisely on it, and makes up his mind to it, without looking elsewhere. . . . Our thoughts are always elsewhere; the hope of a better life stays and supports us, or the hope of our children's worth, or the future glory of our name, or flight from the ills of this life, or the vengeance that threatens those who cause our death. (3.4.632–33)

He is candid about his personal inadequacies: changing the subject, resorting to diversionary interests, humorously embracing the excuse of an authoritative example; so if Caesar said that the quickest and least premeditated death is best, this cannot be cowardice in Montaigne to believe the same (2.13.460). He has the consolation of good company in the philosophers who produce their strained and inept arguments: "I love to see these leading souls unable to shake off our common lot" (3.4.634).

Not the idea of death but the personal details harass Montaigne. In the best Renaissance literature the details search, illuminate, and bring into forms of examinable meaning experiences that can be questioned or accepted, or that induce the further need and prospects for reconciliation. Shakespeare's tragedies have their own ways of making the moment of death intense while not making it the center of life in the play. Lear's death is "public," surrounded by impotent friends who disagree; there is even a brief debate over the conduct of the last moment. Audiences and readers must disagree over details and their meaning. Many find that the death is bounded by a terrible solitude, and the hope that Lear expresses in his last words is either a discovery of hope or a diversion; neither is exempt from the likelihood of being simple illusion. Tichborne, Raleigh, Donne, Herbert, Jonson, Marvell, and Milton make their individual judgments of the problems of living-and-dying. Their idea of death has, at the least, a family resemblance, but details make the messages distinctive. In their poems we hear, see, feel, and renew our sense of the reality of life and the reality of death.

The idea of death has many messengers and other representatives. I shall not undertake to choose among them for their truth or influence, but I single out once more qualifications that the evidence of Renaissance literature shows to have special value: a developed sense of self and the relationships between self and other which make talk about death worth hearing. I take it for granted that in literature the self must convince that it is sentient and there, not a figure of memory; the "other" may be more intellectualized, but the relationships must be felt. Without Cordelia, Lear's death would be deprived of a telling dimension the community of attending friends could not supply. (In a different world, that of Socrates' last day, the story would have been spoiled for all time if the wife and children had been allowed to remain.)

No one capable of love, or capable of ordinary thinking and feeling, can lack means and materials for communing with his own death. I forbear references to previous pages and seek elsewhere for fresh examples, and choose two. When another or others are involved, even those who are unknown strangers or the troops one commands, they help intensify, define, and place in perspective one's own identity in death. I quote the prose translation of a Hebrew poem written in the eleventh century by Samuel Hanagid:

> I billeted a strong force overnight in a citadel laid waste in former days by other generals. There we slept upon its back and flanks, while under us its landlords slept. And I said to my heart: Where are the many people who once lived here? Where are the builders and vandals, the rulers and paupers, the slaves and masters? Where are the begetters and the bereaved, the fathers and the sons, the mourners and the bridegrooms? And where are the many people born after the others had died, in days gone by, after other days and years? Once they lodged upon the earth; now they are lodged within it. They passed from the palaces to the grave, from pleasant courts to dust. Were they now to raise their heads and emerge, they would rob us of our lives and pleasures. Oh, it is true, my soul, most true: tomorrow I shall be like them, and all these troops as well![10]

And now a small, firm item of convincing personal truth, an anonymous old woman's discovery:

> Since Penelope Noakes of Duppas Hill is gone, there is no one who will ever call me Nellie again.[11]

Under the change of times, the old subject changes and remains. The tide of human looking away causes the human invention of the "hospice" and a practical means of recovering for some the benefits of the "tame death." Social history in the making now has an increasing number of those striving to educate the collective unconscious, about which new knowledge has discovered an appropriate instrument of leverage and hope:

> Perhaps public opinion will be aroused and will seize on the subject with the passion it has shown for other vital issues, notably abortion. (Ariès, p. 593)

From time to time catastrophes have provided unprecedented experiences and have exposed an edge of strange knowledge. For instance, among the complex tensions and exchanges between the dying and the witnesses the sense of guilt on both sides was often present but not developed into a distinct and recognizable category of response. The Nazi death camps, however, produced massive traumas of communicable guilt among many who were not chosen when others were, and special traumas that mark the early awareness of a new contagion.[12]

It was an old and valued enterprise to offer rational arguments for the double purposes of making death a helpful servant of life and at the same time making the acceptance of death a conclusion supported by and supporting forms of conscious control. In the recent philosophy of Jaspers, Heidegger, and Sartre, increasing the consciousness of death has been for the most part a side issue but one of considerable importance for approaching problems of existence. Nevertheless, such efforts share many of the standing problems of the old enterprise and make individual contributions to one's understanding of the subject.

But I turn to poets and storytellers, who have their own ways, which I think I understand better. Besides, their examples lend themselves to the brief exhibition I intend. The new seldom is entirely new, not on this subject, but particular intensities and crucial details may quite dominate some of the standard parts of the inherited subject. One recognizes, as one may expect to, traces of an older idea of death, or older habits of thought and their characteristic images, often expressed in altered contexts where old and new confront each other.

Tolstoi was a great nineteenth-century master of the full death scene, with an authoritative power of grasp and a fine sureness of touch. In *Anna Karenina* Nikolay Levin's premonitions and early tactics of evasion finally lead to the stage of the last bed, where the process of evasion intensifies almost as if it were possessed with a life of its own. The medical and clerical roles are at best minor but useful. They accomplish little of what they pretend, but their absence would probably admit further stresses and impede the process that is in motion. They are part of an ambivalent ritual by means of which Nikolay keeps hoping for life while indirectly getting ready to stop hoping. The thoughtful and loving brother, Konstantin, is almost helpless, but his presence is important in ways that do not come under direct scrutiny. The temporary heroine is Konstantin's wife, Kitty, who has all the right instincts and skills. She makes the room, bed, and Nikolay himself comfortable; she chatters pleasantly and entertains him, anticipates and therefore understands his needs, ignores or diverts the disturbing, and makes her company felt. She quickly gets past his suspicious resentment of those well-possessed of life and provides basic human medicine: he likes her and feels himself liked. But her role is ended when internal evidence begins to turn the balance against hope for life. He identifies her cheerfulness with the brief upward swing of his spirits and rejects her when the futility of hope gains a crucial but still contested dominance. Her contribution of human kindness has been to help him through a very difficult stage. No one can help him as much again. Subsequent days of steady pain turn his apprehension, that death is in truth coming, toward a waiting, not without resentment and grumbling, which becomes only at the last a conscious desire for the moment of release. One might be visiting the scene of a "good death" of much earlier times—if one entered the scene very late, believing that the consummation was achieved by the old wisdom and its smoothly running apparatus of preparation. Tolstoi, however, records a sustained conflict between fear of death and hope of life in which the external assistance is chiefly that of practical human kindness to ease suffering and provide support, until nature and the body can teach the inner message, and the dying man acquire a singular kind of consciousness: knowing, resisting, and only at the end accepting, but doing so with a precision of deepened personal knowledge that, like threading a needle too small for others to see, turns into a last corridor of welcomed knowledge. The last two moments are ones of astonishing rightness:

> "He is gone," said the priest, and would have moved away; but suddenly there was a faint stir in the mustaches of the dead man that seemed glued together, and quite distinctly in the hush they heard from the bottom of the chest the sharply defined sounds:
>
> "Not quite . . . soon."
>
> And a minute later the face brightened, a smile came out under the mustaches, and the women who had gathered round began carefully laying out the corpse.[13]

Writing *about the* actual moment of one's death is hard to do, and pretending to do so is encumbered by improbabilities. We have seen (in Chap. 4) some highly motivated but naive and self-betraying efforts. The deathbed scene Donne arranged for himself early in *The Second Anniversary* (discussed in Chap. 13) is not naive but goes to an opposite extreme of willful pretext. (There are brilliant passages in the approaches to and the death scene itself of Camus's abandoned novel, *La mort heureuse* [*A Happy Death*], but these avail themselves of the understood fictional privilege of a writer to enter and speak from the consciousness of his character.) One of Emily Dickinson's remarkable accomplishments was to make the reader willing to receive and enter into her first-person report of the experience of extinction. In "I heard a Fly buzz—when I died—" after that opening line the scene being prepared makes no extreme demands on the reader. Though details and presentations are far from ordinary, the tableau of special waiting is familiar enough to accept while the promise of the mysterious moment collects intensity: the stillness, the tears already wept, the breaths of expectation "For that last Onset—when the King / Be witnessed—in the Room." A brief step backward—that trusted delay of narrative truth—recalls the practical formalities of having already signed away the "Keepsakes" and all of the self that was "Assignable." Then the fly at the window becomes the object of concentrated attention, a veritable Beelzebub of a fly, king and no king, familiar to all stages and corners of life, and after. These thoughts aside, to the speaker the fly becomes part of the external measure of light-and-life. She sees the fly between the light and herself and begins to distinguish the moments of recession in the last moment: the outward parts and then the inward part, the last verifying act of consciousness turning back on itself:

> And then the Windows failed—and then
> I could not see to see.

In *the great* final story of Joyce's *Dubliners,* "The Dead," a small, late episode, bringing to light a personal death years before, affects the disguised face of death represented by the layers of "inauthentic existence" that fill out the bulk of the story. The revealed death was a "beautiful" death of a young man seventeen years old, and Gabriel's wife, Gretta, says, "I think he died for me." That death of another, which still is alive in the wife's feelings, renews in the disturbed husband the believability of the promises of life. Finally, however, the flow of Gabriel's aroused emotion turns his longing into elegiac lyricism, into a strange, compelled celebration of a visionary landscape, which answers the blank futility of his inner life. The beautiful writing and the full measure of sentimentality recreate a *memento mori* of altered appearance. Another alteration is that the message does not come to a sensibility and way of thought trained to receive it as a warning; it comes like a personal last judgment.

To recall for a moment Ariès's model of the Romantic "beautiful" death: its emotions are transferred from self to other and are centered in the feelings of loss while restoring, by the beauty that also controls dangerous emotions, "an extraordinary glamour" to the phenomenon of death. I think one may well be astonished by what Joyce's "details" have done to the recognizable similarities. The "idea of mortality in general" has crept into the idea of life in general, and failures in one's own life become inseparable from the failure of life itself underneath the plastered decorousness of a particular time and place. The older contempt for the illusions of life has been transformed; these are not illusions that may be resisted but are the vanities that we have ourselves become while losing the strength of both desire and hope. The one exception concerns love, which has its own enigmas. Joyce drapes with deliberate beauty the final vision of a darkened land on which the snow is falling, everywhere, and "upon every part of the lonely churchyard on the hill where Michael Furey lay buried. . . . His soul swooned slowly as he heard the snow falling faintly through the universe and faintly falling, like the descent of their last end, upon all the living and the dead." We may notice both similarities and differences when Macbeth's soul, unswooning, responds to a voice of judgment:

> Methought I heard a voice cry, "Sleep no more!
> Macbeth does murther sleep"—the innocent sleep,
> Sleep that knits up the ravell'd sleave of care,
> The death of each day's life, sore labor's bath,
> Balm of hurt minds, great nature's second course,
> Chief nourisher in life's feast.
>
> (2.2.32–37)

Macbeth also speaks a strange, compelled celebration, but it is the anguished praise of unacknowledged prayer and still has the strength of personal, uncrippled desire.

The poet Thomas Hardy abandoned his faith, but he could not forget many of the interests, images, habits of thought, and common resources laid down in his youth and drawn upon by his access to the long memory of the rural folk he knew. There is a great deal of imagined traffic at the grave, both coming and going. Those in residence have individual voices and wonderful things to say when they are moved to sing of present and past, sometimes "all day cheerily, / All night eerily." Revenants with messages or unsatisfied interests are frequent, and they resemble, with some acquired differences, figures long passed away in a literature reserved for antiquaries. My brief samples, however, are intended chiefly to illustrate how durable old attitudes can be in altered contexts.

So in "Overlooking the River Stour"[14] two stanzas of intense, minute description record the life of movement above and on the river. Then the description of an inert meadow takes up a potentiality of the feeling suggested by the repeated lines in each stanza, which sing but also, more to the point, turn back on themselves. The fourth stanza comes to the grief of looking out the window and not turning into the room, "To see the more behind my back." A song of failed love thus translates the innocence of nature into the occasion of a failure of spirit by a rigid act (clearly not the first or the last) of evasion. Back of the poem is a long history of accusing the things of this world of a sinister allurement that misleads mankind and brings about the stupid, willful neglect of the things of the spirit. Images are adaptable.

"During Wind and Rain," a song of the passage of time, with varied refrains, presents a clearly remembered individual scene in each stanza—joyful, painful, the yes and no of it. The poem ends with a standard object recording time more slowly in the present of the title. I quote the last stanza:

> They change to a high new house,
> He, she, all of them—aye,
> Clocks and carpets and chairs
>   On the lawn all day,
> And brightest things that are theirs. . . .
>   Ah, no; the years, the years;
> Down their carved names the raindrop ploughs.
>
> (p. 496)

And last: in "Afterwards" Hardy composes a gentle version of his personal immortality. That is, he asks whether any neighbors will remember, as they see and hear things, how "He was a man who used to notice such things." If he "passes" at a time when the hedgehog "travels furtively over the lawn,"

> One may say, "He strove that such innocent creatures should come to no harm,
> But he could do little for them; and now he is gone."

The last stanza adds a further turn to the good-natured irony:

> And will any say when my bell of quittance is heard in the gloom,
>   And a crossing breeze cuts a pause in its outrollings,
> Till they rise again, as they were a new bell's boom,
>   "He hears it not now, but used to notice such things"?
>
> (p. 553)

The death anticipated throughout Saul Bellow's *Mr. Sammler's Planet*[15] avoids the closure of human engagement. Dr. Elya Gruner, the dying man, centers his resistance on preventing such a family scene, and his calamitous children might be sufficient justification by themselves, but the motives reach beyond them. Gruner is in firm control of his death, as Nikolay Levin was not; so the evasions and contradictions are different and restrained at a deeper level, but they are there. As Mr. Sammler reflects after an intense conversation spoken "factually" and sounding "utterly level":

> Something very odd in Elya's expression. There were tears about, somewhere, but dignity would not permit them. Perhaps it was self-severity, not dignity. But they did not come out. They were rerouted, absorbed into the system. They were subdued, converted into tones. They were present in the voice, in the color of the skin, in the lights of the eye. (p. 164)

In a long soliloquy that comes later, Mr. Sammler goes from trying to think of "mitigating things" to essentials. I quote with many omissions:

> He loved his nephew, and he had something that Elya needed. . . . Elya was a physician and a businessman. . . . And business, in business America, was also a training system for souls. The fear of being unbusinesslike was very great. . . . But at the very end business would not do for Elya. . . . And compassionate utterance was a mortal necessity. Utterance, sounds of hope and desire, exclamations of grief. Such things were suppressed, as if illicit. . . . At this stage of things there was a terrible dumbness. About essentials, almost nothing could be said. Still, signs could be made, should be made, must be made. . . . Elya at this moment had a most particular need for a sign and he, Sammler, should be there to meet that need. (pp. 237–39)

This is followed by a telephone conversation in which Sammler says that he is coming to the hospital and in which all the "signs" are made by Gruner:

"I may have to go down for tests." Elya's voice was filled with unidentifiable tones. Sammler's interpretive skill was insufficient. He was uneasy. "Why shouldn't there be time?" Elya said. "There's time enough for everything." This had an odd ring, and the accents were strange.

"Yes?"

"Of course, yes." . . .

Uneasiness somewhat interfered with Sammler's breathing. Long and thin, he held the telephone, concentrating, aware of the anxious intensity gathered in his face. He was silent. Elya said, "Angela is on her way over."

"I am coming too."

"Yes." Elya lingered somewhat on the shortest words. "Well, Uncle?"

"Goodby, for now."

"Goodby, Uncle Sammler." (p. 240)

Later in the hospital Sammler receives a word of personal farewell transmitted by the attending physician. His own access to an act of farewell is gained by the threat of creating "a bad scene" if he is not taken at once to see his dead nephew. When he uncovers the face, "In the lips bitterness and an expression of obedience were combined." In a "mental whisper" Sammler prays briefly, praises Elya's kindness, and speaks of ("may I be forgiven for this") Elya's desire "to do what was required of him." In the world Gruner and Sammler share, this too is "a good death," because meeting "the terms" of one's "contract" is good. We are witnesses to the reaching out indirectly, to the making of minimal "signs," which are permitted as neither a bad scene nor a good one is. Fulfillment is missing and missed, felt in the tearlessness, the disciplined anguish, the deep ache of an orderly mutilation. At least there would be an autopsy. "Let's find out what went wrong" (pp. 285–86).

Theodore Roethke's death was sudden and mute, but he had prepared his last farewell to himself, a death of his own, and especially in the poems of "North American Sequence." Their meditative ceremonies and celebrations are composed in solitude, making their peace out of the materials of personal and private memory, which has taken in what others have thought; but these are silent presences, a community from whom he has learned how to shape his own solitude. There are traceable affinities, among many differences, to the "tame death," and to the tranquil death of the Renaissance man of good conscience and clear hope, and to the "beautiful death" of the nineteenth century, but like the religious faith the affinities have been transformed into something of his own. We are probably too close to judge whether these poems represent strand or cable, something conscious or unconscious in the spirit of the age.

I seem to be engaging in a long story, but I still intend to be as brief as possible. I settle on one poem, "The Far Field," and single out for special attention one line, an unmarked parenthesis in the final stanza:

> All finite things reveal infinitude:
> The mountain with its singular bright shade
> Like the blue shine on freshly frozen snow,
> The after-light upon ice-burdened pines;
> Odor of basswood on a mountainslope,
> A scent beloved of bees;
> Silence of water above a sunken tree:
> The pure serene of memory in one man, —
> A ripple widening from a single stone
> Winding around the waters of the world. [16]

All the descriptive details from nature compose the harmony of the self changing from "An old man with his feet before the fire" into a revelation of "infinitude." He said, a few lines earlier, "I am renewed by death, thought of my death." The renewal points toward "infinitude," the continuity of life in death, and also toward the other source of the same thought, love of the things of life in life:

> What I love is near at hand,
> Always, in earth and air.

The objects loved in the last stanza are, all but one, things that reveal themselves in still moments of acute vision animated by light and shade, or in movements that become a single movement. They are for the man in love with them parts of the continuity of life in death. But "Odor of basswood on a mountain-slope" has a different kind of animation, marked by the momentary digression of love "near at hand," which expresses love of the things of life in life ("A scent beloved of bees"). The line introducing the bees is mildly errant, moved by the man's loving knowledge a step backward from "infinitude," a barely heard dissonance, a detail that strays, love-drawn, even in the embrace of a commanding vision. It is a marvelous validating touch and is one that reminds me, picking my way through the differences, of what Roethke would have been pleased to hear from me: that this delicate, unruly assertion of self resembles Donne's needing to speak out at the crucial moment of "Hymne to God my God, in my sicknesse" in his own voice to God:

Looke Lord, and finde both *Adams* met in me;
As the first *Adams* sweat surrounds my face,
May the last *Adams* blood my soule embrace.

I *trust that* these retrospective examples have some use in reminding the
reader of the fine differences in Renaissance poems on death and of the
threads of continuity that persevere, however much seems changed.
One last example, a Renaissance poem again, has something further to
tell us about fine differences when a temporal perspective complicates
the relations among things said. My example is the song from the
fourth act of Shakespeare's *Cymbeline,* a dirge for the death (supposed)
of Imogen (disguised). The poem begins:

Fear no more the heat o' th' sun,
Nor the furious winter's rages,
Thou thy worldly task hast done,
Home art gone, and ta'en thy wages.
Golden lads and girls all must,
As chimney-sweepers, come to dust.
(4.2.258–63)

One advantage of quoting these lines after a group of modern
examples is that the reader's temporal perspective will already have had
some useful exercise in making adjustments. One result, I believe, is
that these lines will seem old-fashioned in a special way. They were old-
fashioned when they were first heard on the stage about 1610. The basic
ideas and general orientation are turned away from those "modern"
kinds of attitude and emphasis that individualized death and dying.
What we have now, rather, is a turning back toward the older wisdom
derived from the knowledge, always at hand, that all must die, and
seeming to hold that knowledge with the right kind of untensed readiness. As for the compulsory end, coming to dust: one thing to say is
that so quiet an extreme may well call to mind available alternatives,
such as a powerfully imagined Renaissance scene of Judgment Day or
any assigned part in the crowded, busy spectacle of an ambitious Triumph of Death.

I quote the next two stanzas:

Fear no more the frown o' th' great,
Thou art past the tyrant's stroke;
Care no more to clothe and eat,
To thee the reed is as the oak.
The sceptre, learning, physic, must
All follow this and come to dust.

Fear no more the lightning-flash.
Nor th' all-dreaded thunder-stone.
Fear not slander, censure rash.
Thou hast finish'd joy and moan.
All lovers young, all lovers must
Consign to thee and come to dust.

The second stanza names other privileges of death to be added to the immunity from heat and cold. This last is now figured by the seasonal "rages" of social power; somewhat different is relief from the burden of daily necessities. Finally, a social grouping appears, "The sceptre, learning, physic." Recognized at once, these figures act the part of a regularly constituted allegorical procession; they repeat, as if it were an obligatory ritual, the rule of necessity and thus provide the meager but desired reassurance that all indeed must die, including one's betters as well as one's juniors. Company in death may not be one of the most desired privileges of death, and, construed as a compensation for dying as one should, it may seem like an argument on the verge of bankruptcy—as though one should be promised as a privilege of death to receive from the great a frown turned into a gratifying smile and an arrested stroke turned into the tyrant's companionable wave of hand. But who would argue against the unchallenged reputation of death as the great leveler?

What is effectively in place by the end of the second stanza is an array of old-fashioned responses to death, some of them having been repeated for centuries, on countless schedules and at great length. Still suspended and not aiming at the ready response are some other matters. The release of bodies takes place, but the poem seems unaware of the idea of souls. The representatives of royal power, learning, and the practice of medicine (a modern short list more than a cross-section)—like the "worldly task" and "home" of the first stanza and the "joy and moan" of the third stanza—all share the same habitation, this world. One world, one house of death.

The worst bad news of human certainty, the refrain of "come to dust," is loosely paired with some common ills of life, a sampling from natural and social existence. The pairing is less exact and insistent than it might have been, as the record of some five earlier centuries makes plain. For one thing, none of the bad news encourages hatred of life, and standard opportunities for furthering that cause are ignored. Still, the true end is repeated three times; no alternative is mentioned or intimated; this world or stage seems to have none. All the materials of consolation are derived from the place where the "worldly task" is "done." The consolation is restrained. "Golden lads and girls," "All lovers young, all lovers": these are the only clear candidates for "joy," which is coupled with "moan." Yet a special calm prevails in the graceful flow of energetic pronouncements, and one may remark on a general air of good humor not always found in agreeable messages of cheer. Montaigne's praise of Socrates' view of death seems to describe a quality of Shakespeare's vision here: "He seeks no consolation outside the thing itself. . . . He fixes his gaze precisely . . . without looking elsewhere. . . . Our thoughts are always elsewhere" (3.4.632–33).

In the early seventeenth century many of the images and sentiments would have awakened trusted resonances, among which less familiar matters might have gone unnoticed, for much of the message was very old and had been heard often. Perhaps no one who was interested in poetry would have thought the language itself anything but perfectly current. But at least one part of the message was both old enough and unfamiliar enough to have seemed novel to some. For nothing is said of death that links it with divine punishment for Adam's disobedience, and therefore this death in the poem must be that other kind, derived from pagan thought and explained as a universal law of nature. Like the elegies Shakespeare may well have read in Sidney's *Arcadia*, his poem is based on the fictional privilege of expressing pregospel times. He stretches the privilege greatly when he makes past and present cross each other like fertile similarities and differences. The verses read over Imogen's body create a particular order of imaginative innocence, enchantment, and truth.[17]

As I leave these matters I want to suggest affinities between Shakespeare's song and the modern examples I have offered. I think especially of the relations inherited and made between each past and each present.

In a traditional view frequently expressed in the past, death was imagined as a benevolent agent, a relieving and rewarding friend of the self, supervising the best interests of the self which the reluctant and disagreeing faculties were themselves incapable of deciding but might at last learn. (Though that view is forcefully revised by Tolstoi in the death of Nikolay Levin, it is not canceled.) In the well-remembered image of Aristotle (not unrecognizable still), "The soul rules the body with a despotical rule, whereas the intellect rules the appetites with a constitutional royal rule" (*Politics* 1254b). The recalcitrant, irrational parts of the self might therefore be persuaded or otherwise induced to accept what was in the best "public" interest and in accord with the judgment of royal benevolence. So they might consent to relax, let go, die. Scenarios built on the image engaged standard difficulties with arguments that ran like reliable machinery. Some opportunities for dramatic conflict and hesitation were nevertheless discoverable and often made welcome. On the other hand, debates between the soul as despot and the body as slave required some tempering-tampering in order to make a respectable exhibition piece.

Champions of the body's rights to persuade or command in this matter have been slow to develop the positive side of their arguments. Attacking the claims of mental dominance has been more congenial work. The modern attention to the body may, however, right that balance or come full circle. I quote a recent model by Lewis Thomas, very attractive in its imaginative correspondences between body and sophisticated machines with built-in controls and safety devices:

> There is a pivotal movement at some stage in the body's reaction to injury or disease, maybe in aging as well, when the organism concedes that it is finished and the time for dying is at hand, and at this moment the events that lead to death are launched, as a coordinated mechanism. Functions are then shut off in sequence, irreversibly, and, while this is going on, a neural mechanism, held ready for this occasion, is switched on.[18]

The attentive reader will remember the now quaint images of Ficino and Paracelsus (quoted in Chap. 15)—Ficino to explain why and how the sense of hearing "seizes, and claims as its own, man in his entirety"; and Paracelsus to show how motion, penetration, and celestial bodies cause birthmarks. Their procedures illustrate the Aristotelian rule that the mind is conscious of its thought "along with an image," and they supplement their methods with a kind of narrative sequence for which the old term *fable* was considered appropriate. One can no longer use that term politely to describe serious imaginative efforts to present a conceptual grasp or theory of how important phenomena work, and so I have called Thomas's very interesting account by its proper modern name, a model. It is one that turns away from the formerly believed correspondences between the terrestrial and the supernal worlds to a set of correspondences between the human body as presently understood and some new microcosms of intelligence now being discovered, explored, and invented.[19]

The Aristotelian rule may be pleasant to recognize—especially since here consciousness of thought, bearing and being borne by its image, is not merely an expedient device of rhetorical expression for others but is substantially related to the thought itself, whether or not the thinker is fully aware of what he is doing, and whether he also recognizes that his example is making him an example. And yet, beyond Aristotle, the master spirit of Thomas's model is the Plato of the *Timaeus*.

The machine of my mind, easily activated, calls up images of the urban runners crisscrossing path and pavement, their cardiovascular systems regulated by conscious decisions and sometimes checked, without breaking stride, by newly marketed miniature devices. And though the more graceless joggers produce a composite image I recognize as that of *memento mori,* I admire, as who would not, the strong and stylish runners who are killing time well as they achieve their slow, slow pulse rates.

The winner of the marathon race in the 1984 Olympics, the mature man Carlos Lopes, "Nel mezzo del cammin di nostra vita," was asked by a television reporter, in a standard style of expensive time, whether he had prepared himself specially for the Los Angeles heat and whether he had expected to win. The answer, expressing the consciousness that real alternatives may still have something to say to each other, was that he came prepared to win and prepared to lose. None of the Renaissance writers taken up in these pages would have had any experience with the marathon as an actual event or with the imagistic language by which our present interest expresses itself. Yet all, I believe, would have responded to the words of Lopes, and would have admired their basic design, and would have thought about the meanings under compression.

Notes

CHAPTER I. *What Renaissance Poets Would Have Known*

1. *The Riverside Shakespeare,* ed. G. Blakemore Evans (Boston: Houghton Mifflin, 1974): *Othello,* 5.2.7; *Macbeth,* 5.5.23–28. Numbers refer to act, scene, and line.

2. The *Times* (London), May 10, 1980, p. 14.

3. Jaroslav Pelikan, *The Shape of Death* (New York: Abingdon Press, 1961).

4. *Devotions upon Emergent Occasions,* ed. Anthony Raspa (Montreal: McGill-Queen's University Press, 1975), second prayer (p. 13).

5. Cited in Rosemary Woolf, *The English Religious Lyric in the Middle Ages* (Oxford: Clarendon Press, 1968), p. 296.

6. Origen, *De Principiis,* 3.4.2.

7. *The Four Last Things,* in W. E. Campbell, *The English Works of Sir Thomas More* (1931), 1:468.

8. See the excellent book by Nancy Lee Beaty, *The Craft of Dying: A Study in the Literary Tradition of the "Ars Moriendi" in England* (New Haven: Yale University Press, 1970).

9. See Sr. Mary Catharine O'Connor, *The Art of Dying Well* (New York: Columbia University Press, 1942).

10. Sir Thomas Browne, *Religio Medici,* pt. 1, sec. 58, in *Selected Writings,* ed. Sir Geoffrey Keynes (London: Faber & Faber, 1968), p. 64.

11. To make my point I have omitted some qualifying, partly humorous phrases that do change the emphasis but not, I think, the underlying message. The quotation is from Irving Howe, *A Margin of Hope: An Intellectual Autobiography* (New York: Harcourt Brace Jovanovich, 1982), pp. 347–48.

12. The pioneering book is Louis Martz's *The Poetry of Meditation: A Study in English Religious Literature of the Seventeenth Century* (New Haven: Yale University Press, 1954); 2d ed., rev., 1962. An Augustinian art of meditation is explored in Martz's *The Paradise Within: Studies in Vaughan, Traherne, and Milton* (New Haven: Yale University Press, 1964). In *Donne's "Anniversaries" and the Poetry of Praise* (Princeton: Princeton University Press, 1973), Barbara K. Lewalski presents a distinctively Protestant character of meditation. In my judgment a better-tempered version appears in her very impressive book, *Protestant Poetics and the Seventeenth-Century Religious Lyric* (Princeton: Princeton University Press, 1979).

13. See Camille Wells Slights, *The Casuistical Tradition in Shakespeare, Donne, and Milton* (Princeton: Princeton University Press, 1981).

14. See chap. 4 of Lewalski's *Protestant Poetics* for a brief, authoritative presentation.

15. *Western Attitudes toward Death,* trans. Patricia M. Ranum (Baltimore: Johns Hopkins University Press, 1974); *The Hour of Our Death [L'homme devant la mort,* Paris: Editions du Seuil, 1977], trans. Helen Weaver (New York: Random House, 1982).

CHAPTER 2. *Answers and Questions*

1. I am quoting from an edition printed by John Field in 1662.

2. *The Sermons of John Donne,* ed. G. R. Potter and E. M. Simpson, 10 vols. (Berkeley and Los Angeles: University of California Press, 1953–62), 6:289.

3. *The Historie of the Life and Reigne of that Famous Princesse Elizabeth* (1629), pp. 383–84.

4. James Spedding, R. L. Ellis, and D. D. Heath, *The Works of Francis Bacon* (New York: Hurd & Houghton, 1869), 11:451. This is from the translation of "In Felicem Memoriam Elizabethae," pp. 443–61.

5. In his diary for March 23, John Manningham records information similar in spirit to Camden's report. His entry for the 24th begins: "This morning about 3 at clocke hir Majestie departed this lyfe, mildly like a lambe, easily like a ripe apple from the tree, *cum leve quadam febre, absque gemitu.* Dr. Parry told me that he was present and sent his prayers before hir soule; and I doubt not but shee is amongst the royall saintes in heaven in eternall joyes." A few days later he recorded solemn gossip about a ring from the Earl of Essex which the Queen wore to the day of her death, and this item: "It is certaine the Queene was not embowelled, but wrapt up in cere cloth, and that verry il to, through the covetousnes of them that defrauded hir of the allowance of clothe was given them for that purpose." *The Diary of John Manningham of the Middle Temple, 1602–1603,* ed. Robert Parker Solien (Hanover, N.H.: University Press of New England, 1976), pp. 207, 208, 223.

6. I quote from the translations by Morris Bishop, *Letters from Petrarch* (Bloomington: Indiana University Press, 1966), pp. 288–89.

7. Quoted from Lord Morley's translation of the *Trionfi, Tryumphes of Fraunces Petrarcke,* ed. D. D. Carnicelli (Cambridge: Harvard University Press, 1971), p. 120.

8. I quote from *The Complete Poetry of Ben Jonson,* ed. William B. Hunter, Jr. (Garden City, N.Y.: Doubleday, Anchor, 1963), *Underwood,* 85, lines 61–62. I use this edition throughout.

9. *The Lives* (London: Oxford University Press, 1973), p. 105.

10. Quoted from *The Works of Sir Walter Ralegh* (Oxford, 1829), 8:785.

11. Edward Edwards, *The Life of Sir Walter Ralegh Together with His Letters* (London, 1868), 2:490–91.

12. Quoted from V. T. Harlow, *Ralegh's Last Voyage* (London: Argonaut Press, 1932), p. 310; the quotations above are from pp. 307 and 308.

13. As one might expect, the accounts differ in some details. There seems to be agreement that there were two blows of the axe.

14. Francis Osborne, *Historical Memoires on the Reigns of Queen Elizabeth and King James* (1658), pt. 2, p. 20.

15. David E. Stannard, *The Puritan Way of Death* (New York: Oxford University Press, 1977), pp. 79–80, 83–84.

16. E. Gordon Rupp, *The Righteousness of God* (New York: Philosophical Library 1953), p. 282: "even to the abyss of despair   before I knew how beautiful that despair was, and how near to Grace."

17. Wherever possible I shall cite Bacon from the convenient edition by Hugh G. Dick, *Selected Writings of Francis Bacon* (New York: Random House, 1955). The quotations are from p. 338.

18. This is from *The Wisdom of the Ancients,* the myth of Pan. The text of the translation is quoted from Spedding, Ellis, and Heath, *Works of Francis Bacon,* 13:99.

19. *Works of Francis Bacon,* 13:97.

20. I quote Montaigne from the translation by Donald M. Frame, *The Complete Essays of Montaigne* (Stanford: Stanford University Press, 1958). References are to book, essay, and page.

21. In *A Dialogue of Comfort* (pt. 3, chap. 25) More deals with panic terror in his fable of the hart and the bitch. The answer to the problem is the application of human reasoning, but supported by the necessary grace, which is available if we desire it.

CHAPTER 3. *Donne's Pictures of the Good Death*

1. Some of the following remarks were made July 10, 1977, in the Chelsea Old Church, in commemoration of the 350th anniversary of Donne's sermon.

2. See Astrid Friis, *Alderman Cockayne's Project and the Cloth Trade* (Copenhagen: Levin & Munksgaard, 1927).

3. No doubt such direct quotations touch the feelings of mourners in special ways, as Donne must surely have known. To a reader trying to be objective, the quotations are utterly undistinguished in their triteness. But objectivity is a questionable virtue here, asserting as it does a special privilege of detachment in order to clarify truth, while accepting as a necessary limitation the not-entering into the feelings of the occasion. One must also think that Donne's voice and person presenting those quotations would have given them a force that has faded on the page. Nevertheless, when Donne quoted Lady Danvers directly the difference is instructive. She always hurried her family and household to church "with that cheerful provocation, *For God's sake let's go, For God's sake let's bee there at the Confession*" (8:86). This too is for mourners, but the individual and characterizing words belong to the living family legend. They are not mustered as part of the evidence of a pious death.

4. There is a careful and inconspicuous reservation here, for Donne probably could not yet know whether all of the late financial supplements to the will would be carried out exactly. There is, however, no change in the emphasis upon

Cokayne's individual importance. Such emphasis, one may note in passing, owes little to the typological weight of "witnesses" (who have always counted in the traditions of rhetoric, oratory, and law), or to the volume of evidence that God was with him.

5. Barbara K. Lewalski treats these two sermons from a different point of view, and our interpretations diverge considerably. See *Donne's Anniversaries and the Poetry of Praise* (Princeton: Princeton University Press, 1973), pp. 201–05, 210–12.

6. Faith placed wholly in a merciful God prevents every uncharitable interpretation. Thus, though we cannot trust any evidence that suggests the damnation of a dying man, "wee see often enough to be sory, but not to despaire" (10:240). Donne's faith, however, does not prevent him from entertaining unfavorable "evidence" when human interpretation of the "issue" seeks natural satisfaction in optimism. And so after he comments on our proclivity to comfort ourselves by the testimony that a friend "went away like a *Lambe*," he then adds a brief, grim, alternative interpretation of the apparently peaceful death: "But, *God* knowes, that may bee accompanied with a *dangerous damp* and *stupefaction*, and *insensibility* of his *present state*" (10:240).

CHAPTER 4. Respice Finem

1. A modern text is available in two good anthologies I shall refer to a number of times: J. William Hebel and Hoyt H. Hudson, *Poetry of the English Renaissance* (New York: F. S. Crofts, 1929), pp. 38–39; Norman Ault, *Elizabethan Lyrics* (New York: Capricorn Books, 1960), pp. 27–29.

2. Hebel and Hudson, p. 43; Ault, pp. 10–11.

3. Ault, p. 27.

4. *A Gorgeous Gallery of Gallant Inventions,* ed. Hyder E. Rollins (Cambridge: Harvard University Press, 1926), p. 99; Hebel and Hudson, pp. 192–93.

5. Ault, pp. 491–92.

6. Carleton Brown, *English Lyrics of the Thirteenth Century* (Oxford: Calrendon Press, 1932), no. 71.

7. *Summer's Last Will and Testament,* 1600; Hebel and Hudson, pp. 388–89; Ault, pp. 166–67.

CHAPTER 5. *Death in Earnest: "Tichborne's Elegy"*

1. Hebel and Hudson, pp. 196–97; Ault, pp. 120–21. The poem first appeared in *Verses of Praise and Joy written upon Her Majesty's Preservation,* 1586. The title of the poem, apparently furnished by another hand, was *Tychbornes Elegie, written with his owne hand in the Tower before his execution.* There is no hard evidence that Chidiock Tichborne did write the poem attributed to him, but alternative possibilities have less to go on. His poem, published where it is, makes a special contribution to "Praise and Joy"—so special that it is short-lived

in this sense. The poem becomes an exhibition of the private mental suffering of a convicted traitor, a member of the Babington conspiracy. The youth apparently made a favorable personal impression when he spoke before his execution. The standard mutilation, dismemberment, and protracted dying would have had the normal effect of celebrating without words the queen's escape from danger and a ritualized victory over real enemies. At the same time there must have been some pathos felt, seeing an attractive, helpless youth ending his life in agony.

Alert to modern devices for gaining attention, one may note the calculated effect of *written with his owne hand in the Tower.* The appeal is not, however, any evidence of fraud. The same applies to "T. K's" answer to Tichborne's swan song ("in Cygneam Cantionem"). The aim of the answer is to ridicule by parody anything that might be taken seriously in Tichborne's self-assessment. For example: "Thou soughtst thy death, and found it in desert. / Thou look'dst for life, yet lewdlie forc'd it fade." The answer apparently did not destroy the appeal of Tichborne's poem, which found its way into collections and songbooks—for its own interest, one assumes, no longer a part of "Praise and Joy."

2. I should add that I do not consider myself as having fully explained the lack of religious turn or development in the poem. It is obvious, I assume, that Tichborne's papist loyalties were an important reason for his being recruited for the conspiracy. The letter he wrote his wife from prison contains, as one should expect, many expressions of religious hope and conviction. But in the poem religious thoughts do not emerge directly. What does this mean? We do not find in the poem, and I think we do not consciously miss, any thoughts based on the appointed sequence of events that will produce his death. Tichborne concentrates on the aspects of the subject he has chosen: life, death, and personal time. His mind was also engaged by all the details that were chosen to come together in a poem. That action—may one think?—expresses itself by orderly and other procedures devised along the borders of consciousness, such as between life and death.

No one should expect the interpretation of a poem to explain everything. Tichborne does not mention in the poem any physical details of the death to come; he could scarcely have been unaware of or uninterested in them. Surely, opening his mind to that scene would have interfered mightily with the poem that was taking shape. My interpretation, which is drawn from the materials of the poem and how they are put together, does not enter into other poems that he might perhaps have written. I do not therefore take up or reject the influence of Tichborne's reasonable fear of the savage death he was to receive. There are strange pressures at the edges of the poem, and the concentration, however inspired, may also have served to keep unwanted thoughts at bay.

CHAPTER 6. *Dying in Jest and Earnest: Raleigh*

1. The poetry is quoted, with moderate normalizing of the old spelling, from the edition by Agnes M. C. Latham, *The Poems of Sir Walter Ralegh* (London: Routledge & Kegan Paul, 1951).

CHAPTER 7. *Imagined Dyings: John Donne*

1. For the numbering of the holy sonnets I follow Grierson. For the texts, except where mentioned, I quote from Helen Gardner's edition, *The Divine Poems* (Oxford: Clarendon Press, 1952). Numbers following the two excerpts from "Goodfriday, 1613" on pp. 139 and 140 refer to lines.

2. The quoted words belong to Donne's technical vocabulary for expressing the Christological concept of *kenosis*.

3. The fading trail from Psalm 51 offers no direct invitation to think of Bathsheba and therefore Ann among "those loves," the "all" sacrificed in England, and those "false mistresses" of his ambitious youth. As one of many, Ann means very little in the poem; when we go behind the poem we have to write most of the story ourselves but are not encouraged to make due acknowledgments to the Muse. Having said this much, I turn to simple glossing. The obligation to love God entirely provides the basis for the imputed "jealousy" and has other, formal theological implications not directly applied. Man's unquiet heart, his intellectual endowment, and the urges of entireness are all illustrated in the following: "Grace is not grace to me, till it make me know that I have it. . . . he hath given that soule an appetite, and a holy hunger and thirst to take in more of him; for I have no Grace, till I would have more" (*Sermons*, 8:250). Elsewhere he refers to the notion of "happy excesse," felicitous intoxication, the holy desire that "begets a satiety," that "begets a farther desire" (5:275).

4. In retrospect, it seems more accurate to acknowledge that Donne is consciously allowing special room for common grief. Elsewhere he can write with fine discrimination about imprecation and deprecation and can criticize great men of God for going too far—as when he says of Moses and St. Paul, "There was, if not an irregularity, and an inordinatenesse, at least an inconsideration, not to be imitated by us now, not to be excused in them then" (5:329). R. C. Bald's *John Donne: A Life* (New York: Oxford University Press, 1970), pp. 338–65, tells the facts of the diplomatic trip. They shed little light on the poem.

5. *Devotions upon Emergent Occasions,* Expostulation 17, pp. 87–89.

6. "And therefore God seales his promises with a *Quia*, a reason, an assurance" (*Sermons,* 5:104).

CHAPTER 8. *Entering the History of Death: George Herbert*

1. All quotations from Herbert come from *The Works of George Herbert*, ed. F. E. Hutchinson (Oxford: Clarendon Press, 1941).

CHAPTER 9. *"The Plaudite, or end of life"*

1. *The Complete Poetry of Robert Herrick,* ed. J. Max Patrick (Garden City, N.Y.: Doubleday, Anchor, 1963), p. 132.

2. Another possibility is that Herrick is writing his own special imitation of the death of Augustus, whose friends gathered around the bed were said to

have applauded him for having played his part in life so well. See Bacon, *Selected Writings*, p. 356.

CHAPTER 10. *Introduction*

1. Dedicatory sonnet to Raleigh.
2. *The Prose Works of Sir Philip Sidney*, ed. Albert Feuillerat (reprint, Cambridge: Cambridge University Press, 1968), 2:137–44. Numbers refer to volume and page.
3. Herbert, *A Priest to the Temple*, Hutchinson, p. 238.
4. The quotations, from *Selected Writings*, are from pp. 103, 22, and 20, respectively.
5. This is the opening line of the last elegy for Sidney in *Astrophel*, published in 1595 with Spenser's *Colin Clouts Come Home Again*.
6. Henry King, *Poems, Elegies, Paradoxes and Sonnets*, 1657 (London: Scolar Press Facsimile, 1973), p. 141.

CHAPTER 11. *Lament, Praise, Consolation: Pain/Difficulty, Ease*

1. *The Poems and Letters of Andrew Marvell*, ed. H. M. Margoliouth (Oxford: Clarendon Press, 1927). Numbers refer to lines.
2. See John M. Wallace, *Destiny his Choice* (Cambridge: Cambridge University Press, 1968), pp. 69ff.
3. *The Elegies and The Songs and Sonnets*, ed. Helen Gardner (Oxford: Clarendon Press, 1965), p. 24.
4. Meditation 16, *Devotions*, pp. 82–83.

CHAPTER 12. *The Death of a Loved One: Personal and Public Expressions*

1. *Astrophel*, the contribution by "Clorinda," lines 91–96. In his "Poem upon the Death of O. C.," seven decades later, Marvell repeats the same message. "And in those joyes dost spend the endlesse day, / Which in expressing, we ourselves betray" (lines 297–98).
2. *Underwood*, 14. In his "Elegie for Prince Henry," Donne's "hee is not dead, wee are" is well fortified against the literal meaning.
3. The epitaph appeared in the first edition of the *Reliquae*, with the signature "H. Wotton." In a letter to John Dynely, November 13, 1628, Wotton includes a copy marked "*Authoris Incerti*" for the possible entertainment of the Queen of Bohemia, and "worth her hearing for the passionate plainness" (*Life and Letters*, L. P. Smith (Oxford: Clarendon Press, 1907), 2:34.) One assumes a necessary choice between the pleasure of applying a fine critical phrase to one's own unacknowledged verses and the labor of producing a courteous apology for presuming to send a poor thing of one's own.
4. My interpretation would separate "and my good is dead" from "and to hers." The strained expression would then mean: "She has paid her debt to

Nature, and to her own nature, and (all) my good is dead." Helen Gardner's annotation joins the two phrases: "Death ends the possibility of doing good to oneself or to another." However reasonable this is, in effect it accepts a strained piece of language which seems to have little purpose other than to assert the obvious. In a subsequent printing of her volume, Professor Gardner has omitted the annotation quoted above. In his recent Everyman edition of Donne, C. A. Patrides and I seem to be in agreement.

5. The thirst and the desire to beg derive from God. I have quoted the illustrative text from *Sermons,* 8:250 in n. 3, Chap. 7.

6. Here I follow Grierson's punctuation of the line, "Dost wooe my soule for hers; offring all thine." The "for" I take to mean "for the sake of"; God's offer of love quietly includes Ann and is a gracious act of divine love, not a form of compensation.

7. *The Letters of Marsilio Ficino* (London: Shepheard-Walwyn, 1975), 1:54–55.

8. *The Poems of Thomas Carew,* ed. Rhodes Dunlap (Oxford: Clarendon Press, 1949), pp. 71–74, 64–65.

9. *Silver Poets of the Seventeenth Century,* ed. G. A. Parfitt (London: Dent, 1974), p. 132.

10. See the substantial review of criticism by Douglas Bush, *A Variorum Commentary on the Poems of John Milton* (New York: Columbia University Press, 1972), vol. 2, pt. 2, especially pp. 571ff.

11. *The New Criticism* (Norfolk, Conn.: New Directions, 1941), pp. 323–24.

12. Lord Morley's translation, ed. D. D. Carnicelli, p. 120.

CHAPTER 13. *Episodes in the Progress of Death*

1. I quote from the edition by W. Milgate, *The Epithalamions, Anniversaries, and Epicedes* (Oxford: Clarendon Press, 1978). Numbers refer to lines.

2. I quote from the edition by G. C. Moore Smith, *The Poems of Edward Lord Herbert of Cherbury* (Oxford: Clarendon Press, 1923).

3. Kenneth Allott, *The Poems of William Habington* (London: University of Liverpool Press, 1948), pp. 127–28.

4. Quarles's claim of invention was made by attaching his two "original" stanzas to his *Argalus and Parthenia* (1629) under a title of lofty associations, *Hos ego versiculos.*

5. No. 71 of Carleton Brown's *English Lyrics of the XIIIth Century* (Oxford: Clarendon Press, 1932).

CHAPTER 14. *Preliminary Views*

1. *The Complete Stories,* ed. Nahum N. Glatzer (New York: Schocken Books, 1971), p. 277.

2. 3.4.176, 212; 5.1.187.

3. At the beginning of Chapter 4 of *Urne-Burial*, Sir Thomas Browne puts more directly attitudes like those Donne expresses in meditation: "Christians have handsomely glossed the deformity of death, by careful consideration of the body, and civil rites which take off brutall terminations. And though they conceived all reparable by a resurrection, cast not off all care of enterrment. For since the ashes of Sacrifices burnt upon the Altar of God, were carefully carried out by the Priests, and deposed in a clean field; since they acknowledged their bodies to be the lodging of Christ, and temples of the holy Ghost, they devolved not all upon the sufficiency of soul existence; and therefore with long services and full solemnities concluded their last Exequies" (*Selected Writings*, p. 141).

CHAPTER 15. *Thought and Images*

1. *De genesi ad litteram*, 12.24.51; *Patrologia Latina*, 34:474–75.
2. Quoted by Frances A. Yates, *The Art of Memory* (London: Routledge & Kegan Paul, 1966), p. 71.
3. Bacon demonstrates his effective assimilation of Aquinas's thought on the subject: "Emblem reduceth conceits intellectual to images sensible, which strike the memory more" (*Selected Writings*, p. 299). Bacon seems to be unaware of the intrusion of "a devotional atmosphere" and "a concession to human weakness"—but that raises questions that are not helpful here.
4. Quoted from D. P. Walker, *Spiritual and Demonic Magic from Ficino to Campanella* (London: Warburg Institute, 1958), p. 9.
5. Arthur E. Waite, *The Hermetic and Alchemical Writings of Paracelsus* (New Hyde Park, N.Y.: University Books, 1967), 1:173–74.

CHAPTER 16. *Images of Reflection*

1. For example, *Devotions*, the 19th Expostulation, p. 99; *Sermons*, 2:170–71; 4:179–80; 9:350.
2. Sonnet 32, *Poems and A Defence of Ryme*, ed. Arthur Colby Sprague (reprint, Chicago: University of Chicago Press, 1965), p. 26.
3. *Englands Helicon*, 1600; Latham, p. 16.
4. *Poems*, pp. 8–9.
5. Or response to objects signifying the threat of death, as in Traherne's poem "Wonder," where to the child's innocent eye "Hedges, Ditches, Limits, Bounds" are the enemies of Paradise.
6. Nancy Lee Beaty reports that a high proportion of Parsons's revisions "heighten the fearfulness of the death scene itself" (p. 183).

CHAPTER 17. *Reasoning by Resemblances*

1. Herbert's "Briefe Notes on Valdesso's Considerations," Hutchinson, p. 309.
2. Stoic usage made the language widely familiar. To quote a single exam-

ple, from Seneca's 26th epistle (bk. 3, no. 5): "Incommodum summum est, inquis, minui et deperire et, ut proprie dicam, liquescere. . . . Ecquis exitus est melior quam in finem suum natura solvente dilabi?"

3. As in Plotinus: "For all of the Soul that is in body is asleep and the true getting-up is not bodily but from the body . . . the veritable waking or rising is from corporeal things" (3.6.6: MacKenna's translation).

4. "Morpheus the humble god that dwells," in Parfitt's *Silver Poets,* p. 107.

5. "An Elegy Occasioned by sickness," pp. 141–46.

6. *Poems,* 1616; *The Poems of William Drummond,* ed. W. C. Ward (London: Routledge, n.d.), 1:29; Ault, *Elizabethan Lyrics,* pp. 475–76.

7. Raleigh, *The History of the World* (London, 1614), p. 776.

8. *The Works of Henry Vaughan,* ed. L. C. Martin (Oxford: Clarendon Press, 1957), p. 174.

9. Quoted by Beaty, *Craft of Dying,* p. 175.

10. Donne's "The Good-morrow" and "The Canonization."

11. Henry King, "The Exequy" (p. 54) and "The Boyes answer to the Blackmoor" (p. 7).

12. My intention is only to illustrate a familiar human experience, that to someone in love everything else in the world may appear illusory.

13. Latham, p. 79.

14. Ault, p. 21.

15. Ault, p. 102.

16. *The Complete Poetry of Richard Crashaw,* ed. George W. Williams (Garden City, N.Y.: Doubleday, Anchor, 1970), pp. 123–37, 54, 56.

17. "The Excuse," Latham, p. 10.

CHAPTER 18. *Intricacies*

1. Letter 311 in *Letters of Sigmund Freud,* ed. Ernst L. Freud (New York: Basic Books, 1975), p. 457. The letter was dated December 27, 1938, and was written to Rachel Berdach (Bardi), a German writer born in Budapest, 1878. At the time of Freud's letter she would have been sixty years old.

2. Chapter 15, pp. 190–92.

3. The translation is that of Charles S. Singleton, lines 124–26, from his edition of *The Divine Comedy* (Princeton: Princeton University Press, 1975).

4. *Works,* ed. L. C. Martin, pp. 213 and 312.

5. John Carey, *John Donne: Life, Mind, and Art,* p. 95.

6. Edward Lord Herbert's death as reported by Aubrey is a case in point: "James Usher, Lord Primate of Ireland, was sent for by him, when in his death-bed, and he would have received the sacrament. He sayd indifferently of it, *that if there was good in any-thing 'twas in that,* or *if it did no good 'twould doe no hurt.* The Primate refused it, for which many blamed him. He then turned his head to the other side and expired very serenely" (*Brief Lives,* ed. Oliver L. Dick [London: Secker & Warburg, 1949], p. 135). Aubrey's account, which makes its own disarming claim on art and legend, is breathtakingly different from the art that

narrated the death of Edward's mother. The two decades that separate the death of Magdalen, pictured by Donne, and that of Edward, as reported by Aubrey, seem to belong to two different eras. But no less strange: from the perspective of a century later and the deathbed of Voltaire, how modest is the sense of scandal, especially when blame is distributed in the account, and there is besides the stumbling block of his having died "serenely." But then Herbert had not yet been identified as a "father" of deism. Clearly, there was much more eager attention to the sensational business of Rochester's conversion and death.

7. See, for instance, *Enneads* 4.4.35 and 6.8.4; Hooker, *Laws of Ecclesiastical Polity,* 1.7.3: "Neither is any other desire termed properly will, but that where reason and understanding, or the show of reason, prescribeth the thing desired."

8. *Sermons,* 10:240–41. He continues, p. 241: it is not "the *last word* nor *gaspe* that *qualifies* the *soule.* Stil *pray* wee for a *peaceable life* against *violent death,* and for *time* of *repentance* against *sudden death,* and for *sober* and *modest assurance* against *distemperd* and *diffident death.*" He cites the case of Samson, "subject to interpretation hard enough. Yet the *holy Ghost* hath moved S. *Paul* to celebrate *Sampson* in his *great Catalogue,* and so doth all the *Church.*"

9. A useful commentary is the opening of Donne's sermon on the penitential Psalm 6 (5:364–65). There he speaks of the nature of earnest prayer, which admits importunity, and even "impudency" and violence.

10. See Sermon 17, vol. 7, especially pp. 432–33.

11. *De Miseria Condicionis Humane,* ed. Robert E. Lewis (Athens, Ga.: University of Georgia Press, 1978), p. 134 (1.24).

12. *The Works of Sir John Suckling,* ed. Thomas Clayton (Oxford: Clarendon Press, 1971), pp. 47–48.

13. Dunlap, pp. 49–53.

14. Preface to *Poems* (1656), quoted from *Critical Essays of the Seventeenth Century,* ed. J. E. Spingarn (Oxford, Clarendon Press; reprint, Bloomington: Indiana University Press, 1957), 2:80.

15. *Memoirs of a Tourist,* trans. Allan Seager (Evanston: Northwestern University Press, 1962), p. 133.

16. D. P. Walker, *The Decline of Hell* (Chicago: University of Chicago Press, 1964).

17. In the English Renaissance thoughts of personal annihilation receive little entertainment, as if such thoughts were a vicious residue of paganism. Good words for Epicurus are not frequent. Sir Thomas Browne, however, defends him as "the virtuous heathen, who lived better than he spake," though there is an admitted possibility of his "erring in the principles of himself." (*Urne-Burial,* p. 147). Still, he deserved better treatment than he received from Dante, for "Among all the Set, *Epicurus* is most considerable, whom men make honest without an *Elyzium,* who contemned life without encouragement of immortality, and making nothing after death, yet made nothing of the King of terrours" (p. 146). In his early, full essay on death (1.20), Montaigne heaps up the quotations from Lucretius. At the end of the essay there are eleven, punctuated by a quotation from Manilius and one from Virgil. One imagines that Mon-

taigne was amusing himself by surprising some of his readers with the solid morality contained in the writing of a highly suspect author.

18. See the brilliant study by J. McManners, *Reflections at the Death Bed of Voltaire: The Art of Dying in Eighteenth-Century France* (Oxford: Clarendon Press, 1975).

19. *Works,* ed. Reginald Heber; rev. C. P. Eden, 10 vols. (London: Longman, 1847–54); "A Funeral Sermon . . . Countess of Carbery," 8:488.

20. *John Donne: The Divine Poems,* p. 113.

21. The manuscript of his book *Biathanatos,* which he did not want to publish or to destroy.

22. *St. Thomas More: Selected Letters,* ed. Elizabeth F. Rogers (New Haven: Yale University Press, 1961), p. 253.

23. "Thoughts for the Times on War and Death," *Standard Edition of the Complete Psychological Works,* ed. James Strachey (London: Hogarth Press, 1957), 14:289.

24. Marvell, "A Poem upon the Death of O.C.," lines 7–10.

25. *Ben Jonson,* ed. C. H. Herford and Percy and Evelyn Simpson (Oxford: Clarendon Press, 1947), 8: 597.

26. "Life of Cowley," in G. B. Hill, *Lives of the English Poets* (Oxford:Clarendon, 1905), vol. 1.

27. Denis Meadows, *Elizabethan Quintet* (London: Longmans, Green, 1956), pp. 173–74; cited by Nancy L. Beaty, p. 183.

28. I am indebted to the fine study by Barry Weller. "The Rhetoric of Friendship in Montaigne's *Essais,*" *New Literary History* 9 (1978), 503–23.

CHAPTER 19. *The End*

1. *Selected Writings,* p. 283.

2. Unless otherwise noted, all page references are to *The Hour of Our Death.*

3. The kinds of evidence taken up have different phases of intensity and decline. For instance, the height of interest in the death of the individual may have occurred from the fifteenth to the seventeenth centuries and may have lasted longer in places like New England. Still: "Beginning with the eleventh century a formerly unknown relationship developed between the death of each individual and his awareness of being an individual. Today it is agreed that between the year 1000 and the middle of the thirteenth century 'a very important historical mutation occurred' " (*Western Attitudes toward Death,* p. 51).

4. Geoffrey Gorer, "The Pornography of Death," *Encounter* 5(1955), 49–52; *Death, Grief, and Mourning in Contemporary Britain* (Garden City, N.Y.: Doubleday, 1965). Ariès finds the first definite connections between eroticism and death in some early sixteenth-century paintings. The subject is a large one, even in art. Some less traveled byways are examined in Georges Bataille, *Death and Sensuality: A Study of Eroticism and the Taboo* (New York: Walker & Co., 1962).

5. As in Alexander Solzhenitsyn's *The First Circle*.

6. *The Colloquies of Erasmus,* trans. Craig R. Thompson (Chicago: University of Chicago Press, 1965), p. 143.

7. "The tears of a lackey, the distribution of my old clothes, the touch of a well-known hand, a commonplace phrase of consolation, make me disconsolate and sorry for my self."

8. Jeremy Taylor, *The Rule and Exercises of Holy Dying* (London, 1652), 4.3.179. Subsequent citations will be made in the text; the numbers refer to chapter, section, and page.

9. This is not a matter to argue in passing, and the record in print is always incomplete, and there are many harsh voices proclaiming the higher mercy, but the Renaissance is notable for the learned spokesmen who can argue for human good and felicitously draw reasoning from the usage of common kindness. I think of Robert Burton, and not only the section of his book entitled "Religious Melancholy." But I draw my single illustration from Bacon's *Advancement of Learning,* where he is reviewing the present state of medicine. He criticizes physicians (among many specific deficiencies) for not seeking the skill and taking the care to lessen "the pains and agonies of death." This, as well as the restoration of health, ought to be part of "the office of a physician," to enable a patient "to make a fair and easy passage." He cites famous testimony, the same that Montaigne used, Augustus Caesar's wishing for himself "that same *Euthanasia.*" He goes on to note the successful example of a much-admired ancient, "which was specially noted in the death of Antoninus Pius, whose death was after the fashion and semblance of a kindly and pleasant sleep." In this matter, the recommendation of emperors cannot be imagined as excluding general interest (*Selected Writings,* p. 277).

10. T. Carmi, *The Penguin Book of Hebrew Verse* (New York: Viking Press, 1981), pp. 285–86.

11. W. H. Auden and Louis Kronenberger, *The Faber Book of Aphorisms* (London: Faber & Faber, 1964; reprint, 1974), p. 393.

12. I am thinking of Primo Levi, that patient man, venting his indignation at a fellow prisoner in Auschwitz, an old Jew named Kuhn who found himself not on the list of those chosen to die, and who that night raised his voice in praise to God for his deliverance. A probable indecorum between grateful man and silent God is different from the gross indecorum heard by fellow men, some of whom, also having been spared, are in a position to feel some released emotions. In *Prisoners of Hope* (Cambridge: Harvard University Press, 1983), p. 79, H. Stuart Hughes notes Levi's "sudden breakthrough of passionate revulsion," questions it, and strives to produce an adequate explanation. And yet, whatever the reason, a marvelous patience is here broken through: sensitive, alert, mysteriously good-humored, believably durable.

13. *Anna Karenina,* trans. Constance Garnett (New York: Random House, 1939), 2:583–602.

14. I quote from James Gibson, *The Complete Poems of Thomas Hardy* (New York: Macmillan, 1979), p. 482.

15. Saul Bellow, *Mr. Sammler's Planet* (New York: Viking Press, 1970).

16. *The Collected Poems of Theodore Roethke* (Garden City, N.Y.: Doubleday, 1966), p. 201.

17. I have taken the liberty of disregarding the fourth stanza, which deflects the imaginative action toward the practical present of the immediate stage. The naivety given a dramatic voice in the lyric is one part of the strangeness and the sense of matters unresolved or but partly voiced. One is not, I think, likely to be satisfied by the simple message, taken straight, of the naivety. A poem written only twenty-five years earlier, "Tichborne's Elegy," expresses a naive wonder that is not intended as the dramatic projection of an attitude. But there are similarities between that poem and Shakespeare's "Dirge." The sense of strangeness and reserve in Shakespeare's lyric has its counterpart in the way the inventory of untrustworthy aspects of existence in the world creates, in "Tichborne's Elegy," a momentum that seems to lead toward an opening into familiar religious expression but does not do so.

18. "A Meliorist View of Disease and Dying," *Journal of Medicine and Philosophy* 1 (1976), 212–21. I owe the reference to Sissela Bok, *Lying* (New York: Random House, Vintage, 1979), p. 248.

19. Having made a particular point and having suggested some distant relationships, I have a few further, respectful comments to add. Thomas offers fascinating examples of the body as unwilling host countering intruders with so much zeal that the defense threatens to become fatal to the host. What Donne wrote of Elizabeth Drury, "That one might almost say, her bodie thought," seems like a prophecy, one that would have amazed Donne. For in responding to some infections, the body seems to show intelligence and will. Indeed, out of Thomas's examples a moderately resourceful theologian might make a new kind of case for free will, for individual responsibility for one's own errors, and perhaps for the presence of sin as excess.

Thomas develops another line of thought that will interest readers who have reached this page. He quotes Montaigne's pleasant experience when, after a riding accident, he thought he was dying, letting himself slip away gently and easily; "I hardly ever did anything with less of a feeling of effort." Thomas then cites the memoirs of David Livingstone, the famous explorer of Africa, who was nearly killed by a lion but felt only peaceful calm all the time he was in the lion's jaws. And then, as if to counter centuries of belief in the unnatural pain of the last agony, Thomas quotes a medical authority of splendid credentials and many years spent in hospitals:

> Sir William Osler, who must have seen a great many people die in his time, was quite firmly convinced about this. There was, he maintained, no such state as an agony of death—he had never seen it. (p. 219)

I am pleased to end this note with the reference to Sir William Osler, who, in addition to his more widely known accomplishments, was a learned reader in the period of English literature I have been drawing upon.

Index

Page numbers in boldface type, in references to Donne's *Devotions* and to his *Sermons*, indicate commentary as well as quotation.

Arnold Stein is Professor of English at
the University of Illinois, Urbana-Champaign. He is the author
of five books, including *Johne Donne's Lyrics: The Eloquence of Action,*
George Herbert's Lyrics, and *The Art of Presence.*

THE JOHNS HOPKINS UNIVERSITY PRESS

The House of Death

Designed by Martha Farlow

Composed by the Composing Room of Michigan, Inc., in Bembo

Printed by the Maple Press Company on 50-lb. Sebago Eggshell Cream
offset paper and bound in Holliston Roxite A with Multicolor endsheets

LIBRARY OF CONGRESS CATALOGING-IN-PUBLICATION DATA
Stein, Arnold Sidney, 1915–
The house of death.

Includes index.
1. English literature—Early modern, 1500–1700—History and criticism.
2. Death in literature. I. Title.
PR429.D418S74   1986   820'.9'354   86-45448
ISBN 0-8018-3296-9 (alk. paper)